QUICKB(ONLINE BEGINNERS GUIDE

Simplify Your Business Cash Flow
With QBO. Packed With Step-by-Step
Illustrations and Practical Examples.
Perfect for Small Business Owners

JONAS TURING

Disclaimer

The author and publisher have made every effort to ensure the accuracy of the information contained in this book. However, the content is provided on an "as-is" basis without any guarantees of completeness, accuracy, or timeliness. The information and guidance offered are general in nature and may not apply to all circumstances.

The author and publisher disclaim any liability for any losses or damages caused by the use or misuse of the information provided in this book. Readers are encouraged to consult with a professional accountant or financial advisor to address specific concerns or unique situations related to their business finances.

By reading this book, you agree to use the information at your own risk and release the author and publisher from any liability or claims.

TABLE OF CONTENTS

INTRODUCTION

Welcome to QuickBooks Online for Beginners Guide: Simplify Your Business Cash Flow with QBO. This book is designed to take the stress out of managing your business finances, offering a clear, step-by-step approach to mastering QuickBooks Online (QBO). Whether you're a first-time entrepreneur or a small business owner juggling multiple responsibilities, this guide will empower you to take control of your financial management with confidence.

QuickBooks Online has revolutionized how small businesses manage their accounting. With its user-friendly interface, automated features, and powerful tools, QBO simplifies essential financial tasks like tracking expenses, invoicing, and payroll. However, for many business owners, the software can feel overwhelming at first. This book bridges the gap, breaking down complex processes into manageable steps so that even those with no prior experience can navigate QBO like a pro.

Packed with annotated screenshots, real-world examples, and practical tips, this guide provides everything you need to streamline your bookkeeping and focus on growing your business. Each chapter builds upon the last, guiding you through the setup, customization, and use of QBO's core features. Along the way, you'll also learn best practices, troubleshooting techniques, and ways to leverage QBO for long-term financial planning.

By the end of this book, you'll not only understand how to use QuickBooks Online effectively but also feel empowered to make smarter financial decisions for your business. So let's get started on this journey to financial clarity and success. In the next section, we'll explore why mastering QuickBooks Online is a game-changer for small business owners like you.

Why Mastering QuickBooks Online is Crucial for Small Businesses

For small business owners, managing finances effectively is one of the most critical aspects of ensuring long-term success. Yet, this is also where many entrepreneurs struggle. From tracking expenses to preparing for tax season, financial mismanagement can lead to missed opportunities, unnecessary stress, and costly mistakes. QuickBooks Online (QBO) provides a solution tailored to the needs of small businesses, offering powerful tools to simplify bookkeeping and promote financial clarity. However, to truly reap the benefits, mastering QBO is essential.

1. Financial Organization Saves Time and Reduces Stress

As a small business owner, your time is one of your most valuable assets. Juggling sales, marketing, customer service, and inventory leaves little room for deciphering spreadsheets or manually tracking expenses. QuickBooks Online streamlines financial management by centralizing all your data in one place. With features like automated bank feeds, recurring transactions, and mobile receipt capture, QBO reduces manual entry and ensures your records are always up-to-date.

By mastering QBO, you can efficiently organize your income and expenses, categorize transactions, and generate accurate reports. This not only saves time but also minimizes errors, giving you peace of mind that your financial data is accurate and reliable.

2. Simplifying Tax Preparation and Compliance

One of the most daunting aspects of running a small business is preparing for tax season. Errors or disorganized records can lead to missed deductions, penalties, or even audits. QuickBooks Online eliminates this anxiety by providing tools to track sales tax, record deductible expenses, and generate reports needed for tax filing.

Mastering QBO ensures that your records are always tax-ready. With features like sales tax tracking, automated tax calculations, and the ability to categorize expenses by tax category, you can confidently approach tax season knowing that you've done everything correctly. Additionally, QBO integrates seamlessly with tax software, making the filing process even smoother.

3. Improving Cash Flow Management

Cash flow is the lifeblood of any business. Without a clear understanding of your cash inflows and outflows, you risk running into liquidity problems. QuickBooks Online offers tools like the Cash Flow Planner, which provides a real-time view of your financial health. This allows you to make informed decisions, such as when to reinvest in your business or delay non-essential expenses.

Mastering QBO helps you harness these tools effectively, enabling you to project future cash needs and avoid surprises. For instance, you can set up reminders for upcoming bills, monitor unpaid invoices, and automate recurring payments to ensure your cash flow remains steady.

4. Empowering Business Growth with Financial Insights

One of the greatest advantages of mastering QuickBooks Online is the ability to generate detailed financial reports. These reports, such as profit and loss statements, balance sheets, and cash flow analyses, provide valuable insights into your business's performance.

When used effectively, these insights can guide strategic decisions. For example, by analyzing which products or services are most profitable, you can focus your resources on areas with the highest return on investment. Similarly, identifying areas of overspending allows you to cut costs and boost profitability.

By mastering QBO's reporting features, you can transform raw financial data into actionable strategies that drive business growth.

5. Automating Routine Tasks for Efficiency

Small business owners often wear many hats, and time spent on repetitive financial tasks is time taken away from growing your business. QuickBooks Online offers numerous automation features, such as recurring invoices, payroll processing, and bank reconciliation.

By mastering these automation tools, you can significantly reduce the time spent on bookkeeping while ensuring accuracy. For example, automated reminders for overdue invoices help improve cash flow, while recurring transactions save time by eliminating repetitive data entry.

Automation not only makes your workflows more efficient but also reduces the risk of human error, which can lead to costly mistakes.

6. Enhancing Professionalism and Building Trust

As a small business owner, presenting a professional image is crucial for building trust with customers and vendors. QuickBooks Online helps you create customized, branded invoices, track customer payments, and manage overdue balances seamlessly.

Mastering QBO allows you to leverage these features to their fullest potential. You can personalize templates with your logo and branding, send timely invoices, and even accept payments directly through Quick-Books. This level of professionalism not only improves customer satisfaction but also strengthens relationships with suppliers by ensuring timely payments.

7. Avoiding Common Financial Pitfalls

Many small businesses face challenges like duplicate transactions, missed payments, or unorganized records. These mistakes can snowball into bigger problems, such as inaccurate financial reports or compliance issues.

By mastering QuickBooks Online, you can avoid these pitfalls altogether. Features like bank feeds, reconciliations, and built-in alerts ensure your records are accurate and complete. You'll also learn to troubleshoot common issues, such as resolving discrepancies in your accounts, so that your books always remain in order.

8. Preparing for Future Growth

As your business grows, your financial management needs will become more complex. Mastering QuickBooks Online prepares you for this growth by equipping you with the skills to handle increased transactions, more detailed reporting, and advanced features like inventory tracking and multi-user access.

QuickBooks Online scales with your busi-ness, allowing you to add integrations, advanced reporting tools, and payroll management as needed. By mastering the basics now, you'll be ready to take full advantage of these features when the time comes.

Mastering QuickBooks Online is more than just learning how to use a software tool—it's about empowering yourself to take control of your business finances, reduce stress, and make smarter decisions. From organizing your records to automating repetitive tasks, QBO offers a comprehensive solution for small businesses. By investing time in mastering QBO, you're not just simplifying your bookkeeping; you're setting the foundation for your business's financial success and long-term growth.

Overview of QuickBooks Online Features and Benefits

QuickBooks Online (QBO) is a cloud-based accounting solution that has revolutionized how small businesses manage their finances. Designed to be user-friendly yet robust, it offers a wide array of features that cater to the diverse needs of business owners, from tracking expenses to generating detailed financial reports. Whether you're a sole proprietor or a growing small business, QBO provides tools that help simplify complex accounting processes, save time, and enable smarter financial decision-making. In this section, we'll explore the features and benefits of QuickBooks Online and how they empower small business owners.

1. Cloud-Based Accessibility

One of the standout features of Quick-Books Online is its cloud-based platform, which provides unparalleled accessibility. With QBO, you can manage your finances anytime, anywhere, as long as you have an internet connection. This feature is particularly beneficial for small business owners who often juggle multiple responsibilities and need the flexibility to work from home, the office, or even on the go.

- Feature: Multi-device compatibility (desktop, tablet, and mobile apps).
- Benefit: Real-time access to financial data, ensuring you're always up-to-date, even when traveling or working remotely.

2. Simplified Setup and User-Friendly Interface

Getting started with QBO is straightforward, even for beginners with little or no accounting experience. The intuitive interface is designed with small business owners in mind, offering clear navigation and minimal jargon. The setup process includes guided steps to ensure your accounts are organized correctly from the start.

- Feature: Step-by-step account setup and customizable dashboard.
- Benefit: A smooth onboarding experience that allows users to start managing finances without frustration or confusion.

3. Expense Tracking and Categorization

For any business, understanding where money is being spent is crucial. QuickBooks Online simplifies this by automatically importing transactions from linked bank accounts and credit cards. These transactions can then be categorized into predefined expense types or custom categories, giving you a clear view of your spending patterns.

- Feature: Automatic bank feeds and customizable expense categories.
- Benefit: Eliminates manual data entry, reduces errors, and provides a detailed breakdown of expenses for smarter budgeting.

4. Invoicing and Payment Processing

Invoicing is a critical part of any business, and QBO makes the process seamless. The platform allows you to create professional, customized invoices and send them directly to clients. It also offers options for accepting payments online, making it easier for customers to pay and for you to get paid faster.

- Feature: Branded invoice templates and online payment integration.
- Benefit: Improved cash flow through faster payments and enhanced professionalism with customized branding.

5. Real-Time Financial Reporting

QuickBooks Online's reporting capabilities are one of its most powerful features. The platform provides a range of pre-built reports, such as profit and loss statements, balance sheets, and cash flow statements. These reports can be customized to meet your specific needs and help you gain insights into your business's financial health.

- Feature: Detailed, customizable financial reports.
- Benefit: Informed decision-making through real-time insights into revenue, expenses, and profitability.

6. Cash Flow Management

Cash flow is the lifeblood of any business, and QuickBooks Online helps you keep it under control. The Cash Flow Planner allows you to forecast and plan for future cash needs, ensuring you have enough resources to meet your financial obligations.

- Feature: Cash Flow Planner and automated reminders.
- Benefit: Prevents cash shortages and helps you plan for growth with confidence.

7. Payroll Integration

Managing payroll can be complex and time-consuming, but QuickBooks Online streamlines the process with integrated payroll features. It allows you to calculate employee wages, manage tax filings, and ensure compliance with federal and state regulations.

- Feature: Automated payroll calculations and tax filing.
- Benefit: Saves time, ensures accuracy, and reduces compliance risks.

8. Sales Tax Tracking and Management

For businesses that need to collect and remit sales tax, QuickBooks Online provides tools to simplify this process. The platform automatically calculates sales tax rates based on customer location and tracks collected amounts for accurate reporting.

- Feature: Automated sales tax calculation and tracking.
- Benefit: Minimizes errors and ensures compliance with sales tax laws.

9. Automation of Routine Tasks

Automation is a cornerstone of QuickBooks Online's functionality. The platform allows you to automate repetitive tasks such as sending recurring invoices, setting up payment reminders, and categorizing expenses. These automation tools not only save time but also reduce the risk of errors.

- Feature: Recurring transactions and automated reminders.
- Benefit: Increased efficiency and reduced workload, freeing up time for more strategic tasks.

10. Mobile App for On-the-Go Management

The QuickBooks Online mobile app extends the platform's functionality to your smartphone or tablet, allowing you to manage finances while on the move. From capturing receipts to creating invoices, the app offers nearly all the capabilities of the desktop version.

- Feature: Fully functional mobile app.
- Benefit: Flexibility and convenience for busy business owners.

11. Third-Party App Integrations

QuickBooks Online integrates seamlessly with a wide range of third-party apps, including tools for inventory management, customer relationship management (CRM), and e-commerce platforms. These integrations expand the platform's capabilities, making it a comprehensive solution for small businesses.

- Feature: Integration with apps like Shopify, PayPal, and HubSpot.
- Benefit: Streamlines workflows and eliminates the need for manual data entry across platforms.

12. Scalability for Growing Businesses

QuickBooks Online grows with your business, offering features and plans that scale to meet increasing demands. Whether you need advanced reporting, multi-user access, or additional integrations, QBO has options to accommodate your business's growth.

- Feature: Multiple pricing plans and add-on features.
- Benefit: Long-term value and the ability to adapt as your business evolves.

13. Security and Data Backup

As a cloud-based platform, QuickBooks Online prioritizes data security. All data is encrypted and backed up regularly, ensuring your financial information is safe from loss or unauthorized access.

- Feature: Bank-level encryption and automatic backups.
- Benefit: Peace of mind knowing your data is secure and always recoverable.

14. Collaboration Made Easy

QuickBooks Online supports multi-user access, making it easy to collaborate with your team or accountant. You can assign roles and permissions to ensure everyone has access to the information they need without compromising sensitive data.

- Feature: Multi-user access with customizable permissions.
- Benefit: Enhanced collaboration while maintaining data security.

15. Time-Saving Tools for Tax Season

Tax season is often a stressful time for small business owners, but QuickBooks Online simplifies the process with tools designed to keep your records organized and tax-ready. From categorizing expenses to generating tax-specific reports, QBO helps you stay prepared.

- Feature: Tax reporting and integration with tax software.
- Benefit: Reduced stress and increased accuracy during tax season.

QuickBooks Online is more than just an accounting tool—it's a comprehensive financial management solution designed to meet the unique needs of small businesses. By leveraging its wide array of features, you can save time, reduce errors, and gain valuable insights into your business's performance. From tracking expenses to managing payroll and forecasting cash flow, QBO empowers business owners to take control of their finances and focus on what matters most: growing their business. Whether you're just starting out or scaling your operations, mastering QuickBooks Online is a step toward financial clarity and long-term success.

How This Book Will Help You Manage Your Business Finances

Managing business finances can feel overwhelming for small business owners, especially when juggling multiple responsibilities and lacking a background in accounting. This book, QuickBooks Online for Beginners Guide, is designed to eliminate that overwhelm by providing clear, actionable guidance to help you take control of your financial management. Packed with step-by-step tutorials, real-world examples, and visual aids, this guide is your go-to resource for mastering QuickBooks Online (QBO) and transforming how you manage your business finances.

1. Step-by-Step Guidance for Beginners

Navigating new software can be intimidating, especially for first-time users. This book simplifies the learning process by breaking down complex concepts into easy-to-follow steps. Each chapter is structured to guide you through specific features of QuickBooks Online, starting with the basics and gradually progressing to more advanced tools.

For instance, you'll learn how to:

- Set up your QuickBooks account in just a few steps.
- Customize invoices and forms to reflect your brand.
- Record sales, track expenses, and manage payroll with confidence.

Every chapter includes annotated screenshots and visual callouts to ensure you never feel lost. By the end of the book, you'll have a solid foundation in QBO and the confidence to handle your business finances independently.

2. Practical, Real-World Examples

One of the unique features of this guide is its focus on real-world scenarios that small business owners face every day. Instead of generic examples, you'll encounter practical situations tailored to entrepreneurs like you. For example:

- Learn how to send a professional invoice to a client and track overdue payments.
- Discover how to categorize expenses for tax deductions and reconcile your accounts.
- See how automating payroll can save time and reduce errors.

These relatable examples ensure that what you learn can be immediately applied to your business. Whether you're a sole proprietor or managing a small team, the examples are designed to mirror your day-to-day challenges.

3. Visual Learning with Screenshots and Diagrams

This book is packed with high-quality, annotated screenshots to walk you through the QuickBooks Online interface. Each screenshot highlights important buttons, tabs, and features, making it easy for visual learners to grasp new concepts.

Additionally, workflow diagrams are included to simplify processes like bank reconciliation, sales tax tracking, and invoicing. Visual aids such as callouts and tips ensure you don't miss critical details. These tools make learning intuitive and reduce the time it takes to become comfortable with QBO.

4. Avoiding Common Financial Pitfalls

Many small business owners struggle with common bookkeeping mistakes, such as duplicate transactions, unorganized records, or incorrect categorizations. This book anticipates these pitfalls and provides strategies to avoid them.

For example:

- Learn how to troubleshoot reconciliation errors.
- Discover tips for managing sales tax accurately.
- Understand how to set up reminders for unpaid invoices and upcoming bills.

By following the best practices outlined in this book, you'll keep your financial records clean and error-free, saving time and stress in the long run.

5. Automation Tips to Save Time

Time is a precious resource for small business owners, and this book emphasizes how to use QuickBooks Online to automate repetitive tasks. You'll learn how to:

- Set up recurring invoices and payments.
- Use bank feeds to automatically import and categorize transactions.
- Automate payroll processing for employees and contractors.

By leveraging automation, you'll not only reduce your workload but also minimize the risk of human error. This frees up more time for you to focus on growing your business.

6. Preparing for Tax Season with Confidence

Tax season is often a source of anxiety for small business owners, but this book helps you face it with confidence. You'll learn how to:

- Organize and categorize expenses for maximum deductions.
- Track sales tax and prepare reports for filing.
- Generate financial statements that

provide all the information your accountant needs.

By mastering these skills, you'll eliminate the last-minute scramble for receipts and records, ensuring a smooth and stress-free tax filing process.

7. Insights for Better Financial Decision-Making

Beyond basic bookkeeping, QuickBooks Online offers tools for analyzing your business's financial health. This book helps you unlock those insights by teaching you how to:

- Generate profit and loss statements to evaluate profitability.
- Create budgets and forecasts to plan for the future.
- Use cash flow reports to ensure you're never caught off guard.

Armed with these tools, you'll be able to make smarter financial decisions, such as identifying cost-saving opportunities or determining the right time to reinvest in your business.

8. Troubleshooting and Advanced Tips

Even with the best tools, challenges may arise. That's why this book includes a bonus chapter on troubleshooting common issues. You'll learn how to resolve problems like:

- Bank feed errors or missing transactions.
- Duplicated entries that skew financial reports.
- Setup mistakes that can affect tax calculations.

In addition, advanced users will benefit from tips on using features like custom fields, workflow automation, and app integrations to enhance QuickBooks Online's functionality.

9. Bonus Resources for Ongoing Support

This guide goes beyond the book itself by offering additional resources to help you succeed. You'll gain access to:

- Printable PDF checklists for QuickBooks tasks like month-end reconciliations.
- Video tutorials for visual step-by-step walkthroughs.
- Quick reference guides for common QuickBooks terms and shortcuts.

These resources ensure you have ongoing support as you implement what you've learned.

10. Designed for Your Success

Ultimately, this book is designed to empower small business owners to take control of their finances without relying heavily on external help. Whether you're new to bookkeeping or just looking to refine your processes, this guide offers the tools, techniques, and confidence you need to succeed.

By mastering QuickBooks Online, you'll be able to:

- Simplify your bookkeeping processes.
- Avoid costly financial mistakes.
- Gain a clearer understanding of your business's performance.

This isn't just about learning software—it's about transforming how you manage your business finances, freeing up time, reducing stress, and positioning your business for long-term growth.

This book is more than a tutorial; it's a practical roadmap for financial clarity and efficiency. By the time you finish, you'll have the knowledge and skills to confidently use QuickBooks Online to manage your business finances, avoid pitfalls, and make data-driven decisions.

CHAPTER 1

GETTING STARTED WITH QUICKBOOKS ONLINE

Every small business owner dreams of running a business where finances are organized, tax time is stress-free, and cash flow is always under control. But for many, managing finances can feel like an overwhelming task filled with confusing spreadsheets, stacks of receipts, and endless hours trying to reconcile accounts. That's where Quick-Books Online (QBO) steps in—a powerful, cloud-based accounting tool designed to make financial management easy, efficient, and even enjoyable.

This chapter is your starting point on the journey to mastering QBO and, by extension, your business finances. Whether you're entirely new to bookkeeping or transitioning from a different system, you'll find that QuickBooks Online provides the perfect balance between simplicity and functionality. In this chapter, we'll uncover what QuickBooks Online is, explore its range of subscription plans, and guide you through setting up your account. By the end, you'll be ready to dive into the platform with confidence.

Why QuickBooks Online?

Imagine having all your financial data in one place—accessible anytime, anywhere, on any device. QuickBooks Online makes this a reality. Unlike traditional accounting software, QBO operates entirely in the cloud. This means you no longer need to worry about outdated software or losing critical data stored on a single computer. Instead, QuickBooks Online gives you the freedom to manage your finances on your terms.

Think of it as having a virtual financial assistant. Need to know your current cash flow? It's just a click away. Want to send a professional invoice to a client? QBO handles it seamlessly. Concerned about categorizing your expenses for tax season? QuickBooks Online simplifies the process, automatically syncing with your bank accounts and offering real-time financial insights.

Choosing the Right Plan for Your Business

Before jumping into the setup process, it's essential to choose the QBO plan that best aligns with your business needs. Quick-Books Online offers several subscription tiers, each tailored to a specific type of user. Are you a sole proprietor managing a side hustle? Or perhaps a small business owner with employees and inventory to track? There's a plan for everyone, and this chapter will help you decide which one fits you best.

We'll explore each plan in detail, from the beginner-friendly Simple Start to the robust Advanced plan designed for scaling businesses. With this information, you'll be confident in choosing the subscription that provides the tools you need without overpaying for features you won't use.

The Power of a Proper Setup

Setting up QuickBooks Online is a pivotal step toward gaining control over your finances. A well-organized account ensures that every invoice, expense, and report flows seamlessly, giving you a clear picture of your business's financial health. In this chapter, we'll break the process into ten simple steps. From linking your bank accounts to customizing your invoices, each step is designed to set you up for success.

Mastering the Dashboard

Once your account is ready, the QBO dashboard becomes your command center. This intuitive interface provides a snapshot of your business's financial performance, with colorful charts and graphs showcasing income, expenses, and cash flow. The dashboard also offers quick access to essential tools like invoicing, expense tracking, and financial reports.

As we walk through these features, you'll discover how they work together to simplify your daily tasks. By the end of this chapter, navigating QuickBooks Online will feel second nature, and you'll be ready to unlock its full potential.

Getting started with QuickBooks Online marks the first step in your journey toward financial clarity and business growth. In the following sections, you'll learn how to harness QBO's capabilities to take charge of your bookkeeping, save time, and make informed decisions. Let's dive in and set the foundation for a more organized, stress-free approach to managing your business finances.

What is QuickBooks Online and How Does It Work?

Managing business finances can often feel like solving a never-ending puzzle. Between tracking expenses, sending invoices, rec-

onciling accounts, and preparing for tax season, small business owners face a mountain of responsibilities. QuickBooks Online (QBO) is designed to solve this problem by offering an all-in-one solution for managing finances with ease, efficiency, and accuracy. Whether you're a sole proprietor or a growing business, QBO simplifies bookkeeping and provides powerful tools to help you focus on what matters most: running your business.

An Introduction to QuickBooks Online

QuickBooks Online is a cloud-based accounting platform developed by Intuit, a company known for its trusted financial software. Unlike traditional desktop accounting software that ties you to a single computer, QBO operates entirely in the cloud. This means your financial data is stored securely online, giving you the flexibility to access it anytime, anywhere, and on any device with an internet connection.

At its core, QuickBooks Online is designed to help small businesses manage their money. It streamlines everyday financial tasks like tracking income and expenses, sending invoices, and managing payroll, all while providing real-time insights into your business's financial health. With its intuitive interface and automation features, QBO reduces the time and effort needed to stay on top of your finances, making it an ideal choice for busy entrepreneurs.

The Core Features of QuickBooks Online

QuickBooks Online offers a range of features that cater to the diverse needs of small businesses. These features are designed to work together seamlessly, providing an integrated financial management experience.

1. Expense Tracking: QBO automatically imports transactions from your

linked bank accounts and credit cards. You can categorize expenses with just a few clicks, ensuring accurate records for tax season.

2. Invoicing: With QuickBooks Online, creating and sending professional invoices is simple. You can customize invoices with your logo, track payment status, and even set up recurring invoices for regular clients.

3. Financial Reporting: QBO offers a variety of customizable reports, including profit and loss statements, balance sheets, and cash flow summaries. These reports provide real-time insights into your business's performance.

4. Cash Flow Management: The Cash Flow Planner helps you forecast cash inflows and outflows, allowing you to plan for future expenses and avoid liquidity issues.

5. Payroll Integration: QuickBooks Online integrates seamlessly with QuickBooks Payroll, enabling you to pay employees, calculate taxes, and file necessary forms effortlessly.

6. Sales Tax Tracking: For businesses that collect sales tax, QBO automatically calculates and tracks sales tax payments based on your location and customer transactions.

7. Mobile Accessibility: The QuickBooks Online mobile app provides on-the-go access to your finances, allowing you to manage transactions, send invoices, and capture receipts from your smartphone or tablet.

How QuickBooks Online Works

To understand how QBO works, let's break it down into its core functionalities and workflows.

1. The Cloud-Based Advantage

The key difference between QuickBooks Online and traditional accounting software is its cloud-based nature. This means:

- Accessibility: You can access your financial data from any device with an internet connection—desktop, laptop, tablet, or smartphone.
- Real-Time Updates: All changes are saved automatically in the cloud, ensuring your data is always up to date.
- Collaboration: Multiple users can access the same account simultaneously, making it easier to work with your accountant, bookkeeper, or team members.
- Security: QBO uses bank-level encryption to protect your financial data, along with regular backups to prevent data loss.

This level of flexibility and security makes QBO an excellent choice for modern businesses that value mobility and collaboration.

2. Automation Saves Time

One of QBO's greatest strengths is its ability to automate repetitive tasks. For example:

- Bank Feeds: Once you link your business bank accounts and credit cards, QBO automatically imports transactions, reducing the need for manual data entry.
- Recurring Transactions: You can set up recurring invoices or bills, ensuring you never miss a payment or forget to bill a client.
- Reminders: QBO sends reminders for overdue invoices, helping you maintain healthy cash flow.

By automating these tasks, QuickBooks Online frees up time for you to focus on growing your business.

3. User-Friendly Interface

QuickBooks Online is designed with small business owners in mind, many of whom may not have a background in accounting. The platform features an intuitive dashboard that provides a snapshot of your financial health. Key sections include:

- Income and Expenses: Visual charts show how much money is coming in and going out.
- Profit and Loss: A quick overview of your profitability.
- Bank Accounts: A summary of your account balances and transactions.

Navigation is straightforward, with menus clearly labeled for tasks like invoicing, reporting, and payroll. This simplicity ensures that even beginners can start using the platform with minimal learning curve.

4. Integration with Other Tools

QuickBooks Online integrates with a wide range of third-party apps, making it a central hub for your business operations. For example:

- E-commerce Platforms: Integrate with Shopify or Etsy to sync sales data automatically.
- Payment Processors: Connect with PayPal or Stripe for seamless payment collection.
- CRM Tools: Link with HubSpot or Salesforce to align financial data with customer relationship management.

These integrations eliminate the need for manual data entry and ensure that all your business systems work in harmony.

5. Customization to Fit Your Business

Every business is unique, and QBO acknowledges this by offering customization options. For instance:

- Chart of Accounts: Organize your accounts to reflect the specific needs of your business.
- Invoice Templates: Create professional, branded invoices that match your business identity.
- Reports: Tailor financial reports to focus on the metrics that matter most to you.

This level of customization ensures that QBO works for your business—not the other way around.

6. Scalability for Growing Businesses

As your business grows, your financial needs will evolve. QuickBooks Online is built to scale with you, offering advanced features like inventory management, project tracking, and in-depth reporting in higher-tier plans. You can also add users and integrate more apps as your operations expand.

Why QuickBooks Online is Perfect for Small Businesses

QuickBooks Online stands out as a financial management tool because it simplifies accounting tasks while providing powerful insights. Here's why small businesses love QBO:

- Ease of Use: Designed for non-accountants, QBO's interface is intuitive and beginner-friendly.
- Cost-Effective: Subscription-based pricing ensures you only pay for the features you need.
- Time-Saving: Automation and integrations reduce the time spent on manual tasks.
- Flexibility: Access your finances from anywhere, on any device.
- Scalability: As your business grows, QBO grows with you.

QuickBooks Online is more than just an accounting tool—it's a comprehensive financial management system designed to empower small business owners. With its cloud-based accessibility, automation features, and user-friendly interface, QBO simplifies bookkeeping and provides the insights needed to make informed decisions. By mastering QuickBooks Online, you're not just managing your finances— you're setting the foundation for sustainable growth and long-term success.

Exploring the Different QuickBooks Online Plans

Choosing the right accounting software is a critical decision for any small business owner, and QuickBooks Online (QBO) is designed to cater to a wide range of business needs. Intuit offers multiple subscription plans for QBO, each tailored to specific types of users. Whether you're a freelancer managing a side hustle or a growing business with complex financial requirements, there's a plan that fits your needs. This chapter provides an in-depth exploration of the different QuickBooks Online plans, helping you make an informed choice that aligns with your business's current demands and future goals.

The QuickBooks Online Plan Tiers

QuickBooks Online offers four primary plans: Simple Start, Essentials, Plus, and Advanced. Each plan comes with unique features designed to address different business complexities and sizes. Let's dive into the details of each plan.

Who It's For:

Simple Start is the most basic plan in the QuickBooks Online lineup, making it ideal for freelancers, sole proprietors, and new entrepreneurs who are just starting out. If you're managing a small operation with straightforward financial needs, this plan provides the tools you need without over-whelming you with features you may not use.

Key Features:

- Income and Expense Tracking: Record and categorize income and expenses for a clear picture of your finances.
- Invoicing: Create and send professional invoices to clients and track payment status.
- Tax Deductions: Automatically track deductible expenses to simplify tax filing.
- Mileage Tracking: Use the mobile app to track mileage for business trips.
- Basic Reports: Generate essential financial reports, such as profit and loss statements.
- One User Access: Designed for a single user, with optional access for your accountant.

Limitations:

- No features for bill management or time tracking.
- Limited scalability; not ideal for businesses with employees or multiple users.

Best For:

Freelancers, independent contractors, and small business owners with simple accounting needs who want an affordable solution.

Who It's For:

Essentials is a step up from Simple Start, providing additional tools for businesses that manage employees, work with contractors, or need to handle bills. It's suitable for small businesses looking for basic multi-user access and more robust features.

Key Features:

- Bill Management: Track and pay bills, schedule payments, and keep vendor records organized.
- Multi-User Access: Includes access for up to three users, with customizable permissions.
- Time Tracking: Track billable hours and assign them to clients or projects.
- Recurring Transactions: Automate invoices and bill payments to save time.
- Sales Tax: Automatically calculate and track sales tax based on your location.

Limitations:

- Inventory management and project tracking are not included.
- Some advanced reporting features are missing.

Best For:

Small businesses with a few employees or contractors, as well as businesses that need to manage bills and track time.

Who It's For:

Plus is the most popular QuickBooks Online plan, offering a comprehensive feature set that caters to growing businesses. If you manage inventory, need detailed project tracking, or require advanced financial reporting, this plan is an excellent choice.

Key Features:

- Inventory Tracking: Monitor inventory levels, track costs, and receive alerts when stock is low.
- Project Profitability Tracking: Assign income and expenses to projects to see detailed profitability insights.
- Budgets: Create and manage budgets to track financial performance against goals.
- Multi-User Access: Includes access

for up to five users, with customizable roles and permissions.
- All Features from Essentials: Includes bill management, time tracking, and sales tax capabilities.

Limitations:

- May be more expensive than necessary for businesses that don't need inventory or project tracking.

Best For:

Small to medium-sized businesses that manage inventory, handle multiple projects, or need advanced financial tools to track growth.

Who It's For:

Advanced is the top-tier QuickBooks Online plan, designed for larger organizations with complex accounting needs. If your business is scaling quickly and requires robust tools, dedicated support, and deep integrations, Advanced is the ultimate choice.

Key Features:

- Advanced Reporting: Access highly customizable reporting tools for detailed financial analysis.
- Custom User Roles: Define specific user permissions for enhanced data security.
- Batch Invoicing and Expenses: Save time by processing multiple invoices and transactions at once.
- Integration with Apps: Unlock integrations with premium apps like Salesforce and HubSpot.
- Dedicated Account Manager: Receive priority support and a dedicated account manager for personalized assistance.
- Training and Backup: Access online training and automated data backups.

Limitations:

- The most expensive plan; may not be cost-effective for small or medium-sized businesses.

Best For:

Large businesses, organizations with complex workflows, and businesses that require extensive customization and advanced analytics.

Selecting the right QuickBooks Online plan depends on several factors, including your business size, industry, and accounting needs. Consider the following when making your decision:

1. Assess Your Current Needs

- Are you managing finances for yourself, or do you have employees and contractors?
- Do you need tools for inventory management or project tracking?
- How many users will need access to your account?

For freelancers and sole proprietors, Simple Start is often sufficient. For businesses managing multiple employees or contractors, Essentials or Plus is a better fit. If your business requires advanced reporting or handles large transaction volumes, consider Advanced.

2. Plan for Growth

As your business grows, your accounting needs will evolve. QuickBooks Online allows you to upgrade your plan as your business expands, so it's okay to start with a lower-tier plan and scale up when needed. If you anticipate rapid growth, starting with Plus or Advanced might be more cost-effective in the long run.

3. Evaluate Budget Constraints

While it's important to choose a plan that meets your needs, you should also consider your budget. Overpaying for features you don't use can strain your finances. Compare the monthly cost of each plan with the features you'll actually use to ensure you're getting value for your investment.

4. Take Advantage of Free Trials

QuickBooks Online offers free trials for all its plans. Use this opportunity to explore the platform and test out features before committing to a subscription. This hands-on experience can help you determine whether the plan suits your business.

QuickBooks Online offers a range of plans to suit businesses of all sizes and complexities. From the straightforward simplicity of Simple Start to the robust features of Advanced, each plan is designed to streamline your accounting processes and provide the tools you need to succeed. By understanding your current needs, planning for future growth, and leveraging the unique features of each plan, you can make an informed choice that empowers your business to thrive. Remember, the right QuickBooks Online plan isn't just about managing your finances—it's about giving you the confidence and clarity to focus on what you do best: growing your business.

Setting Up Your QuickBooks Account in 10 Easy Steps

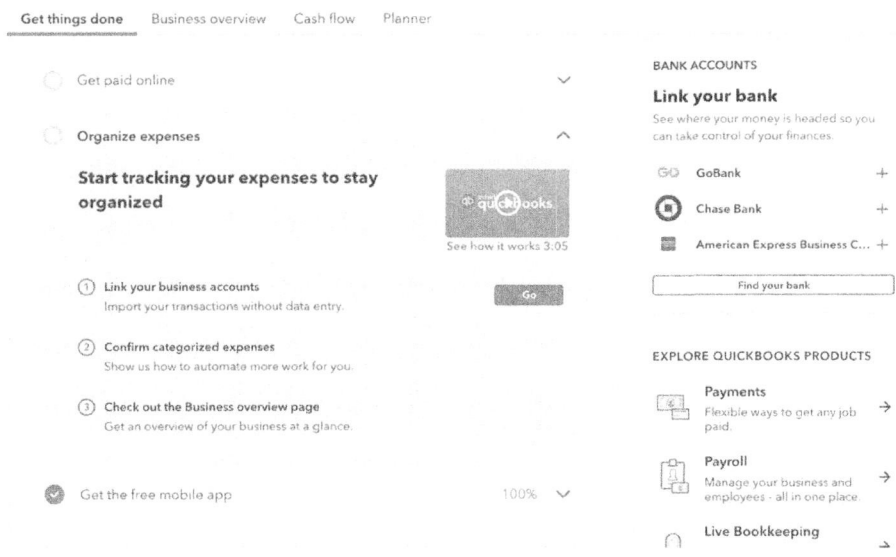

Get things done   Business overview   Cash flow   Planner

Get paid online

Organize expenses

Start tracking your expenses to stay organized

See how it works 3:05

(1) Link your business accounts
Import your transactions without data entry.

(2) Confirm categorized expenses
Show us how to automate more work for you.

(3) Check out the Business overview page
Get an overview of your business at a glance.

Get the free mobile app   100%

BANK ACCOUNTS

Link your bank
See where your money is headed so you can take control of your finances.

GO   GoBank   +

Chase Bank   +

American Express Business C... +

Find your bank

EXPLORE QUICKBOOKS PRODUCTS

Payments
Flexible ways to get any job paid.

Payroll
Manage your business and employees - all in one place.

Live Bookkeeping

Getting started with QuickBooks Online (QBO) is a crucial step toward taking control of your business finances. Proper setup ensures your financial records are accurate, organized, and ready for day-to-day use. This chapter provides a detailed, step-by-step guide to setting up your QuickBooks account. By the end of this process, you'll have a fully configured system tailored to your business needs.

Step 1: Sign Up for a QuickBooks Online Plan

The first step is choosing the right QBO plan for your business. QuickBooks Online offers four subscription tiers: Simple Start, Essentials, Plus, and Advanced.

- Visit the QuickBooks website to compare plans.
- Select the plan that best fits your business's current needs and growth expectations.
- Create your account by entering your email address, password, and basic business details.

Once signed up, you'll gain access to a 30-day free trial, allowing you to explore the platform before committing to a subscription.

Step 2: Provide Basic Business Information

After creating your account, QuickBooks will prompt you to enter essential details about your business:

- Business Name: Enter your official business name as it will appear on invoices and reports.
- Industry: Select your industry to allow QuickBooks to tailor your setup with industry-specific options.
- Business Type: Specify whether you're a sole proprietor, partnership, LLC, or corporation.
- Start Date: If you're transitioning from another accounting system, provide the date you want to start tracking transactions in QuickBooks.

These details help QBO customize your setup for your unique business needs.

Step 3: Link Your Bank and Credit Card Accounts

Connecting your bank accounts and credit cards to QuickBooks Online is a game-changer for simplifying your bookkeeping. This feature automatically imports your transactions, saving you time and ensuring accuracy.

- Go to the Banking menu and click Add Account.
- Search for your bank or credit card provider.
- Enter your login credentials to securely connect the account.
- Choose the date range for importing transactions.

Once connected, QuickBooks will automatically sync transactions, categorizing them based on your preferences.

Step 4: Set Up Your Chart of Accounts

The Chart of Accounts is the backbone of your financial organization. It categorizes your assets, liabilities, income, and expenses, ensuring accurate record-keeping.

- Navigate to the Settings menu and select Chart of Accounts.
- Review the pre-configured categories provided by QuickBooks.
- Add or edit accounts to suit your business needs (e.g., creating categories for specific expense types or revenue streams).

A well-organized Chart of Accounts makes it easier to generate reports and analyze your financial health.

Step 5: Customize Your Invoices

Creating professional invoices is key to maintaining a polished image for your business. QuickBooks Online allows you to customize invoices to align with your brand.

- Go to the Settings menu and select Custom Form Styles.
- Add your business logo, choose your color scheme, and adjust the layout.
- Personalize fields such as payment terms, due dates, and contact information.
- Save your template for consistent, professional invoicing.

Customizing your invoices not only looks professional but also streamlines the billing process.

Step 6: Enable and Configure Sales Tax

If your business collects sales tax, setting up sales tax tracking in QuickBooks Online is essential.

- Navigate to the Taxes menu and click Set Up Sales Tax.
- Enter your business address and QuickBooks will automatically calculate applicable tax rates based on your location.
- Add tax agencies and customize rates for different jurisdictions if necessary.

QuickBooks will track sales tax on invoices and transactions, ensuring compliance and simplifying reporting during tax season.

Step 7: Invite Users and Assign Roles

If you work with a bookkeeper, accountant, or team, QuickBooks allows you to invite multiple users with customized permissions.

- Go to the Settings menu and select Manage Users.
- Click Add User and choose the appropriate role (e.g., Accountant, Standard User, or Admin).
- Enter the user's email address to send an invitation.

Assigning roles ensures that team members

have access to the tools they need without compromising sensitive financial data.

Step 8: Explore App Integrations

QuickBooks Online integrates with a variety of third-party apps, allowing you to streamline operations and eliminate manual data entry.

- Go to the Apps menu to browse available integrations.
- Popular options include Shopify (for e-commerce), PayPal (for payments), and TSheets (for time tracking).
- Connect the apps that align with your business needs.

Integrations save time and ensure consistency across platforms, making your workflows more efficient.

Step 9: Review Your Dashboard and Key Features

The QuickBooks Online dashboard is your command center, offering a snapshot of your financial health. Take a moment to familiarize yourself with its layout and features:

- Income and Expenses: Monitor cash flow with visual charts and summaries.
- Profit and Loss Overview: Get a real-time snapshot of your profitability.
- Bank Accounts: Track balances and review synced transactions.

Spend time exploring the menus for Invoicing, Expenses, and Reports to understand how they interact. This step builds confidence and helps you use the platform effectively.

Step 10: Import Existing Data

If you're transitioning from another accounting tool, importing your historical data ensures continuity in your financial records.

- Navigate to the Settings menu and select Import Data.
- Choose the type of data to import (e.g., Customers, Vendors, Products/Services, Transactions).
- Upload files in compatible formats like Excel or CSV.
- Map the fields to ensure accurate data transfer.

Importing historical data helps you maintain comprehensive records and simplifies year-end reporting.

Setting up your QuickBooks Online account correctly from the beginning has long-term benefits:

- Time Savings: Automating data entry and organizing categories reduces manual work.
- Accuracy: Proper setup ensures accurate reports, minimizing errors and simplifying tax preparation.
- Efficiency: Customized settings and integrations streamline workflows.
- Scalability: A well-structured account can easily adapt as your business grows.

While setting up QuickBooks Online is straightforward, avoiding these common mistakes will ensure a smoother experience:

- Skipping Account Linking: Failing to connect bank accounts reduces automation and increases manual work.
- Neglecting Customization: Generic settings can lead to inconsistent branding and missed opportunities for personalization.
- Overcomplicating the Chart of Accounts: Too many categories can make reporting cumbersome; stick to essentials.

Setting up your QuickBooks Online account is an investment in your business's future. By following these ten steps, you're creating a financial management system that's accurate, efficient, and tailored to your needs. Once your account is fully configured, you'll be ready to leverage QuickBooks Online to streamline your bookkeeping, gain valuable insights, and focus on growing your business. In the next chapter, we'll explore how to navigate the QuickBooks Online dashboard and master its essential features. Let's continue building your financial confidence!

Navigating the Dashboard and Essential Features

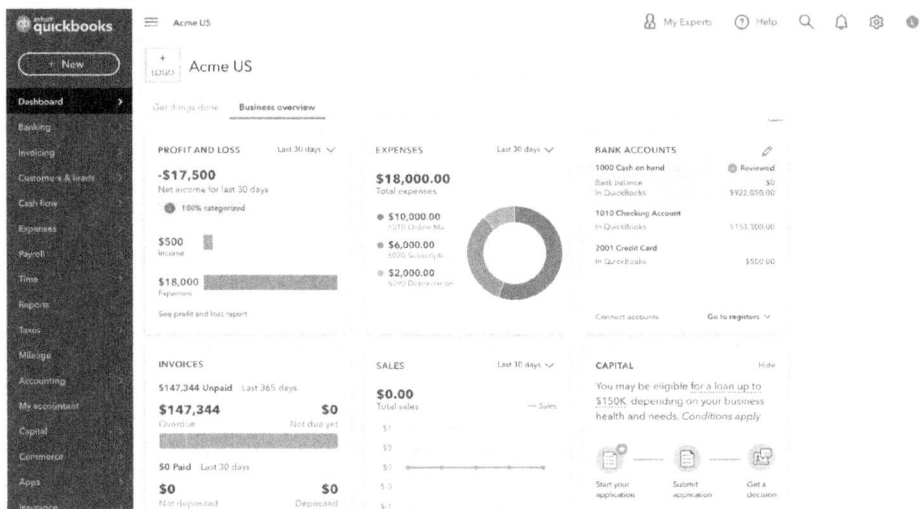

Once your QuickBooks Online (QBO) account is set up, the dashboard becomes your command center for managing your business finances. Intuitive and user-friendly, the dashboard provides an at-a-glance view of your business's financial health while offering easy access to essential features. In this chapter, we'll take a detailed tour of the dashboard, explore its key components, and dive into the essential features that make QBO an indispensable tool for small business owners.

The dashboard is the first thing you see when you log in to QuickBooks Online. It's designed to provide a comprehensive snapshot of your financial data, helping you stay informed and make quick decisions. The dashboard is divided into key sections, each offering valuable insights.

1. Income

The Income section displays a visual breakdown of your revenue over a specified period. This chart shows:

• Invoices sent: The total amount invoiced to clients.

• Payments received: The amount collected from your customers.

This section helps you monitor cash inflows, track overdue payments, and assess your overall revenue trends.

2. Expenses

In the Expenses section, you can view:

- A breakdown of spending by category (e.g., supplies, utilities, marketing).
- Total expenses for the selected period.

This feature helps you identify areas where you're overspending and adjust your budget accordingly.

3. Profit and Loss

The Profit and Loss section summarizes your income and expenses, giving you a snapshot of your profitability. You'll see:

- Net income: Revenue minus expenses for the chosen period.
- A real-time update of your business's financial health.

4. Bank Accounts

This section provides a summary of your linked bank and credit card accounts, showing:

- Account balances: Updated in real time based on synced transactions.
- Uncategorized transactions: Items that need your attention for proper categorization.

The Bank Accounts section simplifies reconciliation and ensures you stay on top of cash flow.

5. Sales

The Sales section shows:

- Outstanding invoices.
- Recent sales activity.
- Upcoming recurring invoices.

This quick overview ensures you never miss a payment or forget to follow up on unpaid invoices.

While the dashboard provides a high-level overview, its true power lies in the features it connects you to. Let's explore these essential tools and how they work.

1. Invoicing

Invoicing is a critical feature for businesses of all sizes, and QBO makes it seamless:

- Create Professional Invoices: Use customizable templates to reflect your brand's identity.
- Track Invoice Status: See which invoices have been sent, paid, or are overdue.
- Set Up Recurring Invoices: Automate billing for regular customers.
- Send Payment Reminders: Gently nudge clients to pay outstanding invoices.

From the dashboard, click on the + New button and select Invoice to create and send professional invoices in just a few clicks.

2. Expense Tracking

QBO's expense tracking tools help you manage your business's spending effortlessly:

- Categorize Expenses: Automatically or manually assign transactions to categories.
- Attach Receipts: Use the mobile app to capture and attach receipts to expenses.
- Monitor Spending: Keep an eye on where your money is going with detailed reports.

The Expenses tab provides access to all recorded transactions, making it easy to review and manage your business's outflows.

3. Bank Reconciliation

Reconciliation ensures that your books match your bank accounts, and QBO simplifies this process:

- Automatically import transactions from linked accounts.
- Match imported transactions with entries in QuickBooks.

- Identify and address discrepancies quickly.

The Banking menu lets you review and reconcile transactions, ensuring accuracy in your financial records.

4. Reports

QuickBooks Online offers a variety of reports to help you understand your business's performance. Some key reports include:

- Profit and Loss Statement: A summary of income and expenses.
- Balance Sheet: An overview of assets, liabilities, and equity.
- Cash Flow Report: A detailed breakdown of cash inflows and outflows.

From the Reports menu, you can customize and generate reports that suit your specific needs, helping you make data-driven decisions.

5. Cash Flow Management

The Cash Flow Planner is a standout feature for managing your business's liquidity:

- Forecast cash inflows and outflows based on historical data.
- Adjust for future expenses or revenue changes.
- Identify potential cash shortfalls in advance.

Accessible from the dashboard, the Cash Flow Planner ensures you're always prepared for financial fluctuations.

6. Sales Tax Management

If your business collects sales tax, QuickBooks Online simplifies compliance:

- Track Sales Tax: Automatically calculate and record sales tax based on location.
- Generate Sales Tax Reports: Summarize collected taxes for easy filing.

- Set Up Multiple Rates: Configure rates for different jurisdictions.

From the Taxes menu, you can manage your sales tax settings and ensure compliance with local regulations.

7. Payroll Integration

For businesses with employees, QuickBooks Online integrates seamlessly with QuickBooks Payroll:

- Calculate Wages: Automate payroll calculations, including deductions and taxes.
- Pay Employees: Set up direct deposits for hassle-free payments.
- File Taxes: Handle payroll tax filings and compliance requirements.

The Payroll menu lets you manage employee payments and track payroll-related expenses efficiently.

8. Mobile Accessibility

The QuickBooks Online mobile app extends the power of the dashboard to your smartphone or tablet. With the app, you can:

- Create and send invoices on the go.
- Capture and categorize expenses using your phone's camera.
- Monitor your financial performance anytime, anywhere.

This level of accessibility ensures you're always connected to your business finances.

To get the most out of your QuickBooks Online dashboard, follow these tips:

1. Customize Your View: Use filters to adjust date ranges and focus on the metrics that matter most to you.
2. Set Alerts: Enable notifications for overdue invoices, uncategorized transactions, or low cash flow.
3. Review Regularly: Spend a few minutes each day reviewing your dashboard to stay informed about your business's financial health.

4. Leverage Insights: Use the trends and data displayed on the dashboard to make informed decisions about spending, investments, or pricing strategies.

While the dashboard is designed to be user-friendly, there are a few common mistakes to watch out for:

- Ignoring Uncategorized Transactions: Always review and categorize transactions promptly to avoid errors in your reports.
- Overlooking Updates: Regularly refresh the dashboard to ensure you're working with the latest data.
- Relying Solely on Visuals: While charts and graphs provide helpful summaries, dive into detailed reports for deeper insights.

By staying proactive, you can avoid these pitfalls and maintain accurate, up-to-date records.

The QuickBooks Online dashboard is more than just a starting point; it's a powerful tool that puts your business's financial health at your fingertips. From tracking income and expenses to generating reports and managing cash flow, the dashboard integrates seamlessly with QBO's essential features, giving you the tools to make informed decisions and streamline your bookkeeping processes. By mastering the dashboard and its capabilities, you'll be equipped to manage your finances confidently and effectively, no matter where your business takes you.

CHAPTER 2

CUSTOMIZING QUICKBOOKS FOR YOUR BUSINESS

One of the most powerful features of Quick-Books Online (QBO) is its ability to adapt to the unique needs of your business. Unlike one-size-fits-all accounting tools, QBO allows you to customize settings, forms, and workflows to align with your specific requirements. By tailoring the platform, you can streamline your processes, enhance your brand identity, and ensure that every aspect of your bookkeeping supports your goals.

This chapter is all about making Quick-Books Online work for you. Whether it's adjusting default settings, designing professional invoices, managing user roles, or integrating third-party apps, customization is key to maximizing efficiency and making the software feel like a natural extension of your business.

Every business operates differently, and your accounting software should reflect that. Customizing QuickBooks Online allows you to:

- Save Time: By automating repetitive tasks and aligning workflows with your operations.
- Improve Accuracy: By setting up default options that reduce manual errors.
- Strengthen Branding: Through personalized forms and templates that showcase your professional identity.
- Enhance Security: By managing user permissions to ensure sensitive data remains protected.

By investing time in customizing your QuickBooks account upfront, you'll save countless hours down the road while creating a system that's tailored to your needs.

In this chapter, we'll guide you through four key areas of customization:

1. Tailoring QuickBooks Settings to Fit Your Needs

QuickBooks Online offers a variety of settings that can be adjusted to suit your business operations. From payment terms to default tax rates, we'll explore how to configure these settings for maximum efficiency and accuracy.

2. Personalizing Invoices, Forms, and Templates

Your invoices and forms are an extension of your brand. We'll show you how to customize templates with your logo, color scheme, and unique fields to create a professional image that leaves a lasting impression on clients.

3. Managing Users and Assigning Permissions

If you work with a team or an accountant, managing user roles is crucial. QuickBooks allows you to assign specific permissions to ensure that everyone has access to the tools they need—without compromising sensitive financial data.

4. Integrating QuickBooks with Apps and Tools for Efficiency

QuickBooks Online integrates seamlessly with a variety of third-party apps, from payment processors to e-commerce platforms. We'll explore how these integrations can save you time, reduce errors, and provide a more comprehensive view of your business operations.

Customization isn't just about aesthetics; it's about creating a system that simplifies your work, enhances your workflows, and aligns with your business's unique needs. By the end of this chapter, you'll have a fully personalized QuickBooks Online account that reflects your business's personality and supports your day-to-day operations. Let's dive in and make QuickBooks truly yours.

Tailoring QuickBooks Settings to Fit Your Needs

Customizing the settings in QuickBooks Online (QBO) is one of the most effective ways to streamline your financial workflows and ensure the software works seamlessly with your business processes. Tailored settings save time, reduce errors, and enhance the overall efficiency of your bookkeeping. This chapter will guide you step-by-step through the customization options available in QBO, from setting up payment terms and tax preferences to automating workflows.

The General Settings in QBO lay the foundation for your account. These options allow you to specify preferences for date formats, numbers, and time zones, ensuring the platform aligns with your regional requirements.

How to Customize General Settings:

1. Navigate to the Settings menu (gear icon) and select Account and Settings.
2. Go to the Company tab to edit:
   - » Business Name and Logo: Ensure your business name appears consistently across forms. Upload your logo for branding.
   - » Company Contact Information: Add your address, phone number, and email so customers can easily reach you.
   - » Time Zone: Set the correct time zone to ensure accurate timestamps on invoices and transactions.

Benefits:

- Accurate regional settings prevent formatting issues on forms.
- Branded contact information boosts professionalism and credibility.

QuickBooks allows you to customize how you record sales, handle payments, and generate invoices. These settings impact how clients interact with your business and how efficiently you track revenue.

How to Configure Sales Preferences:

1. Go to Settings > Account and Settings > Sales.
2. Adjust the following options:
   - » Custom Fields: Add fields for unique invoice details, like PO numbers or project codes.
   - » Preferred Invoice Terms: Set default payment terms (e.g., Net 30) to streamline billing.
   - » Discounts and Deposits: Enable

these features if you offer customer discounts or accept deposits.

» Messages: Customize email templates for invoices and sales receipts to maintain consistent communication.

Benefits:

- Personalized invoices strengthen your brand image.
- Default payment terms reduce confusion and improve cash flow predictability.

Accurate expense tracking is critical for financial management, and QBO offers several options to automate and streamline this process.

How to Customize Expense Settings:

1. Go to Settings > Account and Settings > Expenses.
2. Enable or adjust:

   » Show Item Details on Expense and Purchase Forms: Useful for tracking inventory or itemized costs.

   » Track Expenses by Customer: Assign expenses to specific clients for better project profitability insights.

   » Mark Up Expenses: Automatically add markups to billable expenses.

   » Default Payment Accounts: Select which bank accounts to use for paying bills.

Benefits:

- Enables accurate cost tracking and easier reconciliation with bank statements.
- Simplifies client billing by linking expenses directly to projects.

If your business collects sales tax or pays taxes on goods and services, configuring tax settings in QuickBooks is essential for compliance and accuracy.

How to Customize Tax Settings:

1. Navigate to the Taxes menu and click Set Up Sales Tax.
2. Follow the prompts to:

   » Enter your tax agency and tax rates based on your business location.

   » Add multiple tax rates for different jurisdictions if needed.

3. Review the Account and Settings > Taxes tab to enable automatic tracking for taxable and non-taxable items.

Benefits:

- Accurate sales tax calculations simplify tax filing and compliance.
- Avoids costly errors and penalties associated with incorrect tax reporting.

Automation is one of QBO's most valuable features, saving time and ensuring consistency in your financial processes.

How to Automate Workflows:

1. Enable Recurring Transactions:

   » Go to Settings > Recurring Transactions.

   » Create templates for invoices, bills, or journal entries that occur regularly.

2. Set Up Reminders:

   » Navigate to Settings > Reminders.

   » Configure alerts for overdue invoices, unpaid bills, or other critical tasks.

3. Automate Bank Feeds:

   » Link your bank accounts to QBO for automatic transaction imports.

Benefits:

- Eliminates manual entry, reducing errors.
- Keeps you on top of deadlines with automated reminders.

If your business operates internationally or deals with multiple currencies, enabling QBO's multi-currency feature is essential.

How to Enable Multi-Currency:

1. Go to Settings > Advanced > Currency.
2. Turn on Multi-Currency and add the currencies you'll transact in.
3. Assign default currencies to customers and vendors.

Benefits:

- Tracks exchange rates automatically.
- Simplifies accounting for international transactions.

QuickBooks supports multiple payment methods to provide flexibility for you and your customers.

How to Configure Payment Settings:

1. Go to Settings > Payments.
2. Enable payment processing for credit cards, ACH transfers, or PayPal.
3. Integrate with third-party payment apps if needed.

Benefits:

- Speeds up payments, improving cash flow.
- Offers customers more convenient ways to pay.

Notifications in QuickBooks keep you informed about important events, such as overdue invoices or approaching deadlines.

How to Adjust Notifications:

1. Navigate to Settings > Notifications.
2. Choose which notifications you want to receive, such as:
   » Payment reminders for overdue invoices.
   » Alerts for reconciliation discrepancies.

Benefits:

- Keeps you proactive with financial tasks.
- Reduces the risk of missing critical deadlines.

Advanced settings allow you to fine-tune how QBO records and displays data.

How to Customize Advanced Settings:

1. Go to Settings > Account and Settings > Advanced.
2. Adjust:
   » Fiscal Year Start: Set the start of your fiscal year for accurate reporting.
   » Chart of Accounts Numbers: Enable this feature if you prefer numbered accounts.
   » Automation Preferences: Toggle options for automatically applying credits or categorizing transactions.

Benefits:

- Provides control over data presentation and organization.
- Enhances reporting accuracy.

Although QuickBooks Online automatically saves your data in the cloud, you can enable additional safeguards.

How to Enable Backups:

1. Use QBO's Online Backup and Restore tool.
2. Alternatively, export reports and data manually:
   » Go to Settings > Export Data and download key files.

Benefits:

- Ensures data integrity and recovery in case of errors or cyberattacks.
- Provides peace of mind knowing your records are safe.

Customizing QuickBooks settings creates a platform that fits your unique business processes. It allows you to:

- Save Time: Automation and defaults reduce repetitive tasks.
- Enhance Accuracy: Pre-configured options minimize errors.
- Boost Efficiency: Custom workflows streamline operations.
- Maintain Compliance: Tax and reporting settings ensure you meet regulatory requirements.

While customizing QuickBooks is straightforward, avoid these common errors:

- Skipping Important Preferences: Failing to configure tax settings or expense tracking can lead to inaccuracies.
- Overcomplicating Categories: Keep your Chart of Accounts and expense categories simple and relevant.
- Ignoring Automation: Not using automation features can lead to missed opportunities for efficiency.

Tailoring QuickBooks settings to fit your business is an investment in time-saving efficiency, accuracy, and professionalism. By taking the time to customize everything from payment terms to tax settings, you'll create a streamlined accounting system that supports your unique needs. With your settings optimized, you're now ready to dive deeper into personalizing forms and templates to reflect your brand's identity—covered in the next section of this chapter.

Personalizing Invoices, Forms, and Templates

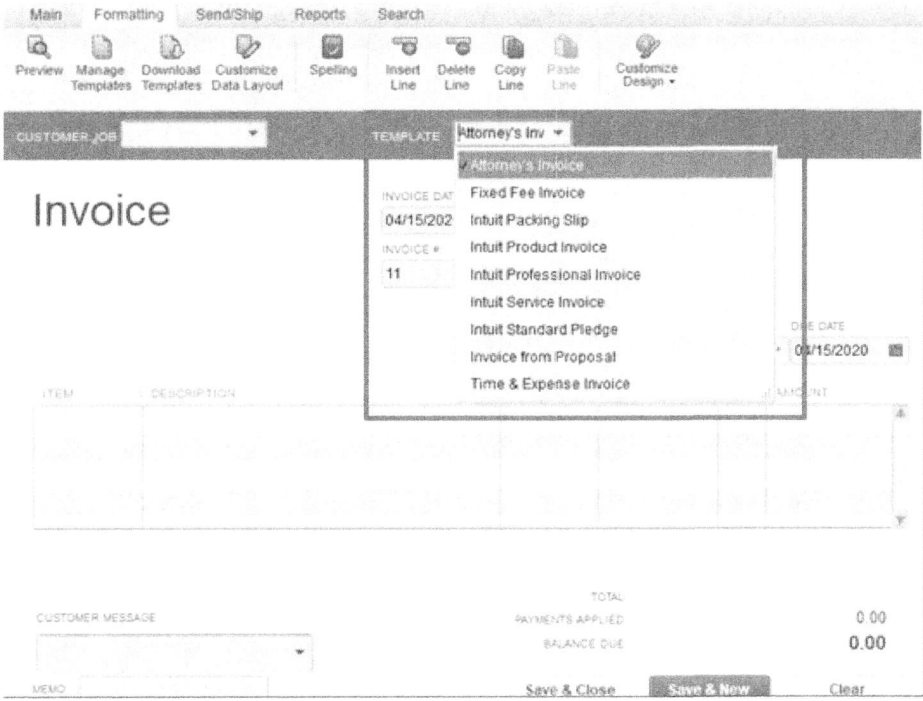

Your invoices, forms, and templates are more than just documents—they are a reflection of your business's professionalism and brand identity. In QuickBooks Online (QBO), customizing these elements is a simple yet impactful way to leave a lasting impression on clients while streamlining your workflows. Personalization not only enhances your brand visibility but also ensures your documents align with your unique operational needs.

This chapter will guide you through the process of personalizing invoices, estimates, sales receipts, and other templates in QBO. By the end, you'll have polished, professional documents that reinforce your brand while making financial transactions seamless.

Personalizing your invoices and forms serves several important purposes:

- Brand Identity: A customized invoice with your logo and colors reinforces your brand image and professionalism.
- Client Clarity: Including all necessary details reduces client confusion and improves payment efficiency.
- Operational Efficiency: Default templates with pre-set fields save time and ensure consistency across transactions.

With these benefits in mind, let's dive into how to customize your invoices and other forms in QuickBooks Online.

Invoices are one of the most commonly used forms in QBO. Customizing them ensures they represent your business effectively.

Step-by-Step Process:

1. Access Customization Settings:

- » Go to Settings (gear icon) > Custom Form Styles.
- » Click the New Style button and select Invoice.

2. Choose a Template:
   - » QBO offers several template designs. Select one that fits your business's aesthetic.
   - » Templates can be previewed to see how they'll look to clients.

3. Add Your Logo and Branding:
   - » Upload your business logo and choose its placement (e.g., top left or center).
   - » Pick colors that align with your brand identity. For example, match your invoice's accent colors to your website or logo.

4. Customize Fields:
   - » Select the fields to include, such as:
   - Invoice number
   - Client name and address
   - Payment terms (e.g., Net 15, Net 30)
   - Due date and payment instructions
   - » Add custom fields if needed, like "Project Name" or "PO Number."

5. Edit Content and Layout:
   - » Adjust the header, footer, and table sections.
   - » Add a personalized message, such as "Thank you for your business!" in the footer.
   - » Organize line items to clearly display descriptions, quantities, and amounts.

6. Save and Apply Defaults:
   - » Save your customized invoice as the default template for future transactions.
   - » Assign the template to specific customers if you use different styles for different clients.

Invoices are just one type of form you'll use in QuickBooks Online. Here's how to customize additional forms to fit your business:

Estimates:

Estimates are used to provide clients with a quote or cost breakdown before work begins. Customizing them adds professionalism to the pre-sale process.

- Follow the same steps as invoice customization.
- Include a note clarifying that the estimate is non-binding or subject to change based on specific terms.

Sales Receipts:

Sales receipts are issued when a transaction is completed. Personalize them to include:

- Payment method (e.g., credit card, cash, check).
- A clear acknowledgment of payment, reinforcing transparency.

Credit Memos:

Credit memos reflect adjustments or refunds. Customize them to include:

- The reason for the credit.
- Clear line-item breakdowns for transparency.

Purchase Orders:

If you work with vendors, customizing purchase orders (POs) ensures they align with your business's communication standards. Add:

- Vendor-specific notes or terms.
- Detailed descriptions of items or services ordered.

Custom fields allow you to include unique information that's relevant to your business or clients. This feature is especially useful for businesses with specialized needs, such as tracking project codes or providing additional instructions.

How to Add Custom Fields:

1. Go to Settings > Custom Form Styles.
2. Click Content and select a section (e.g., header, table, footer) to add the field.
3. Name the field (e.g., "Job Site Address" or "Client Reference Number").
4. Determine if the field is mandatory or optional.

Applications of Custom Fields:

- Add project names or job site locations for contractors.
- Include tax IDs or VAT numbers for international clients.
- Note additional terms or conditions.

Whether your clients receive invoices electronically or in print, ensuring the format is clear and professional is crucial.

For Digital Use:

- Use concise layouts to reduce scrolling.
- Ensure all clickable elements (e.g., payment links) work properly.
- Include your email address or website in the footer for quick client access.

For Print Use:

- Test how the form looks when printed, ensuring it fits on standard paper sizes.
- Use clear fonts and sufficient spacing to improve readability.

One of the best ways to speed up payments is by providing clear, accessible payment instructions directly on your invoices or receipts.

Payment Options to Include:

- Bank Transfers: Include account details for direct deposits.
- Credit Cards: Enable online payment processing through QBO or integrated payment apps.
- PayPal or Venmo: Add links for digital payments.

How to Set Up Payment Links:

1. Navigate to Settings > Payments.
2. Enable payment options and link accounts (e.g., credit card processor, PayPal).
3. Include the payment link directly in the invoice's footer or as a clickable button.

Benefits:

- Clients can pay directly from the invoice, reducing delays.
- Clear instructions prevent confusion about accepted payment methods.

Before rolling out your customized forms, test them to ensure they look and function as intended.

How to Test:

1. Create a sample invoice or form.
2. Send it to yourself or a team member to review the layout, fields, and overall appearance.
3. Print a physical copy to confirm formatting for offline use.

Checklist for Review:

- Is the logo displayed clearly and in the correct size?
- Are all necessary fields included and aligned properly?
- Is the template easy to read and navigate?

For a cohesive brand experience, ensure all forms—from invoices to purchase orders—share consistent design elements. Use:

- The same logo and color scheme.
- Similar layouts for tables and headers.
- Uniform fonts and text sizes.

Consistency reinforces professionalism and makes it easier for clients and vendors to identify your business documents.

As your business evolves, your document needs may change. QBO makes it easy to update templates as needed.

Reasons to Update:

- Adding new branding elements, such as a rebranded logo.
- Changing terms or conditions for specific services.
- Adapting to new regulations, such as tax compliance updates.

How to Update:

1. Return to Custom Form Styles.
2. Select the template you wish to edit.
3. Make changes and save the updated version.

For businesses with recurring clients or transactions, setting default templates saves time and ensures consistency.

How to Set Defaults:

1. Go to Settings > Advanced.
2. Assign specific templates for different transaction types (e.g., invoices, estimates, sales receipts).
3. Save default settings for repeat use.

Customizing your invoices, forms, and templates in QuickBooks Online is an essential step in creating a professional and efficient financial workflow. By personalizing these documents, you not only reinforce your brand identity but also simplify your operations and improve client communication. From branded invoices to tailored purchase orders, your forms will reflect the professionalism and care you bring to every aspect of your business. Take the time to customize today and enjoy the benefits of a polished and streamlined accounting system.

Managing Users and Assigning Permissions in QuickBooks Online

As your business grows, you may find yourself needing to collaborate with others, such as employees, accountants, or bookkeepers, to manage your QuickBooks Online (QBO) account. Granting access to your financial data is an important decision that requires careful control and oversight. QuickBooks Online allows you to add users and assign permissions based on their roles and responsibilities, ensuring your sensitive information remains secure while enabling effective teamwork.

This chapter will explore how to manage users, assign appropriate permissions, and create a system that safeguards your financial data while streamlining collaboration. Whether you're inviting a trusted accountant or delegating tasks to employees, QuickBooks makes it easy to customize access levels to suit your needs.

Managing users and permissions in QuickBooks Online is essential for several reasons:

- Data Security: Limiting access to sensitive financial information reduces the risk of data breaches or unauthorized changes.
- Accountability: By assigning permissions, you can track which user performs specific actions, ensuring transparency and accountability.
- Efficient Collaboration: Customizing permissions ensures users have access to the tools they need without being overwhelmed by irrelevant features.
- Compliance: Controlling access helps maintain compliance with financial and privacy regulations.

Understanding the importance of user management sets the foundation for building a secure and collaborative QuickBooks environment.

QuickBooks Online offers several user roles, each designed for specific tasks. Understanding these roles helps you decide what access to grant based on a user's responsibilities.

User Types:

1. Admin:
   » Full access to all features, settings, and financial data.
   » Can add, remove, and manage other users.
   » Ideal for business owners or primary account managers.

2. Standard User:
   » Access can be customized to include specific features such as sales, expenses, or reports.
   » Does not have access to manage other users or change account settings.
   » Suitable for employees handling specific tasks like invoicing or payroll.

3. Time Tracking Only:
   » Can only track and submit their time for payroll or billing purposes.
   » Ideal for contractors or hourly employees.

4. Reports Only:
   » Access to view reports without the ability to modify data.
   » Useful for business advisors or stakeholders who need financial insights but not editing capabilities.

5. Accountant:
   » Special access designed for external accountants or bookkeepers.
   » Can view and manage all financial data but cannot manage users.

Inviting new users to QuickBooks Online is a straightforward process. Follow these steps to ensure each user has the appropriate access level.

Step-by-Step Process:

1. Navigate to Manage Users:
   » Click the Settings (gear icon) in the top-right corner.
   » Select Manage Users under the Your Company section.

2. Add a New User:
   » Click the Add User button.
   » Choose the user type (Admin, Standard, Time Tracking, Reports Only, or Accountant).

3. Customize Permissions:
   » For Standard Users, customize access by selecting the areas they can access (e.g., Customers, Sales, Vendors, or Reports).
   » Set restrictions if needed, such as viewing without editing or limiting access to specific features.

4. Enter User Details:
   » Provide the user's email address and name.
   » Send the invitation via email. The user will receive a link to accept and set up their account.

5. Review and Confirm:
   » Review the user's access permissions and click Save to finalize the invitation.

Granting the right permissions is critical for protecting your data while ensuring users can perform their tasks effectively. Let's explore how to assign permissions based on common roles.

1. Accountant or Bookkeeper:

- Access Needed:
  » Full access to financial reports, account reconciliation, and tax tools.
- Permissions to Grant:
  » Accountant role (preconfigured for external professionals).
- Why: This role provides comprehen-

sive financial access without admin privileges.

2. Sales Team:

- Access Needed:
  - » Ability to create invoices, track payments, and generate sales reports.
- Permissions to Grant:
  - » Standard User with access to Customers and Sales.
  - » Limit editing of reports or expense-related data.
- Why: Ensures focus on revenue tasks without accessing unrelated financial areas.

3. Payroll Specialist:

- Access Needed:
  - » Access to payroll setup, employee data, and payroll reports.
- Permissions to Grant:
  - » Standard User with access to Payroll and Employees only.
- Why: Provides necessary payroll access while protecting sensitive customer and sales data.

4. Contractors or Hourly Employees:

- Access Needed:
  - » Ability to track and submit time for payroll or billing purposes.
- Permissions to Grant:
  - » Time Tracking Only.
- Why: Restricts access to core financial data while allowing accurate time entry.

Over time, user roles and responsibilities may change. QuickBooks Online makes it easy to update permissions or remove users as needed.

How to Edit User Roles:

1. Navigate to Settings > Manage Users.
2. Select the user whose role you want to edit.
3. Click Edit next to their name.
4. Adjust their permissions or change their role type.
5. Save the changes to update their access.

Removing Users:

If an employee leaves the company or an accountant's services are no longer needed:

1. Go to Manage Users.
2. Locate the user and click Delete next to their name.
3. Confirm the removal to revoke their access.

QuickBooks Online provides tools to monitor user activity, ensuring accountability and transparency.

Audit Log:

- Go to Settings > Audit Log to view a detailed history of user actions.
- See who logged in, edited transactions, or made changes to settings.
- Filter the log by user, date, or activity type for detailed analysis.

Benefits of the Audit Log:

- Identifies errors or unauthorized changes quickly.
- Ensures compliance with company policies.
- Provides a clear record for resolving disputes or tracking issues.

To ensure your QuickBooks account remains secure and efficient, follow these best practices:

1. Grant Access on a Need-to-Know Basis:
   - » Only provide access to the features necessary for a user's role.
   - » Avoid granting full access unless absolutely required.

2. Review User Access Regularly:
   - » Periodically review user roles and permissions to ensure they align with current responsibilities.
   - » Update roles as job functions change.

3. Use the Accountant Role for Financial Professionals:
   - » Instead of creating a new user, use the dedicated Accountant role for external accountants or bookkeepers.

4. Enable Two-Factor Authentication (2FA):
   - » Add an extra layer of security by enabling 2FA for all users. This ensures only authorized individuals can access your account.

5. Remove Inactive Users:
   - » Regularly audit your list of users and remove those who no longer need access.

While managing users in QuickBooks Online is straightforward, avoid these common pitfalls:

- Overgranting Permissions: Giving users more access than necessary can expose sensitive data.
- Failing to Monitor Activity: Regularly review the Audit Log to track user actions.

- Not Revoking Access: Immediately remove access for users who leave the company to prevent unauthorized logins.

Effectively managing users and permissions in QuickBooks Online is a critical aspect of protecting your business's financial data while enabling collaboration. By understanding the different user roles, assigning permissions strategically, and regularly reviewing access, you create a secure and efficient environment for your team. Whether you're working with employees, contractors, or external accountants, QuickBooks Online's flexible user management tools ensure that everyone has the access they need—nothing more, nothing less. With these practices in place, your financial data remains safe, transparent, and well-organized.

Integrating QuickBooks with Apps and Tools for Efficiency

Managing a small business involves juggling various tasks—tracking sales, managing payroll, overseeing inventory, and communicating with clients. While QuickBooks Online (QBO) is a robust accounting platform on its own, its true potential is unlocked through integrations with third-party apps and tools. By connecting QBO to other software, you can automate workflows, eliminate manual data entry, and gain a comprehensive view of your business operations.

This chapter will explore the benefits of integrating QuickBooks Online with external tools and provide a step-by-step guide to setting up integrations. We'll also highlight some of the best apps for specific business needs, ensuring you maximize efficiency and productivity.

Integrating QBO with other apps allows you to create a seamless flow of information between platforms, reducing redundancies and saving time. Here's why integrations are essential:

Efficiency:

- Automatically sync data between platforms, such as sales figures from an e-commerce site or payroll data from a time-tracking app.
- Streamline repetitive tasks like invoicing, inventory updates, or expense tracking.

Accuracy:

- Eliminate manual data entry, reducing errors and ensuring your financial records are up-to-date.
- Consistent data across platforms enhances reporting and decision-making.

Comprehensive View:

- Consolidate data from multiple tools into QBO, providing a single source of truth for your business's financial health.
- Generate detailed reports that combine data from multiple systems.

Scalability:

- As your business grows, integrations ensure your systems remain efficient, supporting new workflows and increased volumes of data.

Connecting QuickBooks Online to third-party apps is straightforward, thanks to its App Marketplace and user-friendly setup process.

Step-by-Step Process:

1. Access the App Marketplace:
   » Log in to your QBO account and click on the Apps menu in the left-hand navigation bar.
2. Browse or Search for Apps:
   » Use the search bar to find specific apps (e.g., Shopify, PayPal, or TSheets).
   » Browse by category, such as e-commerce, time tracking, or expense management.
3. Read Reviews and Features:
   » Click on an app to view its features, user reviews, and pricing.
   » Confirm that the app integrates with your version of QBO.
4. Install the App:
   » Click Get App Now and follow the prompts to connect it to your QBO account.
   » You may need to log in to the app's account or grant permissions to enable the integration.
5. Configure Settings:
   » Customize integration settings based on your business needs (e.g., syncing frequency, data fields to import/export).
   » Test the integration to ensure data flows correctly between platforms.
6. Monitor and Optimize:
   » Periodically review the integration's performance and make adjustments as needed.

QuickBooks Online supports a wide range of third-party apps, catering to various aspects of business operations. Here are some of the best apps for specific needs:

1. E-Commerce:

If you sell products online, integrating QBO with your e-commerce platform is essential for tracking sales, managing inventory, and automating tax calculations.

- Shopify: Syncs sales, refunds, and fees directly with QBO. Automatically tracks inventory and generates sales reports.
- WooCommerce: Integrates seamlessly with QBO to manage orders, track sales tax, and update inventory levels.
- Amazon Seller Central: Imports transactions from your Amazon store, including sales, fees, and reimbursements.

Benefits:

- Simplifies revenue tracking across platforms.
- Reduces manual entry of sales data.
- Ensures accurate inventory and tax reporting.

2. Payment Processing:

QuickBooks Online integrates with payment processors to streamline invoicing and payment collection.

- PayPal: Syncs transactions, including sales, fees, and refunds. Adds PayPal as a payment method for your invoices.
- Stripe: Automatically records payments and fees from Stripe transactions in QBO.
- Square: Imports sales data and fees from your Square POS system.

Benefits:

- Speeds up payment reconciliation.
- Provides customers with multiple payment options.
- Automatically accounts for transaction fees.

3. Time Tracking and Payroll:

For businesses with hourly employees or contractors, time-tracking apps simplify payroll and project billing.

- TSheets by QuickBooks: Tracks employee hours, integrates with payroll, and assigns time to specific projects.
- Clockify: Allows teams to log work hours and syncs time entries with QBO for accurate payroll processing.
- Gusto: Handles payroll, benefits, and HR tasks while syncing payroll data with QBO.

Benefits:

- Ensures accurate time tracking for payroll and client billing.
- Reduces administrative overhead for HR tasks.
- Links labor costs to specific projects for profitability analysis.

4. Expense Management:

Expense tracking apps help manage receipts, categorize expenses, and monitor spending in real-time.

- Expensify: Automatically imports and categorizes expenses, tracks mileage, and generates reports for reimbursements.
- Receipt Bank: Captures receipts and invoices, then syncs them with QBO for seamless expense tracking.
- Fyle: Integrates employee expense reports directly into QBO for approval and reconciliation.

Benefits:

- Automates receipt capture and categorization.
- Improves accuracy in expense tracking and reporting.
- Simplifies reimbursement workflows.

5. Inventory Management:

For businesses that manage physical products, inventory management apps help track stock levels and streamline reordering.

- SOS Inventory: Tracks inventory, orders, and manufacturing workflows while syncing with QBO.
- Fishbowl: Handles advanced inventory needs, such as multi-location tracking and barcode scanning.
- TradeGecko: Offers inventory optimization and demand forecasting integrated with QBO.

Benefits:

- Ensures accurate stock levels and avoids overstocking or stockouts.
- Links inventory costs to financial reports for better decision-making.
- Streamlines order fulfillment processes.

6. CRM (Customer Relationship Management):

Integrating a CRM system with QBO ensures customer data and financial records stay in sync.

- HubSpot: Tracks customer interactions and syncs invoice and payment data with QBO.
- Salesforce: Connects sales pipelines with financial data, automating invoicing and forecasting.
- Zoho CRM: Links customer data, sales transactions, and payments with QBO.

Benefits:

- Provides a holistic view of customer relationships.
- Automates invoicing and follow-ups.
- Aligns sales and accounting data for better decision-making.

To ensure seamless integration and efficient workflows, follow these best practices:

1. Start with Essential Apps:
   » Focus on tools that address your immediate needs, such as e-commerce, payments, or payroll, before expanding integrations.

2. Test Integrations Thoroughly:
   » Run test transactions to verify that data flows correctly between platforms. Identify and resolve errors early.

3. Monitor Performance:
   » Regularly review integrations to ensure they remain functional after software updates or changes.

4. Maintain Consistent Data Entry:
   » Use consistent naming conventions and categories across platforms to avoid mismatched records.

5. Train Your Team:
   » Ensure employees understand how integrations work and how to use them effectively.

While integrations can significantly enhance your efficiency, there are common mistakes to watch out for:

- Overloading Integrations: Avoid connecting too many apps at once, as this can complicate workflows.
- Neglecting Updates: Ensure all integrated apps are updated regularly to avoid compatibility issues.
- Inconsistent Data Mapping: Carefully configure data fields to avoid mismatched or duplicate entries.

Integrating QuickBooks Online with third-party apps and tools is one of the most effective ways to streamline your operations and enhance efficiency. Whether you're syncing sales data from an e-commerce platform, automating payroll with a time-tracking app, or managing inventory across multiple locations, integrations simplify workflows and provide a comprehensive view of your business's financial health. By strategically selecting and maintaining integrations, you can save time, reduce errors, and focus on growing your business with confidence.

CHAPTER 3

MANAGING YOUR CHART OF ACCOUNTS

The Chart of Accounts is the backbone of your financial management system in QuickBooks Online (QBO). It's a comprehensive list of all the accounts your business uses to categorize its financial transactions. From tracking income and expenses to managing assets and liabilities, the Chart of Accounts provides the structure necessary for accurate record-keeping and insightful reporting.

In this chapter, we'll explore the purpose of the Chart of Accounts, how it organizes your financial data, and why it's essential for maintaining a healthy and transparent financial system. Whether you're setting up your accounts for the first time or fine-tuning an existing setup, managing your Chart of Accounts effectively can save you time, reduce errors, and provide a clearer picture of your business's financial health.

Every transaction your business makes—whether it's paying a bill, receiving income, or purchasing supplies—needs a place in your accounting records. The Chart of Accounts serves as the filing system for these transactions, grouping them into categories such as income, expenses, assets, liabilities, and equity. This organization is crucial for:

- Accurate Financial Reporting: A well-structured Chart of Accounts makes it easy to generate reports like profit and loss statements and balance sheets.
- Tax Compliance: Properly categorized transactions simplify tax preparation and help ensure compliance with regulations.
- Informed Decision-Making: Clear financial data empowers you to make smarter business decisions based on your revenue, expenses, and cash flow.

Without a properly managed Chart of Accounts, your financial data can quickly become disorganized, leading to reporting errors, inefficiencies, and costly mistakes.

In this chapter, we'll guide you through the essentials of managing your Chart of Accounts in QuickBooks Online:

1. Understanding the Chart of Accounts and Its Purpose

We'll start with the basics, explaining what the Chart of Accounts is, how it works, and why it's structured the way it is. By understanding its components—such as asset, liability, income, and expense accounts—you'll gain clarity on how it supports your business's financial tracking.

2. Adding, Editing, and Organizing Accounts for Your Business

Next, we'll walk you through creating and customizing accounts to reflect your business's specific needs. You'll learn how to:

- Add new accounts for unique income or expense categories.

- Edit existing accounts to better align with your operations.
- Organize accounts to ensure your financial reports are clear and actionable.

3. Linking Bank and Credit Card Accounts

Connecting your bank and credit card accounts to QuickBooks Online is a game-changer for managing your finances. We'll show you how to link these accounts for seamless transaction syncing, saving you time and improving accuracy.

4. Troubleshooting Common Chart of Account Issues

Finally, we'll address common challenges, such as duplicate accounts, miscategorized transactions, and discrepancies between bank statements and your records. You'll learn practical solutions to keep your Chart of Accounts clean and functional.

Managing your Chart of Accounts effectively is about more than just categorizing transactions—it's about creating a solid foundation for your business's financial management. With a well-organized Chart of Accounts, you'll have the clarity and confidence to monitor your performance, meet compliance requirements, and plan for the future.

Let's dive in and unlock the full potential of your Chart of Accounts, turning it into a powerful tool for your business's success.

Understanding the Chart of Accounts and Its Purpose

The Chart of Accounts (COA) is the cornerstone of any business's accounting system. It serves as an organized framework for categorizing all financial transactions, ensuring that every dollar spent or earned is recorded in the right place. In QuickBooks Online

(QBO), the COA provides the structure needed for accurate record-keeping, clear financial reporting, and insightful decision-making.

This chapter dives into the Chart of Accounts, exploring its purpose, structure, and importance in financial management. Whether you're a small business owner or an accountant, understanding the COA is essential for maintaining a healthy financial system.

The Chart of Accounts is a list of all the accounts a business uses to track its financial transactions. Each account represents a category, such as income, expenses, assets, liabilities, or equity. These accounts serve as a filing system, grouping similar transactions together for easier analysis and reporting.

For example:

Sales Revenue: Tracks income from selling products or services.

Office Supplies: Categorizes expenses for pens, paper, and other office essentials.

Bank Accounts: Records balances and transactions in your business checking or savings accounts.

In QuickBooks Online, the COA is preconfigured with default accounts based on your business type. You can customize it to meet your specific needs, adding new accounts or renaming existing ones.

The Chart of Accounts serves multiple purposes, each crucial for effective financial management.

1. Organizing Financial Data

The COA organizes financial transactions into logical categories, making it easier to track where money is coming from and where it's going. By grouping similar transactions, you can quickly identify patterns, spot discrepancies, and understand your financial performance.

2. Supporting Accurate Financial Reporting

A well-structured COA ensures that your financial reports, such as the Profit and Loss Statement, Balance Sheet, and Cash Flow Statement, are accurate and meaningful. These reports rely on correctly categorized data to provide insights into your business's profitability, assets, and liabilities.

3. Simplifying Tax Preparation

Tax compliance becomes much easier when your transactions are properly categorized. The COA allows you to track deductible expenses, taxable income, and other tax-related data in one place. This reduces the risk of errors and ensures you're claiming all eligible deductions.

4. Enabling Informed Decision-Making

With organized financial data, you can make informed decisions about your business. For instance, you can:

- Identify which products or services generate the most revenue.
- Analyze spending patterns to cut unnecessary costs.
- Forecast cash flow needs based on historical trends.

The Chart of Accounts is divided into five main account types, each serving a specific role in tracking your business's financial activity.

1. Assets

Asset accounts track what your business owns, such as cash, inventory, equipment, or accounts receivable.

- Examples:
  - » Checking Account
  - » Accounts Receivable (money owed to you by customers)
  - » Inventory
  - » Equipment or Vehicles
- Purpose: Asset accounts reflect the resources your business has available to operate and grow.

2. Liabilities

Liability accounts track what your business owes, such as loans, credit card balances, or unpaid bills.

- Examples:
  - » Accounts Payable (bills you need to pay)
  - » Credit Card
  - » Loans Payable
  - » Payroll Liabilities
- Purpose: Liability accounts show your financial obligations and help you manage cash flow to meet those commitments.

3. Equity

Equity accounts represent the owner's investment in the business and retained earnings.

- Examples:
  - » Owner's Capital
  - » Retained Earnings
  - » Drawings (money withdrawn by the owner)
- Purpose: Equity accounts track the net value of the business after liabilities are subtracted from assets.

4. Income

Income accounts track the money your business earns from sales, services, or other sources.

- Examples:
  - » Product Sales
  - » Service Revenue
  - » Rental Income
- Purpose: Income accounts measure your revenue and help determine profitability.

5. Expenses

Expense accounts track the costs of running your business, such as rent, utilities, or supplies.

- Examples:
  - » Rent Expense
  - » Utilities
  - » Advertising
  - » Office Supplies
- Purpose: Expense accounts provide a detailed breakdown of your spending, helping you control costs and plan budgets.

Imagine a small retail business that sells clothing and accessories. Every financial transaction the business makes is categorized using the Chart of Accounts:

- A Sale: When a customer buys a pair of jeans, the transaction is recorded as income under the Product Sales account.
- Paying Rent: The monthly rent for the store is categorized as an expense under the Rent Expense account.
- Purchasing Inventory: Buying a new shipment of jeans is recorded as an increase in the Inventory asset account.
- Credit Card Payment: Paying off a credit card balance is categorized as a

reduction in the Credit Card Liability account.

By categorizing each transaction correctly, the business can easily generate reports, file taxes, and analyze financial performance.

QuickBooks Online allows you to customize your COA to reflect your business's unique operations. This ensures your financial data is organized in a way that makes sense for you.

Adding New Accounts

To add a new account:

1. Navigate to the Settings (gear icon) > Chart of Accounts.
2. Click New.
3. Select the account type (e.g., Income, Expense, Asset).
4. Name the account (e.g., "Social Media Advertising" or "Freight Charges").
5. Save the account.

Editing Existing Accounts

You can rename or merge accounts to keep your COA organized. For example:

- Rename a generic "Miscellaneous Income" account to "Workshop Revenue" for clarity.
- Merge duplicate accounts to simplify reporting.

Organizing Accounts

Group related accounts under subcategories for better organization. For example:

- Group "Electricity" and "Water" under a parent account called "Utilities."

Managing the COA isn't without its challenges, but knowing how to troubleshoot common issues ensures your financial system stays clean and functional.

1. Duplicate Accounts

- Problem: Multiple accounts for the same category (e.g., "Office Supplies" and "Stationery").
- Solution: Merge duplicate accounts to simplify reporting and reduce confusion.

2. Misclassified Transactions

- Problem: Income recorded as a liability or expenses incorrectly categorized.
- Solution: Regularly review transactions and reclassify errors using QuickBooks Online's built-in tools.

3. Overcomplicating the COA

- Problem: Too many accounts make reporting cumbersome.
- Solution: Keep your COA concise and relevant, focusing on accounts that provide actionable insights.

1. Start Simple: Begin with the default COA in QuickBooks and customize only as needed.
2. Review Regularly: Periodically review your COA to ensure it reflects your current operations.
3. Consult a Professional: Work with an accountant to set up or optimize your COA for accuracy and compliance.
4. Use Consistent Naming: Standardize account names for clarity and consistency across transactions.

The Chart of Accounts is a powerful tool that provides the structure necessary for accurate financial management. By understanding its purpose and components, you can ensure every transaction is recorded in the right place, leading to clear reports, smoother tax preparation, and better business decisions. Whether you're setting up your accounts for the first time or refining an existing system, investing time in managing your COA will pay dividends in efficiency and clarity. Now that you understand the foundation, let's explore how to add, edit, and organize accounts in QuickBooks Online to create a system tailored to your business needs.

Adding, Editing, and Organizing Accounts for Your Business

The Chart of Accounts (COA) is the financial backbone of QuickBooks Online (QBO), and customizing it to suit your business is critical for accurate financial tracking and meaningful reporting. Whether you're setting up QuickBooks for the first time or refining an existing system, adding, editing, and organizing accounts ensures that your business transactions are categorized logically and efficiently.

This chapter provides a step-by-step guide on how to add new accounts, edit existing ones, and organize your Chart of Accounts for clarity and accuracy. By the end, you'll have a customized financial structure that reflects your business's unique operations and supports smarter decision-making.

Every business has unique needs, and the default COA in QuickBooks Online might not fully align with yours. Customizing your accounts allows you to:

- Track Key Metrics: Create specific accounts for unique revenue streams, expense categories, or assets.
- Simplify Reporting: Tailor accounts to generate reports that provide actionable insights.
- Maintain Accuracy: Avoid misclassifying transactions by having clear, well-defined accounts.
- Improve Tax Preparation: Categorize transactions in a way that aligns with tax requirements, ensuring compliance and maximizing deductions.

Adding new accounts is a straightforward process that allows you to expand your COA to accommodate your business's operations.

Step-by-Step Guide:

1. Access the Chart of Accounts:
   » Go to Settings (gear icon) in the top-right corner of QuickBooks Online.
   » Select Chart of Accounts under the Your Company section.

2. Create a New Account:
   » Click the New button in the upper right-hand corner.

3. Select Account Type:
   » Choose the appropriate account type from the dropdown menu (e.g., Income, Expense, Asset, Liability, or Equity).

4. Choose a Detail Type:
   » Select a specific category that describes the account more precisely (e.g., Advertising/Promotional under Expenses or Accounts Receivable under Assets).

5. Name the Account:
   » Give the account a clear, descriptive name (e.g., "Digital Marketing Campaigns" or "Office Furniture").

6. Add a Description (Optional):
   » Provide additional details to clarify the account's purpose, especially if multiple users will manage the COA.

7. Set an Opening Balance (If Needed):
   » For new accounts with existing balances (e.g., a bank account), enter the starting balance and the date it was accurate.

8. Save:
   » Click Save and Close or Save and New to add another account.

Best Practices for Adding Accounts:

- Use specific, descriptive names to avoid confusion (e.g., "Social Media Ads" instead of just "Advertising").
- Only add accounts that are necessary to avoid overcomplicating the COA.
- Consult with an accountant or bookkeeper for guidance on tax-related accounts.

Over time, you may need to update account names, merge duplicates, or adjust account settings. QuickBooks Online makes it easy to edit existing accounts.

When to Edit an Account:

- The account name no longer reflects its purpose (e.g., "Miscellaneous Revenue" could be renamed "Workshop Income").
- You've merged two revenue streams and want to consolidate their accounts.
- Tax laws or business changes require you to update categories.

Step-by-Step Guide:

1. Open the Chart of Accounts:
   » Navigate to Settings > Chart of Accounts.
2. Find the Account:
   » Use the search bar or scroll through the list to locate the account you want to edit.
3. Edit the Account:
   » Click the dropdown menu next to the account and select Edit.
4. Make Changes:

   » Update the account name, type, or detail type.
   » Adjust the description or add notes for clarity.
5. Save Changes:
   » Click Save and Close to confirm your updates.

A well-organized COA not only makes your financial system easier to navigate but also improves the quality of your reports. Here's how to organize your accounts effectively:

Group Accounts into Categories:

QuickBooks Online automatically groups accounts by type (e.g., Assets, Liabilities, Income, Expenses). You can further organize these categories by:

- Using Subaccounts: Create subaccounts under a parent account for more detailed tracking. For example:
  » Parent Account: Marketing Expenses
  » Subaccounts: Digital Ads, Print Ads, Event Sponsorships
- Adding Account Numbers (Optional): Assign numbers to accounts for easier sorting and reporting. Enable this feature in Settings > Advanced > Chart of Accounts.

Rearranging Accounts:

While QuickBooks arranges accounts automatically, you can control how they appear in reports by using logical naming conventions and subaccounts.

Archiving Unused Accounts:

If an account is no longer relevant (e.g., a discontinued product line), you can make it inactive:

1. Locate the account in the COA.
2. Click the dropdown menu next to it and select Make Inactive.
3. The account will no longer appear in active lists but can still be reactivated if needed.

To help you structure your COA, here are examples of common accounts for different business types:

Retail Business:

- Income:
  - » Product Sales
  - » Service Revenue
- Expenses:
  - » Cost of Goods Sold
  - » Inventory Purchases
  - » Store Rent
  - » Utilities

Freelancer/Service-Based Business:

- Income:
  - » Client Revenue
  - » Consultation Fees
- Expenses:
  - » Software Subscriptions
  - » Travel Expenses
  - » Marketing and Advertising

E-Commerce Business:

- Income:
  - » Online Sales
  - » Shipping Revenue
- Expenses:
  - » Payment Processing Fees
  - » Shipping Costs
  - » Website Hosting

While managing your Chart of Accounts, it's important to avoid these common pitfalls:

Overcomplicating the COA:

- Problem: Too many accounts make reporting cumbersome and difficult to interpret.
- Solution: Focus on the most relevant categories. Use subaccounts sparingly for additional detail.

Creating Duplicate Accounts:

- Problem: Duplicate accounts lead to inconsistent reporting and confusion.
- Solution: Regularly review your COA for duplicates and merge them when necessary.

Misclassifying Transactions:

- Problem: Incorrect categorization results in inaccurate reports.
- Solution: Train team members on proper categorization and review reports regularly.

Neglecting Updates:

- Problem: Outdated accounts clutter your COA and make it harder to navigate.
- Solution: Periodically review and archive inactive accounts.

To maintain an organized and effective COA, follow these best practices:

1. Start Simple: Use the default QuickBooks COA as a foundation and customize it only when necessary.
2. Use Descriptive Names: Ensure each account name clearly reflects its purpose.
3. Regularly Review and Clean Up: Schedule periodic reviews to remove

unused accounts and update names or categories.

4. Consult Professionals: Work with an accountant or bookkeeper to ensure your COA aligns with tax regulations and best practices.

A well-managed Chart of Accounts is a powerful tool for maintaining accurate financial records and generating meaningful reports. By adding, editing, and organizing accounts to reflect your business's unique operations, you'll create a system that supports efficiency, compliance, and informed decision-making. Taking the time to tailor your COA today will save you hours of work and headaches in the future, allowing you to focus on growing your business with confidence.

Linking Bank and Credit Card Accounts in QuickBooks Online

Accounts payable process workflow

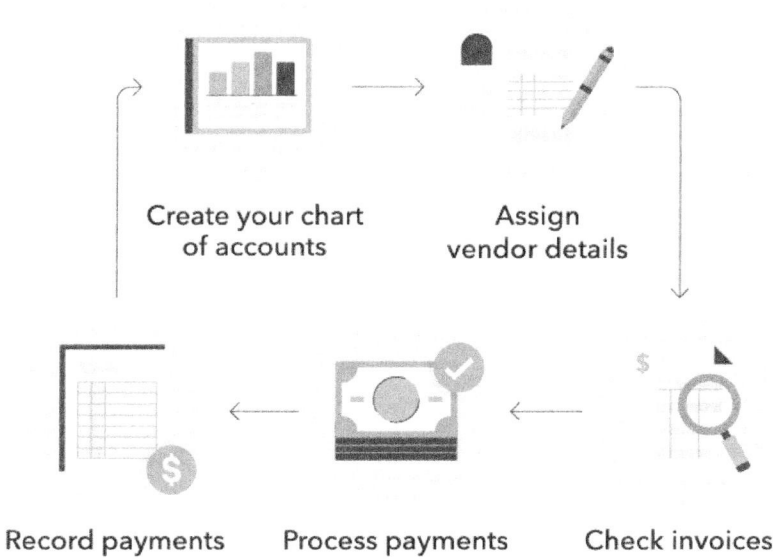

Create your chart of accounts

Assign vendor details

Record payments

Process payments

Check invoices

INTUIT quickbooks

QuickBooks Online (QBO) transforms how small businesses manage their finances, and one of its most powerful features is the ability to link your bank and credit card accounts. By connecting these accounts directly to QBO, you can automate transaction imports, simplify reconciliation, and ensure that your financial records are always up-to-date.

This chapter provides a comprehensive guide to linking your bank and credit card accounts in QuickBooks Online. Whether you're setting up a connection for the first time or troubleshooting existing links, you'll learn how to make the most of this feature to streamline your bookkeeping process.

Linking your accounts to QuickBooks Online offers several significant advantages:

Time Savings:

- Automates the process of importing transactions, eliminating the need for manual entry.
- Speeds up reconciliation by matching imported transactions with entries in your QuickBooks records.

Improved Accuracy:

- Reduces errors that often occur during manual data entry.
- Ensures all transactions, from deposits to payments, are accurately recorded in real time.

Enhanced Insights:

- Provides a comprehensive, up-to-date view of your financial activity.
- Helps you monitor cash flow, spending patterns, and income trends more effectively.

By leveraging these benefits, you can focus more on growing your business and less on tedious bookkeeping tasks.

Before connecting your bank or credit card accounts to QuickBooks Online, there are a few preparatory steps to ensure a smooth setup:

Check Your Bank's Compatibility:

- Most major banks and credit card companies are compatible with Quick-Books Online.
- Visit the Banking menu and search for your financial institution to confirm compatibility.

Gather Login Credentials:

- Have your online banking username and password ready. These credentials will be used to establish the connection securely.

Review Your QuickBooks Setup:

- Ensure your Chart of Accounts includes categories for the accounts you plan to link, such as checking, savings, or credit card accounts.
- If these accounts don't exist yet, create them in Settings > Chart of Accounts.

With these steps completed, you're ready to connect your accounts.

Connecting your bank accounts to QuickBooks Online is straightforward. Follow these steps to get started:

Step-by-Step Process:

1. Navigate to the Banking Menu:
   » Log in to QuickBooks Online.
   » From the left-hand navigation bar, click Banking (or Transactions > Banking).

2. Add a New Account:
   » Click the Link Account button in the upper right-hand corner.

3. Search for Your Bank:
   » Type the name of your financial institution into the search bar.
   » Select your bank from the list of available options.

4. Enter Your Credentials:
   » Log in using your online banking username and password.
   » Depending on your bank, you may need to complete additional

verification steps, such as entering a code sent to your email or phone.

5. Select Accounts to Link:

   » Choose which accounts you want to connect (e.g., checking, savings).
   » Assign each account to its corresponding category in the Chart of Accounts.

6. Set the Date Range:

   » Specify the start date for importing transactions. QuickBooks will download all transactions from this date forward.

7. Complete the Connection:

   » Click Connect to establish the link. Transactions from your selected accounts will begin syncing with QuickBooks Online.

The process for linking credit card accounts is similar to linking bank accounts. However, there are a few additional considerations to keep in mind:

Step-by-Step Process:

1. Access the Banking Menu:

   » From the left-hand navigation bar, go to Banking (or Transactions > Banking).

2. Link a New Account:

   » Click the Link Account button and search for your credit card provider.

3. Enter Your Credentials:

   » Log in with your credit card account username and password.
   » Complete any necessary two-factor authentication.

4. Select the Credit Card Account:

   » Choose the specific credit card account(s) you wish to link.
   » Assign it to the appropriate category in your Chart of Accounts (e.g., Credit Card Liabilities).

5. Import Transactions:

   » Set the date range for transaction imports, ensuring you capture the data you need.

6. Save and Sync:

   » Confirm the connection to start importing transactions from your credit card account.

Once your accounts are linked, QuickBooks Online automatically imports transactions. To maintain accurate financial records, it's essential to categorize and reconcile these transactions regularly.

Categorizing Transactions:

1. Navigate to the Banking menu.
2. Review the list of imported transactions under the For Review tab.
3. Assign each transaction to the appropriate account or category in the Chart of Accounts.
4. Add a description or attach receipts for clarity and documentation.

Matching Transactions:

· QuickBooks may automatically match imported transactions with existing records in your books.
· Review suggested matches and confirm their accuracy by clicking Match.

Reconciling Accounts:

1. Go to Accounting > Reconcile from the left-hand menu.
2. Select the account you want to reconcile.
3. Compare the transactions in QuickBooks to your bank or credit card statement.

4. Resolve discrepancies by adding or editing transactions as needed.

While linking accounts is typically seamless, occasional issues can arise. Here's how to troubleshoot common problems:

Issue 1: Unable to Connect to Bank

- Solution:
    - » Ensure your bank credentials are correct.
    - » Check if your bank's website is down or undergoing maintenance.
    - » Try reconnecting later or contact your bank for assistance.

Issue 2: Missing Transactions

- Solution:
    - » Confirm the selected date range includes the missing transactions.
    - » Manually upload transactions by downloading a CSV file from your bank and importing it into QuickBooks.

Issue 3: Duplicate Transactions

- Solution:
    - » Use the Exclude feature in the Banking menu to remove duplicates.
    - » Regularly reconcile your accounts to catch and resolve duplicates.

Issue 4: Sync Errors

- Solution:
    - » Disconnect and reconnect the account to refresh the connection.
    - » Contact QuickBooks support if the issue persists.

To maximize the benefits of linking your accounts, follow these best practices:

1. Link All Active Accounts:
    - » Ensure all checking, savings, and credit card accounts used for business transactions are connected to QuickBooks.

2. Regularly Review Transactions:
    - » Check imported transactions weekly to keep your books up-to-date and avoid a backlog.

3. Reconcile Monthly:
    - » Reconcile your accounts at the end of each month to catch errors and discrepancies early.

4. Maintain Clear Categories:
    - » Use consistent naming conventions and categories in your Chart of Accounts for accurate reporting.

5. Back Up Data:
    - » Regularly export and save copies of your QuickBooks data to ensure records are protected.

QuickBooks Online offers additional features to enhance your experience with linked accounts:

Automated Rules:

- Create rules to automatically categorize transactions based on descriptions or amounts. For example:
    - » "Office Supplies" for purchases at a specific store.
    - » "Fuel" for gas station charges.

Cash Flow Insights:

- Use the Cash Flow Planner to analyze imported transactions and forecast future cash flow.

Expense Attachments:

- Attach digital receipts to imported transactions for easy documentation and reference.

Linking your bank and credit card accounts to QuickBooks Online is a game-changing feature that automates transaction tracking, improves accuracy, and saves time. By following the steps outlined in this chapter, you can connect your accounts seamlessly and maintain a clear, organized financial system. With regular categorization, reconciliation, and troubleshooting, your linked accounts will provide the foundation for accurate financial reporting and smarter business decisions.

Troubleshooting Common Chart of Account Issues

The Chart of Accounts (COA) in Quick-Books Online (QBO) serves as the foundation of your financial system, organizing your transactions into categories that drive accurate reporting and insightful decision-making. However, like any financial system, challenges can arise. From duplicate accounts to misclassified transactions, issues with the COA can disrupt your records, complicate tax filings, and lead to inefficiencies.

This chapter explores common Chart of Account issues and provides practical solutions to troubleshoot them effectively. Whether you're a small business owner managing your books or an accountant overseeing multiple clients, these strategies will help you maintain a clean, functional COA.

Symptoms:

- Similar transactions appear under multiple accounts.
- Confusion arises when categorizing income or expenses.
- Reports display redundant data, making analysis difficult.

Causes:

- Accounts created with overlapping purposes (e.g., "Office Supplies" and "General Supplies").
- Miscommunication when multiple users manage the COA.

Solutions:

1. Identify Duplicates:
   » Navigate to the Chart of Accounts in QuickBooks Online.
   » Look for accounts with similar names or purposes.

2. Merge Duplicate Accounts:
   » Select the account you want to merge.
   » Click the dropdown arrow next to the account and choose Edit.
   » Change the account name to match the one you're merging it with.
   » Save the changes. QuickBooks will ask for confirmation to merge the accounts.

3. Prevent Future Duplicates:
   » Establish a naming convention for accounts (e.g., "Marketing Supplies" instead of "General Supplies").
   » Train team members to search the COA before creating new accounts.

Symptoms:

- Expenses show up under income accounts or vice versa.
- Reports don't align with actual financial activity.
- Tax preparation becomes confusing due to incorrect categories.

Causes:

- Transactions categorized incorrectly during data entry.
- Accounts mislabeled in the COA.

Solutions:

1. Run a Report to Identify Misclassifications:

   » Go to Reports > Profit and Loss Statement.
   » Review categories for anomalies (e.g., large expenses in income accounts).

2. Reclassify Transactions:

   » Go to Banking > Reviewed or For Review to locate affected transactions.
   » Click on the transaction and select the correct category.
   » Save changes.

3. Edit Account Types:

   » If the issue is due to an incorrectly labeled account, go to the Chart of Accounts, edit the account, and select the correct account type (e.g., Expense instead of Income).

Symptoms:

- Old or inactive accounts appear in reports.
- Errors during reconciliation due to transactions linked to inactive accounts.

Causes:

- Accounts marked inactive without reassigning linked transactions.
- Inactive accounts included in report filters.

Solutions:

1. Review Inactive Accounts:

   » Go to Settings > Chart of Accounts.
   » Filter for inactive accounts to view the list.

2. Reassign Transactions:

   » For accounts that still have transactions, edit the transactions to assign them to active accounts.
   » Delete or merge the inactive account if it's no longer needed.

3. Adjust Report Filters:

   » When generating reports, ensure inactive accounts are excluded from filters.

Symptoms:

- Too many accounts make reports difficult to read.
- Categories overlap, causing confusion during transaction categorization.
- Time wasted navigating a cluttered COA.

Causes:

- Accounts created unnecessarily for minor variations (e.g., "Gas Expenses" and "Fuel Expenses").
- Lack of structure or guidelines when setting up the COA.

Solutions:

1. Consolidate Accounts:

   » Identify accounts with overlapping purposes and merge them into broader categories (e.g., "Office Expenses" instead of "Printer Ink," "Stationery," and "Office Supplies").

2. Use Subaccounts:

   » For detailed tracking, create subaccounts under parent accounts. For example:

   ▪ Parent Account: Marketing

   ▪ Subaccounts: Digital Ads, Print Ads, Event Sponsorships

3. Simplify Naming Conventions:

   » Use clear, concise names that reflect the purpose of each account.

Symptoms:

- Financial reports show incomplete data.
- Bank reconciliation reveals gaps in records.
- Transactions appear in bank statements but not in QuickBooks.

Causes:

- Bank or credit card accounts not linked properly.
- Manual transactions not entered or saved correctly.

Solutions:

1. Check Bank Feeds:

   » Go to Banking > Banking and ensure all bank and credit card accounts are connected and up to date.

2. Manually Import Missing Transactions:

   » Download a CSV or Excel file of transactions from your bank.
   » Go to Banking > Upload Transactions in QuickBooks and follow the import prompts.

3. Review Unmatched Transactions:

   » In the Banking menu, check the For Review tab for transactions that haven't been categorized or matched.

Symptoms:

- Reconciliation discrepancies.
- Reports showing incorrect starting balances for accounts.

Causes:

- Incorrect opening balance entered during account setup.
- Transactions dated before the opening balance were not accounted for.

Solutions:

1. Review Opening Balances:

   » Go to Chart of Accounts, find the affected account, and select View Register.
   » Check the opening balance transaction for accuracy.

2. Adjust the Opening Balance:

   » Edit the opening balance transaction to reflect the correct amount.
   » Ensure adjustments are documented for audit purposes.

3. Reconcile Transactions:

   » After adjusting the opening balance, reconcile the account to verify accuracy.

Symptoms:

- Reports overstate income or expenses.
- Bank reconciliation errors due to mismatched transactions.

Causes:

- Duplicate uploads during manual import.
- Transactions manually entered alongside automated bank feeds.

Solutions:

1. Identify Duplicates:
   » Run the Transaction Detail by Account report.
   » Look for identical transactions with the same amount, date, and description.

2. Delete or Exclude Duplicates:
   » In the Banking menu, go to the For Review tab.
   » Select duplicates and click Exclude.

3. Prevent Future Duplicates:
   » Avoid manual entry for accounts linked to bank feeds.
   » Regularly review the Banking menu for pending transactions.

Symptoms:

- Transactions fail to sync.
- Incorrect balances in linked accounts.
- Missing or delayed updates in financial data.

Causes:

- Bank connections broken or outdated.
- Incorrect account mapping during setup.

Solutions:

1. Reconnect the Account:
   » Go to Banking > Banking.
   » Select the affected account, click the dropdown arrow, and choose Edit Account Info.
   » Re-enter credentials and verify the connection.

2. Verify Account Mapping:
   » Ensure the linked account corresponds to the correct category in the Chart of Accounts (e.g., checking account linked to "Bank Account" category).

3. Test the Connection:
   » Run a test transaction in your bank or credit card account and confirm it syncs with QuickBooks.

1. **Conduct Regular Reviews:**
   » Periodically audit your COA to identify duplicates, inactive accounts, or misclassifications.

2. Train Team Members:
   » Provide training on proper categorization and naming conventions to avoid errors.

3. Work with an Accountant:
   » Consult a professional to ensure your COA is optimized for compliance and reporting needs.

4. Use Automation Tools:
   » Enable features like bank feeds and automated rules to minimize manual errors.

The Chart of Accounts is the backbone of your financial system, and keeping it clean and functional is critical for accurate reporting and efficient bookkeeping. By proactively addressing common issues such as duplicates, misclassifications, and missing transactions, you can ensure your COA remains an asset rather than a source of frustration. Regular maintenance, combined with best practices and troubleshooting strategies, will help you maintain a reliable financial foundation for your business.

CHAPTER 4

RECORDING SALES
AND INCOME

Recording sales and income is at the heart of managing your business's financial health. Whether you're invoicing clients, accepting payments, or generating reports to track revenue trends, accurate record-keeping is essential for maintaining cash flow, identifying growth opportunities, and ensuring compliance during tax season.

In QuickBooks Online (QBO), recording sales and income goes beyond simple bookkeeping. The platform offers powerful tools to streamline these processes, from creating professional invoices and sales receipts to automating recurring transactions. By leveraging these features, you can save time, minimize errors, and focus on building stronger customer relationships.

This chapter will guide you through the key aspects of recording sales and income in QuickBooks Online. You'll learn how to create invoices and sales receipts, manage customer payments, automate recurring transactions, and generate insightful sales reports to understand your revenue trends better. By the end of this chapter, you'll have a clear roadmap for optimizing your sales tracking process and ensuring your financial records are always up-to-date.

Accurate sales tracking is critical for several reasons:

- Cash Flow Management: Recording income helps you monitor your business's cash inflows, ensuring you have enough resources to cover expenses and reinvest in growth.
- Customer Relationships: Properly managing invoices and overdue balances demonstrates professionalism and builds trust with clients.
- Financial Insights: By tracking revenue trends, you can identify top-performing products or services and make informed decisions about pricing and marketing strategies.
- Tax Compliance: Keeping accurate records of your income simplifies tax preparation and ensures compliance with local regulations.

1. How to Create Invoices and Sales Receipts

QuickBooks Online simplifies the process of billing your customers, whether they're paying upfront or on credit. We'll walk you through creating detailed invoices and sales receipts that align with your brand's professionalism. You'll also learn how to customize these forms, add payment terms, and track their status in real time.

2. Managing Customer Payments and Overdue Balances

Once you've billed your clients, managing payments and overdue balances is crucial for maintaining healthy cash flow. We'll explore how to record payments, send reminders for overdue invoices, and apply partial payments or credits to customer accounts. You'll also learn strategies for dealing with late payments professionally and efficiently.

3. Automating Recurring Sales Transactions

For businesses with repeat customers or subscription-based services, automating recurring transactions saves time and ensures consistent cash flow. We'll show you how to set up and manage recurring invoices, so you can focus on other aspects of your business while QuickBooks takes care of billing.

4. Generating Sales Reports to Track Revenue Trends

QuickBooks Online offers a range of sales reports to help you analyze your business's performance. You'll learn how to generate and customize reports like the Sales by Customer Summary or Product/Service Sales Report to gain valuable insights into your revenue streams and customer behavior.

Recording sales and income is more than just a necessary task—it's an opportunity to gain deeper insights into your business's performance and enhance your financial management. By mastering these processes in QuickBooks Online, you'll not only improve your efficiency but also build confidence in the accuracy and reliability of your financial records.

Let's dive in and unlock the full potential of QuickBooks Online to streamline your sales tracking and take your business's financial management to the next level.

How to Create Invoices and Sales Receipts

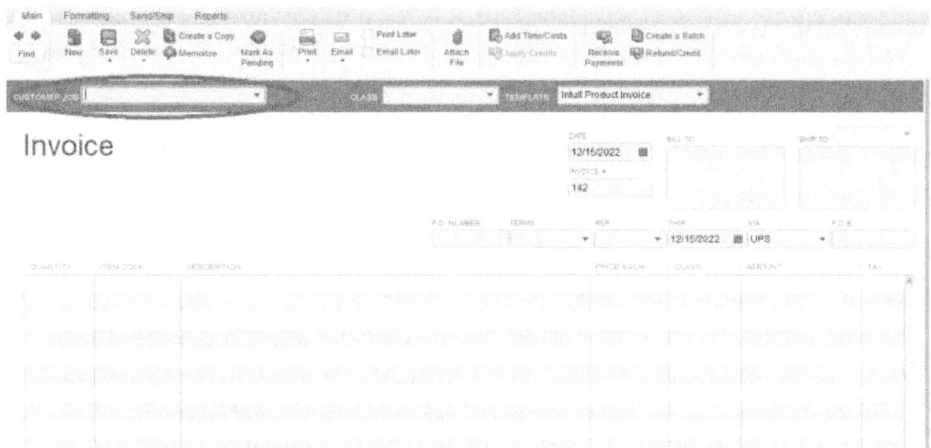

Invoices and sales receipts are essential tools for tracking your business's income and maintaining clear records of customer transactions. QuickBooks Online (QBO) simplifies the process of creating these documents, allowing you to send professional, customized forms to your clients while keeping your books up-to-date. Whether you're billing a client for a service or documenting a completed sale, understanding how to create and manage invoices and sales receipts is key to efficient financial management.

This chapter provides a detailed guide to creating invoices and sales receipts in Quick-

Books Online, covering everything from customization and automation to tips for maintaining professionalism and accuracy.

Before diving into the steps, it's important to understand the distinction between invoices and sales receipts:

- Invoice: Used when a customer agrees to pay you later (on credit). It records the sale and creates an accounts receivable entry, tracking the amount owed by the customer until payment is received.
- Sales Receipt: Used when the customer pays at the time of the sale. It records the payment and the sale simultaneously, ensuring no outstanding balance remains.

Both forms serve distinct purposes and should be used appropriately based on the transaction type.

Creating invoices in QuickBooks Online is simple and customizable, ensuring they reflect your business's professionalism and branding.

Step-by-Step Guide:

1. Navigate to Invoices:
   » Log in to your QuickBooks Online account.
   » Click on + New in the left-hand menu and select Invoice under the Customers section.

2. Choose the Customer:
   » Select an existing customer from the dropdown menu or create a new one by clicking + Add New.
   » Fill in the customer's details, such as name, email, and billing address.

3. Set the Invoice Date and Due Date:
   » The Invoice Date defaults to today's date, but you can adjust it if needed.

   » Select payment terms (e.g., Net 15, Net 30) to calculate the Due Date automatically.

4. Add Line Items:
   » Under the Product/Service column, choose the items or services being billed.
   » Enter a description, quantity, rate, and any applicable discounts or taxes.

5. Include Payment Options:
   » Enable online payment options like credit cards or ACH transfers (if set up in your QBO account).
   » Add clear instructions for offline payments, such as "Payable by check to [Your Business Name]."

6. Customize the Invoice:
   » Click Customize to select a template and add your logo, color scheme, and other branding elements.
   » Add a personalized note in the footer, such as "Thank you for your business!"

7. Review and Send:
   » Double-check all details for accuracy.
   » Click Save and Send to email the invoice to the customer or Save and Print for physical delivery.

Tips for Effective Invoicing:

- Include clear payment terms and due dates to avoid confusion.
- Use professional templates that reinforce your brand identity.
- Regularly monitor invoice statuses (e.g., sent, viewed, paid, overdue) in the Invoices section of QBO.

Sales receipts are ideal for documenting payments received at the point of sale, ensuring both the sale and payment are recorded simultaneously.

Step-by-Step Guide:

1. Navigate to Sales Receipts:
   - » Click + New in the left-hand menu and select Sales Receipt under the Customers section.
2. Choose the Customer:
   - » Select the customer from the dropdown menu or create a new one by clicking + Add New.
3. Set the Sales Receipt Date:
   - » Enter the date of the transaction.
4. Add Payment Details:
   - » Specify the payment method (e.g., cash, credit card, check).
   - » Record the reference number or check number if applicable.
5. Add Line Items:
   - » Choose the products or services sold, including descriptions, quantities, rates, and taxes.
6. Customize the Receipt:
   - » Add your logo and branding elements for a professional look.
   - » Include a thank-you note or other personalized messages in the footer.
7. Save and Deliver:
   - » Click Save and Send to email the receipt or Save and Print for physical delivery.

Tips for Using Sales Receipts:

- Use sales receipts for point-of-sale transactions where payment is immediate.
- Attach copies of receipts to customer records in QBO for easy reference.

Customizing your invoices and sales receipts ensures they reflect your brand identity while providing all necessary details for your customers.

How to Customize:

1. Go to Settings (gear icon) > Custom Form Styles.
2. Click New Style and choose Invoice or Sales Receipt.
3. Add your business logo, color scheme, and preferred fonts.
4. Edit the layout to include or remove fields such as payment terms, due dates, or customer messages.

Key Customization Tips:

- Keep designs simple and professional.
- Use consistent branding across all customer-facing forms.
- Highlight key details like payment terms or late payment fees.

For repeat customers or subscription-based services, automating recurring invoices saves time and ensures consistent billing.

How to Set Up Recurring Invoices:

1. Go to + New > Recurring Transaction.
2. Select Invoice as the transaction type.
3. Choose a template name and customer, then set the recurrence schedule (e.g., weekly, monthly).
4. Add line items and payment terms.
5. Save the recurring invoice.

Benefits of Automation:

- Reduces administrative workload.
- Ensures timely billing for repeat customers.
- Minimizes the risk of missed payments.

After creating invoices and sales receipts, monitoring their statuses is essential for maintaining cash flow and customer relationships.

Invoice Tracking:

- View all invoices in the Sales > Invoices section of QBO.
- Filter by status (e.g., paid, overdue) to prioritize follow-ups.
- Send payment reminders for overdue invoices directly from the platform.

Sales Receipt Tracking:

- Access all sales receipts in the Sales > All Sales section.
- Filter by customer, date, or payment method for quick searches.

Recording Partial Payments or Credits:

- If a customer makes a partial payment, record it by selecting the invoice and entering the amount paid.
- Apply available credits to invoices for accurate tracking.

1. **Use Clear Payment Terms:**
   - » Specify payment due dates and accepted payment methods.
   - » Include late payment fees if applicable.
2. Leverage Automation:
   - » Automate recurring invoices to save time and ensure consistency.
3. Double-Check Before Sending:
   - » Review all details to avoid errors or discrepancies that could delay payment.
4. Maintain Professionalism:
   - » Use polished templates and personalized notes to strengthen customer relationships.
5. Monitor Regularly:
   - » Keep track of unpaid invoices and follow up promptly to maintain cash flow.

Creating invoices and sales receipts in QuickBooks Online is a straightforward yet powerful process that ensures accurate tracking of your sales and income. By understanding when to use each form, customizing them for professionalism, and leveraging automation features, you can streamline your billing processes and focus on growing your business. With these tools at your disposal, managing customer transactions becomes more efficient, helping you maintain healthy cash flow and build strong client relationships.

Send reminder email for 51460

X

To

brad@gmail.com

Subject

Reminder: Invoice [Invoice No.] from Buddy & Dannozo Pet Supplies

Message

Dear Brad Dalmation,

Just a reminder that we have not received a payment for this invoice yet.
Please pay this immediately or if you have any questions please call us to discuss.

Thanks for your business!
Buddy & Dannozo Pet Supplies

Cancel   Send

Managing customer payments and overdue balances is a critical aspect of running a successful business. Efficient payment management ensures healthy cash flow, strengthens customer relationships, and minimizes the risk of financial strain caused by late payments. QuickBooks Online (QBO) offers robust tools to help you track payments, address overdue balances, and maintain accurate financial records.

This chapter provides a detailed guide to managing customer payments and overdue balances in QuickBooks Online. By the end, you'll have a comprehensive understanding of how to record payments, send reminders, handle partial payments, and manage overdue invoices effectively.

When a customer pays an invoice, recording the payment in QuickBooks Online keeps your accounts receivable accurate and ensures that your financial records are up-to-date.

Step-by-Step Guide:

1. Navigate to Receive Payment:

    » Click + New in the left-hand menu

and select Receive Payment under the Customers section.

2. Select the Customer:

    » Choose the customer making

the payment from the dropdown menu.

3. Choose the Invoice:

   » A list of open invoices for the selected customer will appear. Select the invoice(s) being paid.

4. Enter Payment Details:

   » Record the payment method (e.g., cash, check, credit card).
   » If applicable, enter the check number or transaction ID.
   » Specify the deposit location (e.g., checking account or undeposited funds).

5. Save the Payment:

   » Click Save and Close or Save and New to record the payment and close the invoice.

Tips for Recording Payments:

- Always match payments to the correct invoice to avoid discrepancies.
- Attach payment receipts to the transaction in QBO for easy reference.
- Use the Undeposited Funds account for payments that will be grouped in a single bank deposit.

When customers fail to pay invoices on time, it's essential to address overdue balances promptly to maintain cash flow and reduce the risk of bad debts. QuickBooks Online provides tools to track overdue invoices and communicate with customers professionally.

How to Identify Overdue Invoices:

1. Navigate to Sales > Invoices in the left-hand menu.
2. Use the filters to display overdue invoices.
3. Review the Status column to see how many days past due each invoice is.

Sending Payment Reminders:

1. Open the overdue invoice in QBO.
2. Click the Send Reminder button.
3. Customize the reminder message with polite but firm language, such as:

   » "We hope this serves as a friendly reminder that Invoice #12345 is overdue. Please let us know if you need any assistance completing the payment."

4. Send the email directly from QuickBooks.

Automating Reminders:

- Set up automated payment reminders in Settings > Reminders to reduce manual follow-ups.
- Customize the frequency and timing of reminders (e.g., one day before the due date, one week overdue).

Customers may occasionally make partial payments toward an invoice. QuickBooks Online allows you to record these payments while keeping the invoice open for the remaining balance.

How to Record a Partial Payment:

1. Go to + New > Receive Payment.
2. Select the customer and open invoice.
3. Enter the amount paid in the Amount Received field.
4. Save the payment. The invoice will remain open with the outstanding balance displayed.

Tips for Managing Partial Payments:

- Include notes in the invoice about the partial payment and remaining balance.
- Send updated copies of the invoice to the customer to ensure clarity.
- Set reminders for the remaining balance if payment terms allow.

Sometimes, you may need to apply credits or adjustments to customer accounts due to overpayments, discounts, or refunds.

Issuing a Credit Memo:

1. Click + New and select Credit Memo under the Customers section.
2. Choose the customer and add the reason for the credit (e.g., discount, returned items).
3. Save and apply the credit to an open invoice.

Adjusting Balances:

- Use Journal Entries to adjust accounts receivable balances if necessary.
- Consult with an accountant for complex adjustments to ensure compliance.

After receiving customer payments, depositing them into your bank account keeps your records accurate and your bank reconciliation smooth.

How to Deposit Payments:

1. Navigate to + New > Bank Deposit.
2. Select the payments recorded in the Undeposited Funds account.
3. Choose the bank account for the deposit.
4. Verify the deposit total and click Save and Close.

Benefits of Using the Undeposited Funds Account:

- Groups multiple payments into a single deposit, matching your bank statement.
- Reduces errors during reconciliation.

Payment disputes can arise due to incorrect invoices, missed discounts, or customer dissatisfaction. Resolving these issues promptly is crucial for maintaining good relationships.

Steps to Resolve Disputes:

1. Identify the Issue:
   » Review the invoice and payment terms to understand the customer's concern.
2. Communicate Professionally:
   » Reach out to the customer to discuss the issue.
   » Offer solutions, such as correcting the invoice or providing additional information.
3. Document the Resolution:
   » Record any adjustments in QuickBooks Online (e.g., issuing a credit or creating a revised invoice).

Tracking your accounts receivable ensures you have a clear view of outstanding invoices and overdue balances.

Generating Accounts Receivable Reports:

1. Go to Reports > Accounts Receivable Aging Summary.
2. Review overdue balances categorized by time frame (e.g., 1-30 days overdue, 31-60 days overdue).
3. Use the report to prioritize follow-ups with customers.

Analyzing Trends:

- Identify customers with a history of late payments and adjust payment terms if needed.
- Monitor the percentage of overdue invoices to gauge your collection efficiency.

For businesses with repeat customers or subscription services, automating payment processing can save time and reduce overdue balances.

Setting Up Automatic Payments:

- Enable recurring payments for customers with consistent billing schedules.
- Use QuickBooks Payments or third-party integrations to process payments securely.

Benefits of Automation:

- Reduces manual follow-ups.
- Ensures timely payments, improving cash flow.

To maintain efficient payment management, follow these best practices:

1. Establish Clear Payment Terms:
   - » Define due dates, late fees, and accepted payment methods in every invoice.
   - » Communicate payment policies upfront to avoid confusion.

2. Follow Up Promptly:
   - » Send reminders for overdue invoices as soon as they pass the due date.
   - » Be polite but firm in your communications.

3. Offer Flexible Payment Options:
   - » Accept multiple payment methods, including credit cards, bank transfers, and digital wallets.

4. Maintain Accurate Records:
   - » Regularly reconcile payments to ensure your accounts match your bank statements.
   - » Document all communications and adjustments for reference.

5. Build Strong Customer Relationships:
   - » Address payment issues professionally and collaboratively.
   - » Reward timely payments with discounts or incentives when feasible.

Managing customer payments and overdue balances is vital for sustaining cash flow and building strong client relationships. QuickBooks Online provides the tools to track payments, handle overdue invoices, and resolve disputes efficiently. By following best practices and leveraging QBO's features, you can maintain accurate financial records, minimize overdue balances, and ensure your business remains financially stable. With a clear process in place, you'll spend less time chasing payments and more time focusing on growing your business.

Automating Recurring Sales Transactions

Running a business often involves repetitive tasks that consume valuable time. Automating recurring sales transactions in QuickBooks Online (QBO) is one of the simplest ways to reduce manual effort and ensure consistency in your financial processes. Whether you're billing clients for subscription services, ongoing contracts, or repeat purchases, automation helps you maintain accurate records, streamline cash flow, and enhance customer satisfaction.

This chapter provides an in-depth guide to automating recurring sales transactions in QBO, including the setup process, customization options, and best practices for leveraging this feature effectively. By automating recurring invoices, sales receipts, and other sales-related tasks, you can focus more on growing your business and less on administrative chores.

Automation is not just about convenience—it delivers tangible benefits that positively impact your business operations:

Time Savings:

- Eliminates the need to manually create invoices or receipts for repeat transactions.
- Frees up time for other business priorities, such as customer service or strategic planning.

Consistency:

- Ensures invoices and receipts are sent on schedule, reducing the risk of missed or delayed billing.
- Promotes reliable cash flow by maintaining a predictable billing cycle.

Improved Customer Experience:

- Enhances customer trust by ensuring timely, accurate invoices.
- Allows for tailored communications, such as adding personalized messages or payment terms.

Error Reduction:

- Minimizes data entry errors that can occur during manual invoicing or sales recording.

By automating these processes, you create a more efficient and professional workflow.

QuickBooks Online supports automation for several types of sales transactions. The most common include:

Recurring Invoices:

- Used for customers who pay on credit or are billed periodically for goods or services (e.g., monthly subscription fees, ongoing service contracts).

Recurring Sales Receipts:

- Ideal for customers who pay upfront or have payments automatically debited (e.g., gym memberships, SaaS subscriptions).

Recurring Estimates:

- Useful for businesses that provide regular quotes for ongoing projects or services.

Each type serves a unique purpose, and you can customize them to suit your business's needs.

QuickBooks Online makes it easy to automate recurring transactions. Follow these steps to set up recurring sales transactions:

Step-by-Step Guide:

1. Navigate to Recurring Transactions:
   - » Log in to QuickBooks Online.
   - » Click Settings (gear icon) in the top-right corner and select Recurring Transactions under the Lists menu.

2. Create a New Template:
   - » Click the New button to start creating a recurring transaction.
   - » Choose the transaction type (e.g., Invoice, Sales Receipt, Estimate) from the dropdown menu.

3. Choose a Template Name:
   - » Enter a descriptive name for the template (e.g., "Monthly Subscription for Customer A").

4. Select the Customer:
   - » Assign the template to an existing customer or create a new one.

5. Set the Recurrence Schedule:
   - » Choose how often the transaction

will repeat (e.g., weekly, monthly, annually).

» Specify the start date and, if applicable, the end date.

6. Add Line Items:

» Include the products or services being billed, along with quantities, rates, and applicable taxes.

» Add detailed descriptions to ensure clarity.

7. Customize Payment Terms:

» For invoices, set payment terms (e.g., Net 15, Net 30).

» For sales receipts, specify the payment method (e.g., credit card, ACH transfer).

8. Save the Template:

» Review all details for accuracy.

» Save the template to activate automation.

Personalization ensures your recurring transactions align with your brand and meet customer expectations.

Customizable Fields:

• Template Name: Use meaningful names to easily identify templates in your Recurring Transactions list.

• Messages: Add custom messages to invoices or receipts, such as "Thank you for your continued business!"

• Attachments: Include contracts, terms of service, or other relevant documents for each transaction.

Editing Recurring Transactions:

• To make changes to an existing template, go to Settings > Recurring Transactions.

• Select the template, click Edit, and update the necessary fields.

Using Dynamic Fields:

• Use placeholders like {Customer Name} to automatically populate customer-specific details.

Automation doesn't mean you can set it and forget it—regular monitoring ensures everything runs smoothly.

Viewing Recurring Transactions:

• Go to Settings > Recurring Transactions to view all active templates.

• Check the schedule and last transaction date to verify accuracy.

Monitoring Status:

• Ensure templates are set to active. If a template is paused or deactivated, transactions will not process.

• Use the Activity Log in the Recurring Transactions menu to track recent activity.

Handling Modifications:

• For changes in pricing, quantities, or service terms, edit the recurring transaction template to reflect updates.

• Notify customers of significant changes to avoid confusion.

For businesses that accept online payments, integrating payment automation with recurring transactions further streamlines the process.

Setting Up Online Payments:

• Enable QuickBooks Payments or a third-party processor to accept credit cards or ACH transfers.

• Link the payment method to the recurring sales receipt template.

Benefits of Payment Automation:

• Reduces delays in payment collection.

• Simplifies reconciliation, as payments are automatically recorded in QBO.

Handling Payment Failures:

- Set up notifications for failed transactions to address issues promptly.
- Reach out to customers to update payment methods if necessary.

To maximize the benefits of automation, follow these best practices:

1. Communicate with Customers:
   - » Notify customers before setting up recurring transactions to ensure transparency.
   - » Provide clear payment terms and expectations.

2. Keep Records Up-to-Date:
   - » Regularly update customer details, such as billing addresses and payment methods.
   - » Audit recurring transactions to ensure they align with current pricing or service terms.

3. Review Templates Periodically:
   - » Check active templates for accuracy and relevance.
   - » Archive templates for inactive customers to keep your list organized.

4. Test Automation:
   - » Run a trial transaction to verify that everything works correctly before activating a recurring schedule.

5. Leverage Reports:
   - » Use sales reports to monitor income generated from recurring transactions.
   - » Analyze customer trends to identify opportunities for upselling or cross-selling.

Despite its reliability, automation may occasionally encounter hiccups. Here's how to address common issues:

Missed Transactions:

- Cause: The template may be paused or deactivated.
- Solution: Reactivate the template and check the schedule.

Incorrect Amounts:

- Cause: Outdated pricing or service terms.
- Solution: Edit the template to reflect accurate amounts.

Customer Complaints:

- Cause: Lack of communication about recurring charges.
- Solution: Provide detailed invoices and communicate changes proactively.

For Business Owners:

- Saves time by automating repetitive tasks.
- Improves cash flow predictability with consistent billing.

For Customers:

- Provides convenience through timely, error-free billing.
- Enhances trust by maintaining clear, professional communication.

Automating recurring sales transactions in QuickBooks Online is a game-changing feature that streamlines billing, improves cash flow, and enhances customer satisfaction. By following the steps outlined in this chapter, you can set up and manage recurring invoices, sales receipts, and other transactions with ease. Regularly monitoring and customizing templates ensures that your automation remains accurate and aligned with your business's needs. With these tools, you'll spend less time on administrative tasks and more time focusing on growing your business.

Generating Sales Reports to Track Revenue Trends

Understanding your business's sales performance is crucial for making informed decisions, identifying growth opportunities, and staying ahead in a competitive market. QuickBooks Online (QBO) simplifies this process by offering a range of customizable sales reports that provide insights into revenue trends, customer behavior, and product or service performance.

This chapter explores how to generate and interpret sales reports in QuickBooks Online. Whether you're looking to analyze your top customers, identify seasonal revenue spikes, or evaluate the success of specific products or services, QBO's reporting tools make it easy to track and act on key metrics.

Sales reports serve as a roadmap for your business's financial health and growth strategy. By analyzing revenue trends, you can:

- Monitor Cash Flow: Understand when and where revenue is coming from to plan for future expenses.
- Identify Top Customers: Focus on building relationships with loyal customers who contribute the most to your bottom line.
- Evaluate Products or Services: Determine which offerings generate the most revenue and which may need improvement or discontinuation.
- Track Seasonal Trends: Identify patterns in sales activity to optimize inventory, marketing, and staffing.

QuickBooks Online provides a variety of sales reports, each designed to highlight specific aspects of your revenue. The most commonly used reports include:

1. Sales by Customer Summary

- Shows total sales revenue grouped by customer.
- Helps identify top customers and track their purchasing behavior over time.

2. Sales by Product/Service Summary

- Displays sales performance by product or service.
- Useful for analyzing which offerings contribute the most to revenue.

3. Sales by Month

- Breaks down sales data month by month, revealing seasonal trends or growth patterns.

4. Profit and Loss Statement

- Provides a high-level overview of your income and expenses.
- Highlights how sales revenue contributes to overall profitability.

5. Invoice and Receipts Report

- Tracks payments received against invoices and sales receipts.
- Useful for monitoring cash flow and overdue balances.

Each report can be customized to meet your specific needs.

QuickBooks Online makes it easy to generate sales reports with just a few clicks. Follow these steps to access and customize your reports:

Step-by-Step Guide:

1. Navigate to Reports:
   » Log in to QuickBooks Online.
   » Click on the Reports menu in the left-hand navigation bar.

2. Search for the Desired Report:
   » Use the search bar to find specific sales reports (e.g., "Sales by Customer Summary").
   » Alternatively, browse the Sales and Customers category.

3. Customize the Report:
   » Click the Customize button to adjust filters, such as date range, customer, or product/service.
   » Add or remove columns to include relevant data fields (e.g., quantities, tax amounts, discounts).

4. Run the Report:
   » Click Run Report to generate the report with your customizations.

5. Export or Print:
   » Use the Export button to download the report as a PDF or Excel file.
   » Print the report for physical record-keeping or presentations.

Once you've generated your sales reports, the next step is interpreting the data to gain actionable insights. Here's how to analyze the most common sales reports:

1. Sales by Customer Summary

- What to Look For:
  » Identify your top-performing customers based on revenue.
  » Spot customers with declining sales for targeted re-engagement strategies.

- Actionable Insights:
  » Offer loyalty discounts or incentives to top customers.
  » Reach out to customers with declining sales to understand and address their needs.

2. Sales by Product/Service Summary

- What to Look For:
  » Identify which products or services contribute the most to revenue.
  » Spot low-performing items that may need re-evaluation.

- Actionable Insights:
  » Focus marketing efforts on high-revenue items.
  » Consider discontinuing or improving underperforming products.

3. Sales by Month

- What to Look For:
  » Analyze seasonal trends or periods of growth and decline.
  » Compare monthly revenue to past years for long-term trend analysis.

- Actionable Insights:
  » Plan seasonal promotions or sales during high-revenue months.
  » Adjust inventory and staffing based on anticipated demand.

4. Profit and Loss Statement

- What to Look For:

- » Evaluate how sales revenue compares to expenses.
- » Identify areas where expenses may be outpacing income.
- Actionable Insights:
  - » Set sales targets to improve profitability.
  - » Reduce unnecessary expenses in low-margin areas.

5. Invoice and Receipts Report

- What to Look For:
  - » Track overdue payments and unpaid invoices.
  - » Identify payment trends to predict future cash flow.
- Actionable Insights:
  - » Follow up on overdue invoices promptly.
  - » Offer flexible payment terms for customers with consistent payment delays.

Customization is a powerful feature in QuickBooks Online, allowing you to tailor reports to your unique business needs. Here's how to make the most of it:

Filters:

- Adjust date ranges to focus on specific periods, such as quarterly or yearly performance.
- Filter by customer, product, or region to narrow down the data.

Columns:

- Add columns for metrics like gross profit, discounts, or tax amounts to gain a more comprehensive view.

Grouping and Sorting:

- Group data by categories such as product type or sales rep to identify patterns.
- Sort by revenue to highlight top-performing items or customers.

Memorizing Reports:

- Save customized reports by clicking Save Customization.
- Access saved reports easily from the Custom Reports tab in the Reports menu.

To save time and ensure consistent tracking, automate the generation of your sales reports.

How to Automate:

1. Customize a report to fit your needs.
2. Click Save Customization and name the report.
3. Set up a recurring schedule to receive the report via email (e.g., weekly, monthly).
4. Use automation to monitor revenue trends without manually generating reports.

Benefits of Automation:

- Keeps you informed about sales performance without additional effort.
- Reduces the risk of forgetting to track key metrics.

Sales reports are not just for record-keeping—they're tools for driving growth and making strategic decisions. Here are some ways to use the insights from your reports:

Pricing Strategy:

- Adjust prices based on high-demand periods or top-selling products.

Marketing Focus:

- Allocate marketing resources to products, services, or customers that generate the most revenue.

Inventory Management:

- Optimize stock levels by analyzing product performance trends.

Goal Setting:

- Set realistic sales targets based on historical data.

Customer Retention:

- Develop loyalty programs for top customers and strategies to re-engage dormant ones.

To get the most out of your sales reports, follow these best practices:

1. Review Reports Regularly:
   » Schedule time to review sales reports weekly or monthly to stay updated.
2. Compare Against Benchmarks:
   » Compare current performance against past periods or industry standards.
3. Involve Your Team:
   » Share insights from sales reports with your team to align on strategies and goals.
4. Integrate with Other Data Sources:
   » Combine sales data with metrics from marketing or inventory tools for a holistic view.
5. Act on Insights:
   » Use the data to make informed decisions, such as revising sales strategies or improving customer outreach.

Generating and analyzing sales reports in QuickBooks Online is a vital part of tracking revenue trends and making informed business decisions. By leveraging tools like the Sales by Customer Summary, Profit and Loss Statement, and other key reports, you can gain valuable insights into your business's performance. Regularly reviewing and customizing these reports ensures you're always equipped with the data you need to drive growth, optimize resources, and maintain a healthy financial outlook. With these strategies, your sales reports will become more than just numbers—they'll be a roadmap for your business's success.

CHAPTER 5

TRACKING EXPENSES AND BILLS

Managing expenses and vendor payments is a critical part of running a successful business. Staying on top of your bills ensures that you maintain good relationships with suppliers, avoid late fees, and keep a clear view of your company's financial health. QuickBooks Online (QBO) provides powerful tools to track expenses, categorize them appropriately, and streamline the process of managing vendor transactions.

This chapter focuses on how to effectively track and manage your business expenses and bills in QuickBooks Online. By the end of this chapter, you'll have a solid understanding of how to record transactions, automate recurring expenses, capture receipts, and reconcile vendor payments with accuracy and ease.

Tracking expenses goes beyond simply paying your bills—it's about understanding where your money is going, ensuring compliance, and improving your financial decision-making. Here's why it matters:

- Financial Insights: Categorized expenses help you identify where you're spending the most and reveal opportunities to reduce costs.
- Tax Compliance: Properly recorded and categorized expenses simplify tax preparation and help you claim all eligible deductions.

- Cash Flow Management: Staying aware of your upcoming bills and recurring payments helps you plan your cash flow and avoid surprises.
- Vendor Relationships: Timely payments ensure good standing with your suppliers, fostering stronger business relationships.

With QBO's tools, tracking and managing expenses becomes a seamless process, giving you more time to focus on growing your business.

1. Recording Vendor Transactions and Categorizing Expenses

Understanding how to record and categorize vendor transactions is the foundation of expense management. You'll learn how to input bills, payments, and credits while categorizing them into the appropriate accounts in your Chart of Accounts. This ensures accurate record-keeping and reliable financial reports.

2. Setting Up Recurring Expenses and Payment Reminders

Recurring expenses, such as rent or subscriptions, can be automated in QBO, saving time and reducing the risk of missed payments. We'll guide you through setting up recurring transactions and enabling payment reminders to keep your business running smoothly.

3. Capturing Receipts with the QuickBooks Online Mobile App

Managing receipts is often a tedious task, but QBO's mobile app simplifies the process. You'll learn how to use the app to capture, store, and link receipts to their corresponding transactions, ensuring accurate expense tracking and easy retrieval during audits.

4. Reviewing and Reconciling Vendor Payments

Reconciliation is a key step in maintaining accurate financial records. We'll show you how to reconcile your vendor payments with your bank statements, ensuring that your books match your actual transactions.

Effective expense tracking is about more than just recording payments—it's about creating a system that reduces errors, saves time, and provides valuable insights. With QuickBooks Online, you can automate repetitive tasks, organize your financial data, and gain a clear picture of your business's spending habits.

In this chapter, we'll cover practical strategies and tools to help you master expense and bill management. Let's dive in and take control of your expenses to keep your business on the path to financial success!

Recording Vendor Transactions and Categorizing Expenses

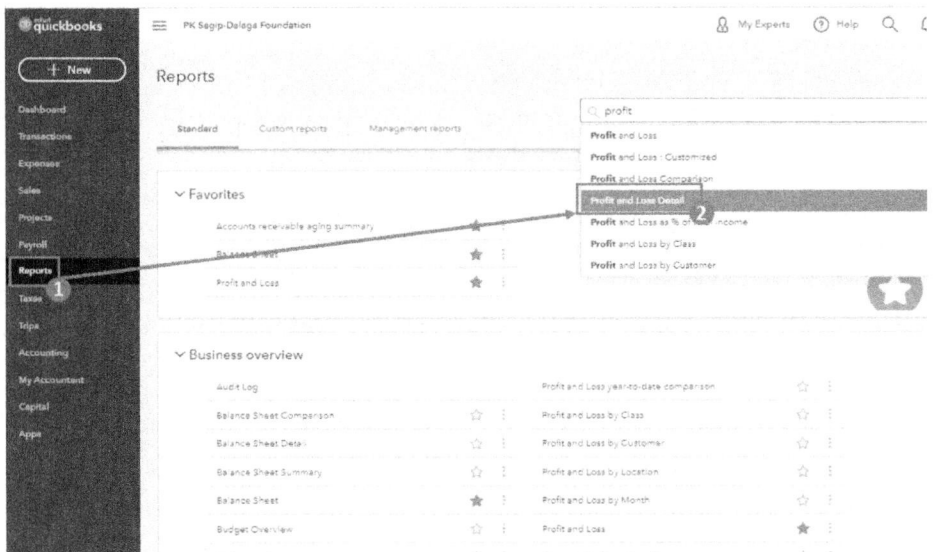

Effective expense management is a cornerstone of any well-run business. Recording vendor transactions and categorizing expenses in QuickBooks Online (QBO) ensures that your financial records are accurate, your spending is well-organized, and your financial reports provide meaningful insights. Whether you're paying for office supplies, utility bills, or contractor services, accurate tracking and categorization of expenses helps you maintain control over your finances and prepares you for tax season.

This chapter provides a detailed guide on how to record vendor transactions, categorize expenses accurately, and use QBO's tools to streamline the process.

Recording vendor transactions and categorizing expenses correctly is essential for several reasons:

- Accurate Financial Reporting: Proper categorization ensures your Profit and Loss (P&L) statements and Balance Sheets reflect your business's true financial position.
- Cash Flow Management: Tracking expenses helps you monitor your spending and plan for upcoming payments, preventing cash flow issues.
- Tax Compliance: Categorizing expenses correctly ensures that you claim all eligible deductions while remaining compliant with tax laws.
- Budgeting and Decision-Making: Clear expense data allows you to analyze spending patterns and make informed decisions about cost-cutting or investments.

With QBO, these processes are streamlined and integrated, making it easier to stay on top of your business expenses.

Vendor transactions typically involve bills, payments, and credits. QuickBooks Online provides a straightforward process for recording each type of transaction.

Step-by-Step Guide to Recording Bills:

1. Navigate to the Bills Section:
   - » Click + New in the left-hand menu and select Bill under the Vendors section.
2. Enter Vendor Information:
   - » Choose the vendor from the dropdown menu or add a new vendor by clicking + Add New.
   - » Include the billing address and terms of payment (e.g., Net 30, Net 15).
3. Input Bill Details:

- » Enter the bill date, due date, and reference number (if applicable).
- » Add line items for the goods or services purchased, specifying the Category, Description, Amount, and Tax.
4. Save and Close:
   - » Review the details for accuracy and click Save and Close or Save and New to continue entering additional bills.

Recording Payments to Vendors:

After entering bills, you can record payments when they are made.

1. Go to Pay Bills:
   - » Click + New and select Pay Bills under the Vendors section.
2. Select the Vendor:
   - » Choose the vendor whose bill you're paying.
3. Choose Payment Method and Account:
   - » Specify the payment method (e.g., check, credit card, ACH transfer).
   - » Select the account from which the payment will be made.
4. Apply the Payment:
   - » Choose the bills to pay and enter the payment amount.
   - » Click Save and Close to complete the transaction.

Applying Vendor Credits:

If a vendor issues a credit (e.g., for a return or overpayment), you can record it as follows:

1. Go to Vendor Credits:
   - » Click + New and select Vendor Credit.
2. Enter Credit Details:

» Select the vendor, add the credit amount, and categorize it appropriately.

3. Apply the Credit:

» Use the credit when paying future bills from the same vendor.

Proper categorization is crucial for maintaining organized financial records and ensuring that your reports provide meaningful insights.

How to Categorize Expenses in QuickBooks Online:

1. Select the Correct Expense Category:

» Choose a category from the Chart of Accounts (e.g., Office Supplies, Rent, Advertising).

» If the appropriate category doesn't exist, create a new one under Settings > Chart of Accounts.

2. Use Detailed Descriptions:

» Add a clear description for each transaction to provide context and ensure clarity.

3. Split Categories When Necessary:

» For transactions that include multiple expense types (e.g., a single receipt for supplies and shipping costs), use the Split feature to allocate amounts to different categories.

4. Review and Adjust Categorization:

» Regularly review categorized expenses to ensure accuracy and make adjustments if needed.

Best Practices for Expense Categorization:

• Be Consistent: Use the same categories consistently to avoid confusion in reports.
• Avoid Miscellaneous Categories: Min-imize the use of "Other" or "Miscellaneous" categories, as they obscure details in financial reports.
• Consult an Accountant: For complex transactions, seek guidance to ensure proper categorization.

QuickBooks Online offers several features to simplify the process of recording and categorizing expenses.

Expense Tracking with Bank Feeds:

1. Connect Bank Accounts:

» Link your business bank and credit card accounts to QBO for automatic transaction imports.

2. Categorize Transactions:

» Go to the Banking menu, review imported transactions, and assign categories.

Rules for Automation:

• Create rules to automate expense categorization based on transaction details (e.g., categorize all payments to a specific vendor as "Office Supplies").

Receipt Management:

• Use the QBO mobile app to capture and attach receipts to transactions.
• Automatically match uploaded receipts to expenses in QBO.

Mistakes in recording vendor transactions or categorizing expenses can lead to inaccurate reports and potential compliance issues. Here's how to avoid common pitfalls:

Duplicate Entries:

• Issue: Entering the same transaction multiple times.
• Solution: Use bank feeds and recon-

ciliation tools to identify and remove duplicates.

Misclassification:

- Issue: Categorizing expenses incorrectly, such as recording a fixed asset purchase as an operating expense.
- Solution: Double-check categories and consult an accountant for complex transactions.

Ignoring Tax Implications:

- Issue: Failing to track sales tax or VAT on purchases.
- Solution: Enable tax tracking in QBO and categorize tax-related expenses accurately.

Once your expenses are recorded and categorized, you can use QBO's reporting tools to analyze spending patterns and make informed decisions.

Key Reports:

1. Profit and Loss Report:
   - » Review total expenses by category to identify high-cost areas.
2. Expenses by Vendor Summary:
   - » Track spending by vendor to evaluate supplier relationships and negotiate better terms.
3. Transaction Detail by Account:
   - » Drill down into specific expense categories for a detailed view.

Using Insights to Improve Finances:

- Identify areas where costs can be reduced.
- Negotiate bulk discounts or better payment terms with top vendors.
- Adjust budgets based on historical spending trends.

Recording vendor transactions and categorizing expenses accurately in QuickBooks Online is essential for maintaining organized financial records and gaining valuable insights into your business's financial health. By following the steps and best practices outlined in this chapter, you can streamline your expense management processes, reduce errors, and make more informed financial decisions. With QBO's tools and features, expense tracking becomes a seamless and integral part of your business's success.

Setting Up Recurring Expenses and Payment Reminders

Managing recurring expenses efficiently is a vital part of maintaining a healthy cash flow and staying on top of your financial obligations. Whether it's rent, utility bills, software subscriptions, or vendor contracts, automating these payments and setting up reminders in QuickBooks Online (QBO) reduces manual effort and ensures you never miss a payment.

In this chapter, we'll explore how to set up recurring expenses and payment reminders in QBO. You'll learn the step-by-step process for creating recurring transactions, automating reminders, and using these tools to streamline your expense management. By automating recurring expenses, you can focus on growing your business while keeping your finances organized and stress-free.

Automating recurring expenses in QBO provides several significant advantages:

1. Time Savings:

- Reduces manual entry for repeated transactions.
- Frees up time for more strategic tasks, such as financial analysis or customer service.

2. Consistency:

- Ensures expenses are recorded accurately and on time, eliminating the risk of missed payments or late fees.

3. Cash Flow Management:

- Allows you to anticipate and plan for regular outflows, helping you maintain a balanced cash flow.

4. Reduced Errors:

- Automates calculations and categorization, minimizing the risk of data entry mistakes.

5. Compliance:

- Ensures accurate record-keeping for tax purposes by consistently tracking recurring expenses.

Recurring expenses typically fall into a few broad categories. Automating these types of transactions in QBO ensures that they are always accounted for:

- Fixed Expenses: Payments with a consistent amount and frequency, such as rent, insurance, or loan repayments.
- Variable Expenses: Payments with fluctuating amounts, such as utility bills or credit card payments.
- Subscription-Based Services: Recurring payments for software, memberships, or other subscription-based services.

Setting up recurring expenses in QBO is a straightforward process. Follow these steps to automate your regular payments:

Step-by-Step Guide:

1. Navigate to Recurring Transactions:

   » Log in to your QuickBooks Online account.
   » Click Settings (gear icon) in the top-right corner and select Recurring Transactions under the Lists section.

2. Create a New Recurring Expense:

   » Click the New button.
   » Choose Expense or Bill as the transaction type, depending on your needs.

3. Choose a Template Type:

   » Scheduled: Automatically records the transaction on a specific schedule.
   » Reminder: Sends a notification prompting you to review and record the transaction manually.
   » Unscheduled: Saves the template for on-demand use without setting a specific schedule.

4. Set Up Vendor Details:

   » Select the vendor associated with the recurring expense.
   » Add or verify the vendor's contact details for accuracy.

5. Input Payment Details:

   » Enter the payment amount, category (e.g., utilities, office supplies), and any applicable taxes.
   » If the amount varies, leave it blank and fill it in manually when the transaction is processed.

6. Specify the Recurrence Schedule:

   » Choose the frequency of the expense (e.g., daily, weekly, monthly).
   » Set the start date and, if applicable, the end date for the recurring transaction.

7. Assign the Payment Method:

   » Select the payment method (e.g., check, credit card, ACH transfer).

8. Save the Template:

» Review all details for accuracy and click Save Template to activate the recurring transaction.

Payment reminders in QBO help you stay on top of due dates and avoid late fees. They are especially useful for recurring expenses that require manual review or approval.

Step-by-Step Guide to Setting Up Payment Reminders:

1. Go to Settings:

» Click the Settings (gear icon) in the top-right corner.
» Navigate to Reminders under the Tools section.

2. Enable Payment Reminders:

» Turn on reminders for expenses or bills as needed.
» Customize when reminders are sent (e.g., 3 days before the due date).

3. Set Up Specific Reminders for Vendors:

» Go to Expenses > Vendors and select a specific vendor.
» Click Set Reminder and define the frequency and timing of the reminders.

4. Customize Reminder Messages:

» Personalize the message to include details such as the invoice number, due date, or payment amount.
» Ensure the tone is professional and clear.

Once your recurring expenses and reminders are set up, regular monitoring ensures that your automated system is working as intended.

Viewing Active Recurring Transactions:

· Navigate to Settings > Recurring Transactions to view all active templates.
· Check the next scheduled date and status to confirm that transactions are processing correctly.

Editing or Updating Templates:

· To make changes to an existing template, click Edit next to the template.
· Update details such as the amount, schedule, or category.

Pausing or Deactivating Templates:

· If an expense is no longer relevant, pause or deactivate the template to stop automated processing.

For recurring expenses with fluctuating amounts, such as utility bills, QBO's rule feature helps you automate categorization while allowing for manual adjustments.

Setting Up Rules:

1. Go to Banking > Rules.
2. Click New Rule and set conditions for the transaction (e.g., vendor name, amount range).
3. Assign a category and specify how the transaction should be recorded.

Benefits of Rules:

· Automates categorization for variable expenses.
· Saves time by reducing manual entry for common transactions.

Reconciliation ensures that your recurring expenses match your bank statements, keeping your records accurate.

Steps for Reconciliation:

1. Navigate to Accounting > Reconcile.

2. Select the account associated with the recurring expenses.

3. Compare each transaction in QBO to your bank statement and resolve discrepancies.

Despite its efficiency, automation may occasionally encounter issues. Here's how to resolve them:

Issue: Duplicate Transactions

- Cause: A manual entry overlaps with an automated recurring transaction.
- Solution: Review and delete duplicates in the Expenses menu.

Issue: Missed Payments

- Cause: A paused or deactivated template.
- Solution: Reactivate the template and ensure the schedule is correct.

Issue: Incorrect Categorization

- Cause: Outdated templates or rules.
- Solution: Update the template or rule to reflect accurate categories.

To make the most of automation, follow these best practices:

1. Review Regularly:
   » Periodically review active templates to ensure accuracy and relevance.

2. Communicate with Vendors:
   » Notify vendors of automated payments to avoid confusion or disputes.

3. Monitor Cash Flow:
   » Use QBO reports to track recurring expenses and plan for upcoming payments.

4. Set Alerts:
   » Use reminders to stay informed about upcoming transactions.

Automating recurring expenses offers significant advantages for both your workflow and your bottom line:

- Efficiency: Saves time by reducing manual effort.
- Accuracy: Minimizes errors in recording and categorization.
- Consistency: Ensures payments are made on time, preserving vendor relationships.
- Insight: Provides a clear view of recurring costs, aiding in budget planning and financial analysis.

Setting up recurring expenses and payment reminders in QuickBooks Online is a powerful way to streamline your expense management and maintain financial accuracy. By automating fixed and variable expenses, you can reduce manual work, avoid missed payments, and gain better control over your cash flow. Regular monitoring and adherence to best practices ensure that your automated system continues to operate effectively, freeing you to focus on growing your business. With these tools in place, recurring expense management becomes a seamless and efficient part of your financial operations.

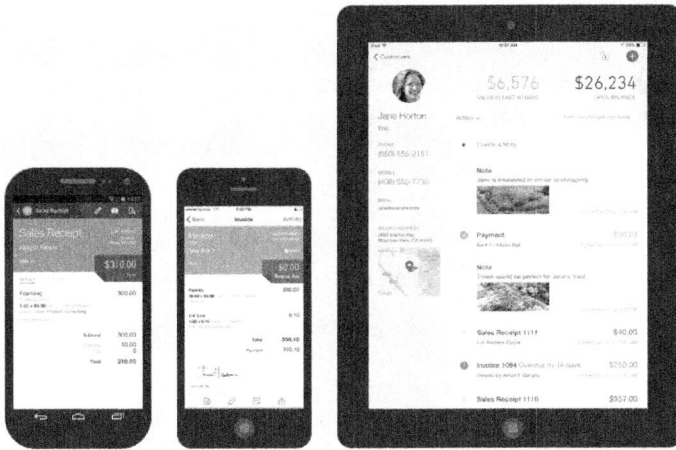

Managing receipts is a crucial aspect of expense tracking and financial management. Whether it's a meal expense during a business trip, office supplies purchased on the go, or any other business-related purchase, receipts provide proof of the transaction and are often required for tax deductions. However, manually organizing and storing receipts can be time-consuming and prone to errors.

The QuickBooks Online Mobile App simplifies receipt management by allowing you to capture, upload, and attach receipts directly to their corresponding transactions. This not only streamlines your record-keeping but also ensures your expenses are accurately tracked and categorized.

This chapter explores how to use the QuickBooks Online Mobile App to manage receipts effectively. You'll learn step-by-step how to capture, upload, and match receipts, as well as the best practices for maintaining a well-organized digital archive.

Tracking receipts is essential for several reasons:

1. Tax Compliance:

- Receipts serve as evidence for expense claims and tax deductions.
- Proper documentation ensures compliance with tax regulations, reducing the risk of audits or penalties.

2. Accurate Record-Keeping:

- Linking receipts to transactions provides a clear audit trail, improving financial transparency and accuracy.

3. Simplified Reconciliation:

- Matching receipts with transactions helps ensure that your records align with your bank and credit card statements.

4. Improved Organization:

- A centralized, digital archive of receipts eliminates the clutter of physical documents and minimizes the risk of lost paperwork.

The QuickBooks Online Mobile App is available for both iOS and Android devices. Before diving into receipt management, ensure you have the app installed and linked to your QuickBooks Online account.

Steps to Set Up the App:

1. Download the App:
   - » Visit the App Store (iOS) or Google Play Store (Android) and search for "QuickBooks Online."
   - » Download and install the app.

2. Log In:
   - » Open the app and log in using your QuickBooks Online credentials.

3. Access the Receipt Management Feature:
   - » Navigate to the Expenses or Receipts tab in the app's main menu to begin managing your receipts.

Capturing receipts with the QuickBooks Online Mobile App is quick and straightforward. Follow these steps to ensure your receipts are accurately uploaded and linked to transactions:

Step-by-Step Guide:

1. Open the Receipts Feature:
   - » Navigate to the Receipts tab in the app.

2. Capture a New Receipt:
   - » Tap the + Add Receipt button and select Take Photo.
   - » Use your device's camera to capture a clear, high-resolution image of the receipt.
   - » Ensure the entire receipt is visible and legible, including the vendor name, date, amount, and payment method.

3. Upload an Existing Receipt:
   - » If you already have a digital copy of the receipt, tap Upload Receipt and select the file from your device's gallery.

4. Save the Receipt:
   - » Once captured or uploaded, the receipt will be saved in the Receipts tab for further processing.

QuickBooks Online automatically scans uploaded receipts and attempts to match them to existing transactions in your account. Here's how the process works:

Automatic Matching:

- QuickBooks uses information from the receipt (e.g., vendor, date, and amount) to find a matching transaction.
- If a match is found, you'll see a notification or prompt to confirm the match.

Manual Matching:

If QuickBooks does not automatically match the receipt, you can manually link it to a transaction:

1. Go to the Receipts tab and select the uploaded receipt.
2. Review the details and choose the appropriate transaction from the list of potential matches.
3. Click Match to link the receipt to the transaction.

Once a receipt is uploaded and matched, you can use it to categorize the expense appropriately.

Steps to Categorize Expenses:

1. Open the matched transaction in QuickBooks Online.
2. Confirm or update the Category field to reflect the nature of the expense (e.g., Office Supplies, Travel, or Meals).
3. Save the changes to ensure the expense is accurately recorded.

Best Practices for Categorization:

- Use consistent categories to maintain clarity in your financial reports.
- Avoid using generic categories like "Miscellaneous" unless absolutely necessary.

The QuickBooks Online Mobile App includes Optical Character Recognition (OCR) technology, which automatically extracts key information from receipts. This reduces manual data entry and speeds up the process of recording expenses.

How OCR Works:

- When you upload a receipt, OCR scans the image for details such as vendor name, date, amount, and payment method.
- These details are automatically populated in the transaction fields, saving you time.

Tips for Best Results with OCR:

- Ensure the receipt is clear and not crumpled or faded.
- Capture the receipt in good lighting for maximum legibility.
- Verify the extracted data before saving the transaction.

Maintaining an organized digital archive of receipts is crucial for efficient expense tracking and compliance.

Viewing Saved Receipts:

- Access all uploaded receipts in the Receipts tab of the app or in the Receipts section of the web version of QuickBooks Online.

Searching and Filtering:

- Use filters (e.g., date range, vendor, or category) to quickly locate specific receipts.

Archiving or Deleting Receipts:

- Archive old receipts that are no longer active but still need to be retained for records.
- Delete duplicate or unnecessary receipts to keep your archive clutter-free.

QuickBooks Online enables you to generate reports that include receipts, making it easy to audit your expenses.

How to Generate Receipt Reports:

1. Go to the Reports section in QuickBooks Online.
2. Select a report type, such as Expenses by Vendor Summary or Transaction Detail by Account.
3. Filter the report to include transactions with attached receipts.

Benefits of Receipt Reports:

- Provides a clear audit trail for expenses.
- Simplifies the process of preparing for tax season or external audits.

Here are some common challenges and how to address them:

Issue: Missing or Faded Receipts

- Solution: Capture receipts immediately after a transaction to avoid losing or damaging them.

Issue: Duplicate Uploads

- Solution: Regularly review uploaded receipts to identify and delete duplicates.

Issue: Misfiled Receipts

- Solution: Use consistent naming conventions and categories to keep receipts organized.

To get the most out of the QuickBooks Online Mobile App, follow these best practices:

1. Capture Receipts Immediately:
   - » Upload receipts as soon as the transaction occurs to avoid forgetting or misplacing them.
2. Review OCR Data:
   - » Double-check extracted data to ensure accuracy before saving transactions.
3. Use Consistent Categories:
   - » Maintain consistency in categorization to simplify reporting and analysis.
4. Store Backup Copies:
   - » Consider saving digital receipts in cloud storage as an additional backup.
5. Regularly Audit Receipts:
   - » Schedule periodic reviews to ensure all expenses are properly documented and categorized.

Capturing and managing receipts with the QuickBooks Online Mobile App transforms what was once a tedious task into a seamless, automated process. By leveraging features like receipt capture, OCR technology, and automatic transaction matching, you can maintain accurate financial records, simplify tax preparation, and gain better control over your expenses. With these tools and best practices, managing receipts becomes a hassle-free part of your overall financial workflow, allowing you to focus on growing your business.

Reviewing and Reconciling Vendor Payments

Effective management of vendor payments is crucial for maintaining healthy relationships with suppliers and ensuring the accuracy of your business's financial records. Reviewing and reconciling vendor payments in QuickBooks Online (QBO) allows you to verify that all payments are accurately recorded, prevent duplicate or missed payments, and ensure your accounts match your bank or credit card statements.

This chapter provides a step-by-step guide to reviewing and reconciling vendor payments in QBO. By the end, you'll understand how to ensure your records align with actual transactions, troubleshoot discrepancies, and maintain an organized and error-free accounting system.

Reviewing and reconciling vendor payments offers several key benefits:

1. Accuracy in Financial Records:

- Verifies that vendor payments are recorded correctly, reducing the risk of errors in your books.

2. Prevention of Duplicate or Missed Payments:

- Ensures vendors are paid accurately and on time, avoiding late fees or strained relationships.

3. Improved Cash Flow Management:

- Helps you monitor outgoing payments and plan for future expenses.

4. Tax Compliance:

- Ensures expenses are accurately categorized and supported by proper documentation for tax deductions.

5. Audit Preparedness:

- Creates a clear audit trail by linking vendor payments to invoices and receipts.

Before reconciling accounts, it's important to review vendor payments to ensure they are recorded and categorized correctly.

Step-by-Step Guide:

1. Access the Expense Menu:
   - » Navigate to Expenses > Vendors in the left-hand menu.

2. Select a Vendor:
   - » Click on the vendor whose payments you want to review. This will display all associated transactions, including bills, payments, and credits.

3. Filter Transactions:
   - » Use filters (e.g., date range, transaction type) to focus on the payments you want to review.

4. Check Payment Details:
   - » Open individual transactions to verify the amount, payment method, and categorization.
   - » Confirm that each payment is linked to the correct bill or expense.

5. Resolve Unapplied Payments:
   - » Look for payments that are not matched to any bills and link them to the appropriate transactions.

Best Practices for Reviewing Payments:

- Review vendor payments weekly or monthly to catch errors early.
- Use detailed descriptions and notes in each payment for clarity.

Before starting the reconciliation process, gather the necessary information to ensure a smooth workflow:

What You Need:

- Bank or credit card statements for the account being reconciled.
- A list of vendor payments recorded in QBO.
- Supporting documentation, such as receipts or invoices, for each payment.

Setting Up Reconciliation in QBO:

1. Go to Accounting > Reconcile in the left-hand menu.
2. Select the account you want to reconcile (e.g., checking or credit card account).
3. Enter the Beginning Balance and Ending Balance from your bank or credit card statement.
4. Set the reconciliation Date Range to match your statement period.

Reconciliation involves comparing transactions in QBO to your bank or credit card statement to ensure they match.

Step-by-Step Guide:

1. Start Reconciliation:
   - » After entering the beginning and ending balances, click Start Reconciling.
2. Match Payments:
   - » Review each vendor payment in QBO and match it to a cor-

responding transaction on your bank or credit card statement.

» Verify the transaction amount, date, and vendor name.

3. Mark Matched Transactions:

» Check the box next to each transaction in QBO that matches a statement entry.

» The reconciliation summary will update to reflect the remaining difference between your records and the statement balance.

4. Investigate Unmatched Transactions:

» For any payments that don't match, review supporting documents or contact the vendor for clarification.

» Common issues include:

▪ Missing transactions: Add the missing payment to QBO.

▪ Duplicate entries: Delete one of the duplicates.

▪ Incorrect amounts: Edit the transaction to reflect the correct amount.

5. Finalize Reconciliation:

» Once all transactions are matched and the difference is $0, click Finish Now.

Reconciling vendor payments isn't always straightforward. Here are some common issues and how to resolve them:

1. Missing Transactions:

- Cause: A vendor payment wasn't recorded in QBO.
- Solution: Add the missing transaction in QBO and link it to the appropriate bill.

2. Duplicate Transactions:

- Cause: The same payment was recorded twice in QBO.
- Solution: Identify the duplicate entry and delete it.

3. Incorrect Payment Amounts:

- Cause: A payment was recorded with the wrong amount.
- Solution: Edit the payment in QBO to reflect the correct amount.

4. Timing Differences:

- Cause: Payments recorded in QBO may not have cleared the bank by the statement date.
- Solution: Exclude uncleared payments from the current reconciliation and include them in the next cycle.

After reconciling vendor payments, ensure they are categorized correctly in QBO to maintain accurate financial records.

Steps for Categorization:

1. Open each payment in QBO.
2. Verify that the payment is assigned to the correct account (e.g., Utilities, Rent, Supplies).
3. Adjust categories if necessary and save changes.

Tips for Categorization:

- Use consistent categories to simplify reporting and tax preparation.
- Consult with an accountant for complex transactions.

QuickBooks Online offers several reports to help you analyze vendor payments and track expenses.

Key Reports:

1. Expenses by Vendor Summary:

» Provides a breakdown of total payments made to each vendor.

» Helps identify top vendors and monitor spending trends.

2. Transaction Detail by Account:

» Lists all transactions in a specific account, including vendor payments.

» Useful for auditing and troubleshooting discrepancies.

3. Profit and Loss Statement:

» Shows how vendor payments contribute to overall expenses and profitability.

Customizing Reports:

• Filter reports by date range, vendor, or category to focus on specific data.

• Save customized reports for regular use.

To maintain accurate and organized financial records, follow these best practices:

1. Reconcile Monthly:

» Perform reconciliation at the end of each month to stay up-to-date.

2. Keep Supporting Documents:

» Attach receipts or invoices to each vendor payment for a clear audit trail.

3. Automate Payment Tracking:

» Use QBO's recurring transaction feature for regular vendor payments.

4. Monitor Cash Flow:

» Use QBO reports to analyze outgoing payments and plan for future expenses.

5. Involve Your Accountant:

» Consult with an accountant or bookkeeper for complex reconciliations or discrepancies.

Regularly reviewing and reconciling vendor payments in QuickBooks Online offers long-term benefits for your business:

• Improved Accuracy: Minimizes errors and discrepancies in financial records.

• Stronger Vendor Relationships: Ensures timely and accurate payments, fostering trust with suppliers.

• Enhanced Financial Insights: Provides a clear understanding of expenses, helping you make informed decisions.

Reviewing and reconciling vendor payments in QuickBooks Online is an essential part of maintaining accurate financial records and ensuring smooth vendor relationships. By following the steps outlined in this chapter, you can identify and resolve discrepancies, streamline your reconciliation process, and gain valuable insights into your expenses. With regular reviews and reconciliations, you'll have a reliable foundation for managing your business finances effectively and efficiently.

CHAPTER 6

PAYROLL AND EMPLOYEE MANAGEMENT

Running a business with employees or contractors is both rewarding and challenging, especially when it comes to managing payroll. Ensuring that everyone is paid accurately and on time while staying compliant with tax regulations can feel like a juggling act. Mistakes, even small ones, can lead to unhappy employees, penalties, or unnecessary stress. That's where QuickBooks Online (QBO) steps in to make payroll and employee management seamless.

Imagine the ease of knowing that payroll is handled automatically, taxes are calculated correctly, and filings are just a few clicks away. With QuickBooks Online's powerful payroll features, you can focus on building your business while it takes care of the heavy lifting. Whether you're running payroll for a growing team or managing payments for independent contractors, QBO provides the tools to simplify the process.

In this chapter, we'll dive into the essentials of setting up and managing payroll in QuickBooks Online. You'll learn how to configure payroll settings to suit your business needs, onboard employees with ease, and manage payroll taxes without breaking a sweat. From generating detailed payroll reports to filing essential tax forms like W-2s and 941s, QuickBooks ensures you stay compliant and organized.

For businesses that rely on contractors, we'll explore how to handle payments and prepare 1099 forms, ensuring that your records are accurate and tax-ready. By the end of this chapter, you'll feel confident navigating payroll and employee management, transforming what was once a daunting task into an efficient and stress-free process.

With QuickBooks Online as your partner, payroll becomes more than just a necessary chore—it's an opportunity to strengthen your team, streamline your operations, and keep your business running smoothly. Let's get started!

Setting Up Payroll in QuickBooks Online

Setting up payroll in QuickBooks Online (QBO) is a critical step for businesses with employees or contractors. Payroll is more than just paying your team—it involves tracking hours, calculating taxes, and ensuring compliance with local, state, and federal laws. With QuickBooks Online Payroll, the process becomes intuitive, streamlined, and adaptable to your business's unique needs.

This chapter walks you through the step-by-step process of setting up payroll in QBO, from choosing the right payroll plan to configuring essential settings. By the end, you'll have a fully functioning payroll system that saves you time, reduces errors, and ensures your employees are paid accurately and on time.

QuickBooks Online Payroll simplifies payroll processing, offering features that benefit businesses of all sizes:

1. Automation:

- Automates calculations for wages, taxes, and deductions.
- Schedules payments to employees and tax authorities automatically.

2. Compliance:

- Helps ensure compliance with tax laws by calculating, filing, and paying payroll taxes on time.
- Provides forms like W-2s and 1099s at year-end.

3. Efficiency:

- Tracks employee hours, benefits, and deductions in one place.
- Generates detailed payroll reports for better financial oversight.

4. Integration:

- Syncs seamlessly with your QuickBooks Online account, ensuring payroll and accounting records are always aligned.

Before setting up payroll, it's essential to select the payroll plan that best fits your business. QuickBooks Online offers three primary payroll plans:

1. Core Plan:

- Basic payroll management with automatic tax calculations and direct deposit.
- Ideal for small businesses with straightforward payroll needs.

2. Premium Plan:

- Includes everything in the Core Plan plus time tracking and HR support.
- Suitable for businesses with hourly employees or more complex payroll processes.

3. Elite Plan:

- Offers tax penalty protection and a dedicated payroll expert.
- Designed for larger businesses or those seeking advanced payroll services.

Compare these plans carefully and choose one that aligns with your current and future payroll requirements.

Once you've chosen a payroll plan, it's time to set up payroll in QuickBooks Online. Follow these steps to get started:

Step 1: Access Payroll Settings

1. Log in to QuickBooks Online.
2. Click on Payroll in the left-hand navigation menu.
3. Select Get Started to begin the setup process.

Step 2: Enter Company Information

1. Provide your business's legal name, address, and Employer Identification Number (EIN).
2. Verify your state and federal tax details, including tax filing frequencies and deposit schedules.

Step 3: Configure Payroll Preferences

1. Choose the pay schedule(s) for your employees (e.g., weekly, biweekly, or monthly).
2. Set up payment methods, such as direct deposit or paper checks.

Step 4: Add Bank Account Details

1. Enter your business bank account information to facilitate payroll payments and tax deposits.
2. Verify your bank account by following QuickBooks' prompts (e.g., confirming micro-deposit amounts).

Adding employees to your payroll system ensures that they're paid accurately and their taxes are calculated correctly.

Step 1: Gather Employee Information

Before entering employee details into QuickBooks, collect the following:

- Full name, address, and Social Security Number (SSN).
- Employment details, such as hire date and job title.
- Pay rate, including hourly or salary amounts.
- Tax withholding information from the employee's W-4 form.
- Benefits or deductions, such as health insurance or retirement contributions.

Step 2: Input Employee Details

1. Navigate to the Payroll menu and select Employees.
2. Click Add Employee.
3. Enter the employee's personal and employment details.

Step 3: Set Up Pay Information

1. Specify the pay schedule (e.g., weekly, biweekly).
2. Enter the pay rate and any additional earnings, such as bonuses or overtime.
3. Configure tax withholding and deductions based on the employee's W-4.

Step 4: Save Employee Profile

Once all details are entered, save the employee profile. Repeat the process for additional employees.

Payroll taxes are a critical component of your payroll system. QuickBooks Online simplifies tax management by calculating, filing, and paying taxes on your behalf.

Step 1: Verify Tax Settings

1. Confirm your federal and state tax details during the payroll setup process.
2. Ensure your EIN is accurate and up to date.

Step 2: Configure Tax Payments

1. Enter your tax payment schedule based on your tax filing frequency.
2. Link your bank account to facilitate automatic tax payments.

Step 3: Enable Automatic Tax Filing (Optional)

QuickBooks Online Payroll allows you to enable automatic filing and payment of payroll taxes. Turn this feature on for added convenience and peace of mind.

To ensure your payroll system meets your business needs, customize the following settings:

1. Pay Types:

- Add pay types such as overtime, commissions, or bonuses if applicable.

2. Benefits and Deductions:

- Set up employee benefits like health insurance, retirement plans, or flexible spending accounts.
- Configure pre-tax and post-tax deductions as needed.

3. Time Tracking:

- If your payroll plan includes time tracking, integrate tools like TSheets to track employee hours directly in QuickBooks.

Before running your first payroll, test the system to ensure everything is set up correctly.

Steps to Test Payroll:

1. Run a test payroll for one or two employees to verify calculations.
2. Confirm that paychecks or direct deposits are processed accurately.
3. Check tax calculations and ensure they align with current tax rates.

Once your payroll system is set up and tested, you're ready to process your first payroll.

Step-by-Step Guide:

1. Go to the Run Payroll tab in the Payroll menu.
2. Select the pay period and pay date.
3. Review employee hours, earnings, and deductions.
4. Confirm payment amounts and processing method (e.g., direct deposit or check).
5. Submit the payroll.

QuickBooks will handle the rest, including generating pay stubs, recording payroll expenses, and calculating taxes.

Even with QuickBooks Online's user-friendly interface, you may encounter challenges during setup. Here are some common issues and their solutions:

1. Bank Account Verification Delays:

- Solution: Check for micro-deposit confirmation emails and ensure the entered bank details are correct.

2. Incorrect Employee Information:

- Solution: Double-check employee profiles and update errors before processing payroll.

3. Tax Configuration Errors:

- Solution: Consult with a tax professional or QuickBooks Payroll support to verify tax settings.

Follow these best practices to ensure a smooth payroll setup process:

1. Gather Information Early:
   - » Collect all necessary employee and tax details before starting the setup.
2. Test Before Launch:
   - » Run test payrolls to catch errors and verify accuracy.
3. Leverage Support:
   - » Use QuickBooks Online's customer support and help resources for guidance.
4. Stay Up to Date:
   - » Keep payroll tax rates and employee information updated regularly.

Setting up payroll in QuickBooks Online is an essential step toward efficient employee management and accurate financial reporting. By following the detailed process outlined in this chapter, you can ensure your payroll system is configured correctly, saving you time and reducing the risk of errors. With QuickBooks handling the heavy lifting, payroll becomes less of a chore and more of a streamlined process that supports your business's success.

Adding Employees and Managing Payroll Taxes

INFORMATION FOR **Doe, Jane**

| Personal |
| Address & Contact |
| Additional Info |
| Payroll Info |
| Employment Info |
| Workers' Comp |

LEGAL NAME | Mr./Ms./ | Jane | M.I. | Doe

PRINT ON CHECKS AS | Jane Doe

SOCIAL SECURITY NO.

GENDER | Male

DATE OF BIRTH | 02/03/1990

MARITAL STATUS | Single

U.S. CITIZEN | Yes

ETHNICITY | White

DISABILITY

DISABLED | No

DISABILITY DESCRIPTION

I-9 FORM

ON FILE

WORK AUTHORIZATION EXPIRES

MILITARY

U.S. VETERAN

STATUS

☐ Employee is inactive   OK   Cancel   Help

Managing payroll is one of the most essential, yet intricate, aspects of running a business. Whether you're hiring your first employee or managing a growing team, adding employees to your payroll system and handling payroll taxes accurately are critical to maintaining compliance and fostering a positive work environment. QuickBooks Online (QBO) simplifies these tasks, providing tools to streamline employee onboarding and automate tax calculations, filings, and payments.

This chapter will guide you through the step-by-step process of adding employees to your payroll system, managing their pay and benefits, and ensuring payroll taxes are calculated and paid correctly. By mastering these features in QBO, you'll save time, avoid costly errors, and ensure that your employees and tax obligations are handled seamlessly.

Before diving into the details, it's important to understand why precise employee and payroll tax management is essential:

For Employees:

* Ensures employees are paid correctly and on time, boosting satisfaction and trust.
* Tracks benefits and deductions accurately, including health insurance, retirement plans, and other withholdings.

For Tax Compliance:

* Meets federal, state, and local payroll tax requirements, avoiding penalties or audits.
* Prepares accurate tax filings, such as W-2s and 941 forms, for submission to tax authorities.

For Business Operations:

- Maintains organized financial records for budgeting and decision-making.
- Reduces administrative workload by automating recurring payroll tasks.

QuickBooks Online Payroll makes it easy to onboard employees and record their pay and tax details. Follow these steps to add employees to your payroll system:

Step 1: Gather Employee Information

Before adding an employee, ensure you have the necessary details:

- Full name, address, and Social Security Number (SSN).
- Employment details, including job title, hire date, and employment type (full-time, part-time, or seasonal).
- Pay rate and schedule (hourly, salary, or commission-based).
- Tax withholding details from the employee's W-4 form.
- Benefits and deductions, such as health insurance or retirement contributions.

Step 2: Add Employee Information

1. Navigate to Payroll > Employees in the left-hand menu.
2. Click Add Employee to begin the set-up process.
3. Enter the employee's personal details, including name, address, and SSN.
4. Specify their employment type and hire date.

Step 3: Configure Pay Details

1. Choose the employee's pay schedule (e.g., weekly, biweekly, monthly).
2. Enter the pay rate and any additional earnings, such as overtime or bonuses.
3. Set up benefits, deductions, or garnishments as applicable.

Step 4: Input Tax Information

1. Use the employee's W-4 form to input their federal and state tax withholding details.
2. Specify allowances, additional withholdings, or exemptions, if applicable.

Step 5: Save and Review

Once all information is entered, review the employee's profile for accuracy and save the details. Repeat the process for additional employees.

QuickBooks Online Payroll takes the complexity out of payroll taxes by automating calculations, filings, and payments. Here's how to set up and manage payroll taxes effectively:

Step 1: Set Up Payroll Tax Details

1. Navigate to Taxes > Payroll Taxes in the left-hand menu.
2. Click Set Up Taxes and provide your business's tax details:
   - » Employer Identification Number (EIN).
   - » Federal and state tax rates.
   - » Filing and deposit schedules.
3. Link your business bank account to enable automatic tax payments.

Step 2: Enable Tax Automation

1. Turn on Automatic Tax Payments and Filings in the payroll settings. This feature ensures that QuickBooks calculates, files, and pays your payroll taxes on time.
2. Verify that tax rates and filing fre-

quencies are accurate based on your location and business type.

Step 3: Review Tax Calculations

QuickBooks automatically calculates payroll taxes each time you run payroll. These calculations include:

- Employee Withholding: Federal income tax, Social Security, and Medicare.
- Employer Contributions: Social Security, Medicare, and unemployment taxes (FUTA and SUTA).

Review these calculations during payroll processing to ensure accuracy.

QuickBooks Online streamlines tax filing and payment, ensuring you meet compliance deadlines effortlessly.

Step 1: Access Tax Forms

1. Go to Taxes > Payroll Taxes and select the appropriate form, such as:

   » Form 941 for quarterly federal tax returns.
   » Form W-2 for annual wage and tax statements.

2. QuickBooks generates these forms automatically based on your payroll data.

Step 2: Submit Tax Forms

1. Review the generated form for accuracy.
2. Submit the form electronically through QuickBooks or print it for manual filing.

Step 3: Schedule Tax Payments

1. Go to Taxes > Payroll Taxes > Pay Taxes.
2. Select the tax type (e.g., federal, state, or local) and the payment amount.

3. Schedule the payment date and confirm the transaction.

Payroll taxes often intersect with employee benefits and deductions, which must be accurately managed to avoid discrepancies.

Setting Up Benefits:

1. Navigate to Payroll Settings > Benefits and Deductions.
2. Add employee benefits such as health insurance, retirement contributions, or commuter benefits.
3. Specify whether the benefit is pre-tax or post-tax.

Adjusting Payroll Taxes:

For adjustments, such as correcting overpaid or underpaid taxes:

1. Go to Payroll > Employees.
2. Edit the affected payroll run to adjust taxes or deductions.
3. Save changes and reconcile any discrepancies.

Despite automation, payroll tax management may occasionally encounter challenges. Here's how to address common issues:

Issue 1: Tax Calculation Errors

- Cause: Incorrect employee tax details or outdated tax rates.
- Solution: Verify employee profiles and update tax rates in payroll settings.

Issue 2: Missing Tax Payments

- Cause: Bank account verification delays or failed transactions.
- Solution: Confirm that your bank account is linked and funded appropriately.

Issue 3: Late Filings

- Cause: Missed deadlines or incomplete filings.
- Solution: Use QuickBooks' automated filing feature and set reminders for manual filings.

QuickBooks Online Payroll includes reports to help you monitor payroll taxes and ensure accuracy.

Key Reports:

1. Payroll Summary: Provides an overview of wages, taxes, and deductions for each pay period.
2. Tax Liability Report: Lists upcoming payroll tax payments and filing deadlines.
3. Employee Earnings Report: Breaks down wages, taxes, and benefits for individual employees.

Customizing Reports:

- Filter reports by date range, employee, or tax type for detailed insights.
- Export reports to Excel or PDF for record-keeping.

To ensure smooth payroll tax management, follow these best practices:

1. Double-Check Employee Information:
   - » Ensure all employee profiles are accurate and up to date.
2. Review Tax Settings Regularly:
   - » Update tax rates and filing frequencies as needed.
3. Leverage Automation:
   - » Enable automatic tax payments and filings to reduce manual workload.
4. Keep Records Organized:
   - » Store copies of tax forms, payments, and correspondence for easy access during audits.

Adding employees and managing payroll taxes in QuickBooks Online is a critical process that, when done correctly, ensures compliance, accuracy, and efficiency. By following the steps outlined in this chapter, you can streamline employee onboarding, automate payroll tax calculations, and confidently handle filings and payments. With QuickBooks Online as your payroll partner, you'll have the tools and insights needed to keep your team and tax authorities happy while focusing on the growth and success of your business.

Running Payroll Reports and Filing Tax Forms

Payroll is a significant aspect of managing a business, involving not just paying employees but also ensuring accurate reporting and compliance with tax regulations. Payroll reports and tax forms are essential tools that help you track wages, taxes, and deductions while preparing you for tax filing and audits. QuickBooks Online (QBO) simplifies these tasks by providing a suite of payroll reports and automated tax form filing capabilities.

In this chapter, we'll explore how to run payroll reports, interpret the data, and use QBO to file key tax forms like W-2s, 941s, and 1099s. With these insights, you'll be equipped to maintain accurate records, meet filing deadlines, and avoid potential penalties.

Payroll reports and tax forms are crucial for several reasons:

1. Accurate Record-Keeping:

- Payroll reports provide a detailed breakdown of employee earnings, taxes, and deductions, ensuring your records are comprehensive and accurate.

2. Compliance:

- Filing tax forms like W-2s and 941s is a legal requirement for businesses with employees.
- Accurate forms ensure compliance with federal, state, and local tax laws.

3. Business Insights:

- Payroll reports help you understand labor costs, monitor tax liabilities, and make informed financial decisions.

4. Audit Preparedness:

- Payroll reports and tax filings create a clear audit trail, reducing the risk of fines or penalties during tax audits.

QuickBooks Online offers several payroll reports to help you track payroll activity, taxes, and employee earnings:

1. Payroll Summary Report:

- Provides an overview of wages, deductions, taxes, and net pay for a specific time period.
- Ideal for understanding overall payroll costs.

2. Payroll Details Report:

- Breaks down payroll data by employee, including hours worked, wages, and deductions.
- Useful for verifying individual employee payments.

3. Tax Liability Report:

- Displays total payroll taxes owed to federal, state, and local authorities.
- Helps you track upcoming tax payments.

4. Employee Earnings Report:

- Summarizes earnings, taxes, and deductions for each employee.
- Useful for employee-specific inquiries or year-end reviews.

5. Payroll Tax Payments Report:

- Tracks payroll tax payments made, including dates and amounts.
- Ensures all tax payments are accounted for.

Running payroll reports in QuickBooks Online is straightforward and customizable. Follow these steps to generate and interpret reports:

Step-by-Step Guide:

1. Navigate to Reports:
   - » Log in to QuickBooks Online and click on Reports in the left-hand menu.

2. Search for Payroll Reports:
   - » Use the search bar to find specific payroll reports, such as "Payroll Summary" or "Tax Liability."

3. Customize the Report:
   - » Adjust filters for date range, employees, or specific payroll items to tailor the report to your needs.

4. Run and Review:
   - » Click Run Report to generate the report.
   - » Review the data for accuracy, focusing on key metrics like wages, taxes, and net pay.

5. Export or Print:
   - » Use the Export button to download the report as a PDF or Excel file.

» Print the report for physical record-keeping or presentations.

QuickBooks Online Payroll automates the process of generating, filing, and submitting payroll tax forms. Here's how to file key tax forms using QBO:

Step 1: Set Up Tax Filing Preferences

1. Navigate to Taxes > Payroll Taxes in the left-hand menu.
2. Ensure your business's Employer Identification Number (EIN) and other tax details are accurate.
3. Turn on Automatic Tax Payments and Filings to let QuickBooks handle the filings on your behalf.

Step 2: Review Tax Forms

1. Go to Taxes > Payroll Tax > Forms.
2. Select the tax form you need, such as:
   » Form W-2: Reports annual wages and taxes for employees.
   » Form 941: Reports quarterly federal payroll taxes.
   » Form 940: Reports annual federal unemployment taxes.
3. Review the form for accuracy, ensuring all employee and payroll data is correct.

Step 3: File the Tax Form

1. Click File Now to submit the form electronically through QBO.
2. For manual filings, print the form and mail it to the appropriate tax authority.

Step 4: Track Filing Status

1. Monitor the status of your filings under Taxes > Payroll Tax > Filings.

2. Ensure forms are accepted and payments are processed on time.

Here's a closer look at the key payroll tax forms you'll need to file:

1. Form W-2 (Wage and Tax Statement):

- Filed annually to report employee wages and taxes withheld.
- Due to employees by January 31 and to the IRS by the end of February.

2. Form 941 (Employer's Quarterly Federal Tax Return):

- Filed quarterly to report income tax withheld and Social Security/Medicare taxes.
- Due on the last day of the month following the end of the quarter.

3. Form 940 (Employer's Annual Federal Unemployment Tax Return):

- Filed annually to report unemployment taxes paid under FUTA.
- Due by January 31.

4. Form 1099-NEC (Nonemployee Compensation):

- Filed annually for contractors paid $600 or more during the year.
- Due to contractors by January 31 and to the IRS by February 28.

Even with QuickBooks Online's automation, you may encounter occasional challenges. Here's how to address common issues:

Issue 1: Missing or Incorrect Data in Reports

- Cause: Employee profiles or payroll entries are incomplete or inaccurate.
- Solution: Review employee profiles and payroll data for errors, then rerun the report.

Issue 2: Rejected Tax Forms

- Cause: Mismatched EINs, incorrect tax amounts, or submission errors.
- Solution: Correct the errors and resubmit the form. Consult QuickBooks support for assistance if needed.

Issue 3: Late Filings

- Cause: Missed deadlines or incomplete setups.
- Solution: Set reminders for filing deadlines and ensure your tax filing preferences are configured in QBO.

Payroll reports aren't just for compliance—they also provide valuable business insights. Here's how to leverage payroll reports for better decision-making:

1. Monitor Labor Costs:

- Use the Payroll Summary Report to analyze labor costs as a percentage of revenue.
- Identify opportunities to optimize staffing or reduce overtime expenses.

2. Track Tax Liabilities:

- Review the Tax Liability Report to anticipate upcoming tax payments and plan cash flow accordingly.

3. Employee Performance Analysis:

- Use the Employee Earnings Report to evaluate compensation and performance trends.

4. Budgeting and Forecasting:

- Incorporate payroll data into your budgeting process to ensure accurate cost projections.

To ensure smooth payroll reporting and tax filing, follow these best practices:

1. Run Reports Regularly:
   - » Generate payroll reports after each pay period to catch errors early.
2. Double-Check Tax Data:
   - » Verify employee and tax information before filing forms to avoid rejections.
3. Leverage Automation:
   - » Enable automatic tax payments and filings to reduce manual effort and ensure compliance.
4. Keep Records Organized:
   - » Store copies of filed tax forms and payroll reports for at least seven years.
5. Consult Professionals:
   - » Work with an accountant or tax professional for complex filings or compliance questions.

Running payroll reports and filing tax forms in QuickBooks Online is a seamless process when done correctly. By leveraging QBO's powerful reporting tools and automated tax filing features, you can maintain accurate records, meet compliance requirements, and gain valuable insights into your business's financial health. With these processes in place, payroll and tax management becomes less of a burden, freeing you to focus on growing your business with confidence.

Handling Contractor Payments and 1099s

As your business grows, you may find yourself working with independent contractors. Unlike employees, contractors are not subject to the same payroll tax rules, but managing their payments and ensuring proper tax reporting is just as important. QuickBooks Online (QBO) simplifies the process of handling contractor payments and preparing 1099 forms, ensuring compliance with IRS regulations while keeping your records accurate and organized.

This chapter provides a comprehensive guide to managing contractor payments and filing 1099 forms in QuickBooks Online. By following these steps, you'll streamline the process of working with contractors, meet your tax reporting obligations, and maintain a clear record of your business expenses.

Who is a Contractor?

A contractor is an independent worker who provides goods or services to your business under terms specified in a contract. Contractors are not employees and are responsible for paying their own taxes, including income tax and self-employment tax.

Why File 1099 Forms?

The IRS requires businesses to report payments made to contractors if:

- The total payments during the calendar year are $600 or more.
- The contractor is not a corporation (exceptions apply, such as for attorneys).

The 1099-NEC (Nonemployee Compensation) form is used to report payments to contractors.

Before you can pay contractors or generate 1099 forms, you need to add them to your QuickBooks Online account.

Step-by-Step Guide:

1. Navigate to the Contractor Section:
   - » Click on Payroll > Contractors in the left-hand menu.
2. Add a Contractor:
   - » Click Add a Contractor.
   - » Enter the contractor's name, email, and payment details.
   - » If you need their tax information, send them an email invitation to complete their W-9 form directly through QuickBooks.
3. Collect Tax Information:
   - » Contractors must complete a W-9 form to provide their Taxpayer Identification Number (TIN) and other details.
   - » Store the W-9 securely for your records.
4. Save the Contractor Profile:
   - » Once all details are entered, save the profile. Repeat this process for additional contractors.

Paying contractors in QuickBooks Online is straightforward and can be done through various methods, such as checks, direct deposit, or ACH transfers.

Step 1: Record a Payment

1. Click + New in the left-hand menu.
2. Select Expense or Check, depending on the payment method.
3. Enter the contractor's name and payment details, including:
   - » Date of payment.
   - » Amount.
   - » Category (e.g., Professional Services).

Step 2: Use Direct Deposit (Optional)

If you have a QuickBooks Online Payroll subscription, you can enable direct deposit for contractors:

1. Go to Payroll > Contractors.
2. Click on the contractor's name and enable direct deposit.
3. Enter the contractor's bank account details.
4. Process payments directly from QuickBooks.

Step 3: Save the Payment

After entering the payment details, click Save and Close to record the transaction.

To keep your records organized and ensure you meet 1099 reporting requirements, track all payments made to contractors in QuickBooks Online.

Using Reports:

1. Navigate to Reports in the left-hand menu.
2. Search for the 1099 Transaction Detail Report to view all contractor payments.
3. Filter the report by date range, contractor, or category to focus on specific details.

Monitoring Payment Thresholds:

QuickBooks automatically tracks payments to contractors and notifies you when they reach the $600 reporting threshold.

At the end of the calendar year, you'll need to prepare and file 1099 forms for all contractors who meet the reporting criteria.

Step 1: Verify Contractor Details

1. Go to Payroll > Contractors.
2. Review each contractor's profile to ensure their tax information (TIN, address) is complete and accurate.

Step 2: Run a 1099 Report

1. Navigate to Taxes > 1099 Filings.
2. Click Prepare 1099s.
3. Review the list of contractors and payments, ensuring all relevant transactions are included.

Step 3: Map Accounts for 1099 Reporting

1. Assign expense categories (e.g., Professional Services, Rent) to the appropriate boxes on the 1099-NEC form.
2. Save the mapping to ensure accurate reporting.

Step 4: Generate 1099 Forms

1. Click E-File for Me or Print and Mail to generate the 1099 forms.
2. QuickBooks will automatically e-file the forms with the IRS if you choose the electronic filing option.

Step 5: Distribute 1099s to Contractors

- Contractors must receive their 1099 forms by January 31.
- QuickBooks will mail or email the forms directly to contractors if you select the e-file option.

Even with QuickBooks Online's automation, you may encounter challenges when managing contractor payments and 1099 forms. Here's how to resolve common issues:

Issue 1: Missing or Incorrect Contractor Information

- Solution: Contact the contractor to update their W-9 form and correct any errors in their profile.

Issue 2: Misclassified Payments

- Solution: Run the 1099 Transaction Detail Report to identify and reclassify miscategorized expenses.

Issue 3: Duplicate Payments

- Solution: Review payment records and delete duplicates in the contractor's transaction history.

Issue 4: Late or Missing 1099s

- Solution: File 1099s as soon as possible. If you miss the deadline, consult with the IRS about penalties and submit the forms promptly.

To streamline contractor payments and 1099 filing, follow these best practices:

1. Request W-9 Forms Early:
   » Collect W-9 forms from contractors before issuing their first payment to avoid delays during tax season.
2. Review Payments Regularly:
   » Run monthly reports to monitor contractor payments and ensure all transactions are recorded correctly.
3. Use Direct Deposit:
   » Enable direct deposit for contractors to simplify payments and reduce administrative workload.
4. Map Expense Categories:
   » Consistently assign contractor payments to the correct categories to avoid errors during 1099 preparation.
5. File 1099s Electronically:
   » E-file 1099 forms through Quick-Books Online to save time and ensure compliance with IRS deadlines.

QuickBooks Online simplifies contractor management in several ways:

- Automation: Tracks payments and prepares 1099 forms automatically, reducing manual effort.
- Accuracy: Ensures contractor payments are recorded and categorized correctly.
- Compliance: Keeps you in line with IRS regulations by filing forms on time and maintaining accurate records.
- Convenience: Allows you to manage contractor profiles, payments, and tax forms from a single platform.

Handling contractor payments and 1099s in QuickBooks Online is a straightforward process that ensures compliance with tax regulations while keeping your financial records organized. By following the steps outlined in this chapter, you can streamline payments, monitor expenses, and prepare accurate 1099 forms with ease. With Quick-Books Online as your partner, managing contractors becomes a seamless part of your business operations, allowing you to focus on what matters most—growing your business.

CHAPTER 7

SALES TAX AND COMPLIANCE

Managing sales tax is a critical responsibility for any business that sells products or services subject to taxation. Whether you operate in one state or across multiple jurisdictions, staying compliant with sales tax regulations can be a complex task. QuickBooks Online simplifies this process by providing tools to configure sales tax settings, track payments, and generate reports to ensure accurate filings.

Sales tax compliance goes beyond calculating the correct amount at the point of sale. It involves tracking collected taxes, filing returns accurately, and maintaining organized records for audits or tax season. Errors or missed deadlines can result in penalties, making it essential to establish a reliable system for managing sales tax.

In this chapter, we'll explore how to configure sales tax settings in QuickBooks Online to align with your business's needs. You'll learn how to track and report sales tax payments, prepare for tax season with organized records, and avoid common filing errors that could jeopardize your compliance. By leveraging QuickBooks Online's automation and reporting tools, you'll save time, reduce stress, and ensure your business remains on the right side of tax laws.

1. Configuring Sales Tax Settings in QuickBooks Online: Learn how to set up and customize sales tax settings based on your location and business requirements.

2. Tracking and Reporting Sales Tax Payments: Understand how to track collected taxes and generate accurate reports for filing.

3. Preparing for Tax Season with Organized Records: Discover strategies to keep your records audit-ready and streamline the tax filing process.

4. Avoiding Common Tax Filing Errors: Explore tips to prevent common mistakes and ensure smooth sales tax compliance.

With these tools and insights, you'll master sales tax management and maintain compliance with confidence. Let's get started!

Configuring Sales Tax Settings in QuickBooks Online

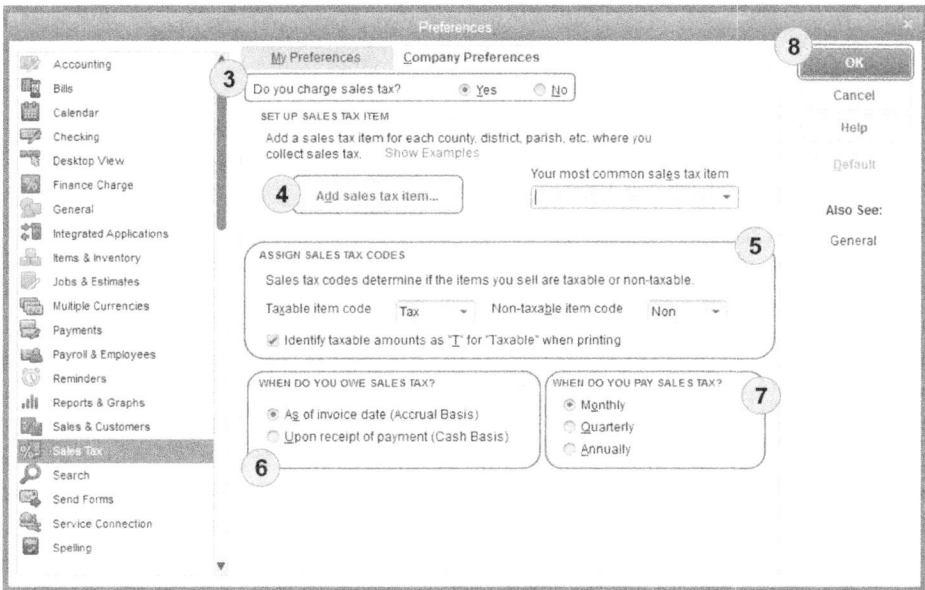

Sales tax compliance is an integral part of managing your business finances. Whether you operate in a single state or across multiple jurisdictions, configuring your sales tax settings correctly in QuickBooks Online (QBO) is essential to ensure accurate calculations, reporting, and filing. QBO provides robust tools to streamline sales tax management, from setting up tax rates to automating the tracking and reporting process.

This chapter provides a comprehensive guide to configuring sales tax settings in Quick-Books Online. By following these steps, you'll create a system that reduces manual effort, minimizes errors, and keeps your business compliant with sales tax regulations.

Before configuring sales tax in QBO, it's essential to understand how the platform manages it:

- Automatic Calculations: QBO calculates sales tax based on your business location, customer location, and the products or services sold.
- Tax Agency Integration: QBO tracks taxes owed to various tax agencies and organizes payments and filings.
- Customizable Settings: QBO allows you to add custom rates for specific jurisdictions or special cases.

Sales tax management in QBO is designed to adapt to your business's unique require-ments, ensuring accurate and compliant processes.

Step 1: Enable Sales Tax

1. Access the Tax Center:
   » Log in to QBO and click on Taxes in the left-hand menu.
2. Set Up Sales Tax:
   » Click Set Up Sales Tax.
   » Follow the prompts to configure the tax setup wizard.

Step 2: Specify Business Location

1. Enter your business's physical address to determine the applicable sales tax rate.
2. QBO uses your address to calculate taxes based on state, county, and city requirements.

Step 3: Add Tax Agencies

1. Select the tax agencies your business collects taxes for (e.g., state tax department, local municipalities).
2. Enter the agency's name and filing frequency (e.g., monthly, quarterly, annually).

QBO automatically calculates tax rates for most jurisdictions, but there may be cases where you need to add or adjust rates manually.

Adding Custom Tax Rates:

1. Go to Taxes > Sales Tax Settings.
2. Click Add Rate and Agency.
3. Enter the following details:
   » Name of the custom rate (e.g., "City of Denver Special Tax").
   » Tax rate percentage.
   » Associated tax agency.
4. Save the custom rate for future transactions.

Managing Exemptions:

- If certain customers or products are tax-exempt, configure exemptions in QBO:
  » Navigate to Taxes > Sales Tax Settings.
  » Add exemptions by specifying the customer or product/service category.

One of QBO's standout features is its ability to automate sales tax calculations, reducing manual effort and ensuring accuracy.

Enable Automatic Sales Tax:

1. Go to Taxes > Sales Tax Settings.
2. Turn on Automated Sales Tax.
3. Review and confirm your business address and tax agency details.

How Automated Sales Tax Works:

- When you create an invoice or sales receipt, QBO calculates the correct tax based on:
  » Your business location.
  » Customer location (shipping address or point of sale).
  » Product or service taxability.

Benefits of Automation:

- Reduces human error in tax calculations.
- Updates rates automatically to reflect changes in tax laws.

Not all products and services are taxable, and some may be taxed at different rates. Assigning tax categories ensures QBO calculates the correct tax.

Step 1: Categorize Products and Services

1. Go to Sales > Products and Services.
2. Select a product or service and click Edit.
3. Under the Sales Tax section, choose whether the item is:
   » Taxable (standard rate applies).
   » Non-taxable.
   » Taxable at a custom rate.

Step 2: Apply Tax Categories to Transactions

- When creating an invoice or sales receipt, QBO will automatically apply the assigned tax category for each item.

Some customers may qualify for sales tax

exemptions based on their status or location.

Step 1: Mark Customers as Tax-Exempt

1. Go to Sales > Customers.
2. Select the customer's profile and click Edit.
3. Under Tax Info, check the box for This customer is tax-exempt.
4. Add a reason for the exemption (e.g., resale certificate, nonprofit status).

Step 2: Apply Tax Settings to Invoices

- When creating an invoice or sales receipt, QBO will exclude sales tax for tax-exempt customers.

Once sales tax is configured, QBO automatically tracks taxes owed to each tax agency.

View Sales Tax Liabilities:

1. Go to Taxes > Sales Tax.
2. Review the Sales Tax Owed dashboard, which shows:

   » Total sales tax collected.
   » Amounts owed to each tax agency.
   » Filing deadlines.

Run Sales Tax Reports:

1. Navigate to Reports > Sales Tax Liability Report.
2. Customize the report by date range or tax agency to review details.

QuickBooks Online makes it easy to file and pay sales taxes, ensuring compliance with filing deadlines.

Step 1: Prepare Sales Tax Filing

1. Go to Taxes > Sales Tax.
2. Select the tax agency and click Prepare Return.
3. Review the collected tax amounts and confirm accuracy.

Step 2: File and Pay Taxes

1. Choose the payment method (e.g., e-payment or check).
2. File the return electronically through QBO or submit manually based on agency requirements.
3. Record the payment in QBO to update your liabilities.

Even with automated tools, sales tax management can present challenges. Here's how to resolve common issues:

Issue 1: Incorrect Tax Rates

- Cause: Outdated business location or custom rate errors.
- Solution: Verify and update your business address and tax rate settings in QBO.

Issue 2: Missing Sales Tax on Transactions

- Cause: Incorrect product or customer tax settings.
- Solution: Check the tax category for the product or customer and update as needed.

Issue 3: Unfiled Taxes

- Cause: Missed filing deadlines or incomplete filings.
- Solution: Set reminders in QBO for upcoming due dates and regularly review liabilities.

To maintain accurate sales tax management, follow these best practices:

1. Verify Settings Regularly:

   » Periodically review your business address, tax agency details, and rates to ensure accuracy.

2. Update for Changes:

> » Monitor tax law changes in your jurisdiction and update QBO settings accordingly.

3. Use Reports for Review:

> » Run sales tax reports monthly to catch discrepancies before filing.

4. Keep Records Organized:

> » Maintain digital copies of filings and correspondence with tax agencies for audit purposes.

Configuring sales tax settings in QuickBooks Online is an essential step toward accurate and compliant tax management. By automating calculations, categorizing products and customers, and integrating tax agency requirements, QBO simplifies the complexities of sales tax management. With these settings in place, you can confidently track, file, and pay sales taxes, freeing up time to focus on growing your business.

Tracking and Reporting Sales Tax Payments

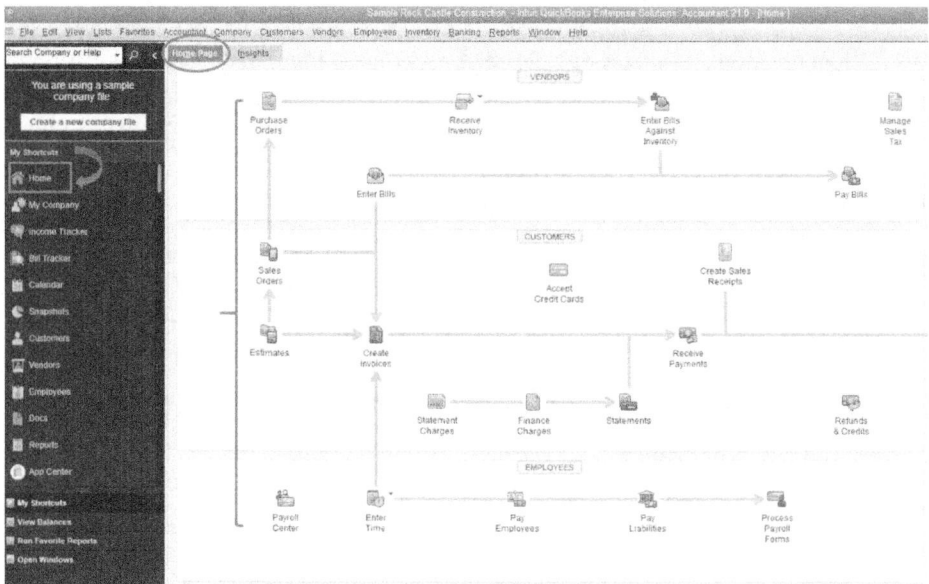

Accurately tracking and reporting sales tax payments is a crucial aspect of managing your business's financial obligations. Sales tax compliance requires businesses to monitor taxes collected from customers, ensure they are properly recorded, and report them to the appropriate tax agencies. QuickBooks Online (QBO) simplifies this process by providing tools to automate tracking, generate detailed reports, and streamline payment submissions.

This chapter offers a step-by-step guide to tracking and reporting sales tax payments in QBO. By mastering these features, you'll ensure compliance with tax laws, maintain accurate records, and minimize the risk of penalties or audits.

1. Legal Compliance:

- Sales tax laws vary by state, county, and city. Accurate tracking ensures compliance with all applicable regulations.

2. Avoiding Penalties:

- Late or incorrect tax filings can result in fines or interest charges. Proper tracking helps you meet filing deadlines.

3. Audit Preparedness:

- Maintaining accurate records of collected and paid sales tax creates a clear audit trail.

4. Financial Management:

- Understanding sales tax liabilities provides a complete picture of your business's financial obligations.

QBO offers an automated system to track sales tax collected from transactions, making it easy to monitor liabilities and prepare for reporting.

Step 1: Enable Sales Tax Tracking

1. Go to Taxes in the left-hand menu and click Set Up Sales Tax (if not already configured).
2. Follow the prompts to specify your business location, tax agencies, and filing frequencies.

Step 2: Automatic Sales Tax Calculation

1. When creating an invoice or sales receipt, QBO automatically calculates sales tax based on:

   » Your business location.
   » The customer's shipping or billing address.
   » Taxability of the products or services sold.

2. Review the tax amount displayed on the transaction to ensure accuracy.

Step 3: View Sales Tax Liabilities

1. Navigate to Taxes > Sales Tax.
2. The Sales Tax dashboard displays:

   » Total sales tax collected.
   » Taxes owed to each agency.
   » Upcoming filing deadlines.

Before reporting or paying sales taxes, it's important to review the transactions contributing to your liabilities.

Step 1: Run Sales Tax Reports

1. Go to Reports in the left-hand menu.
2. Search for and select the Sales Tax Liability Report.
3. Customize the report by:

   » Date range (e.g., monthly, quarterly).
   » Tax agency (e.g., state, local).
   » Customer or product.

Step 2: Verify Transactions

1. Review individual transactions included in the report to ensure they are categorized correctly.
2. Check for any discrepancies, such as:

   » Missing tax amounts.
   » Incorrect tax rates.
   » Transactions assigned to the wrong tax agency.

Step 3: Adjust Errors

1. Edit transactions directly in QBO to correct errors.
2. Re-run the Sales Tax Liability Report to confirm the adjustments.

Once your sales tax liabilities are tracked and reviewed, you're ready to prepare and file sales tax reports with the appropriate tax agencies.

Step 1: Access the Tax Center

1. Navigate to Taxes > Sales Tax.
2. Select the tax agency for which you need to file a return.

Step 2: Prepare the Sales Tax Return

1. Click Prepare Return.
2. Review the tax amounts owed, broken down by jurisdiction (e.g., state, county, city).
3. Ensure that all sales, exemptions, and adjustments are accurately reflected.

Step 3: Generate the Return

1. Use QBO to generate the sales tax return based on the data in your account.
2. Download the return if needed for manual submission to the tax agency.

Step 4: Submit the Return

1. Submit the sales tax return electronically through QBO (if supported by your tax agency) or manually on the agency's website.
2. Record the filing in QBO to update your tax liabilities.

After filing your sales tax return, the next step is to pay the taxes owed.

Step 1: Schedule the Payment

1. In the Tax Center, click Pay Sales Tax.
2. Select the tax agency and the amount owed.
3. Choose the payment method (e.g., bank transfer, check).

Step 2: Record the Payment

1. QBO automatically records electronic payments made through the platform.
2. For manual payments, record the payment by selecting Taxes > Record Tax Payment.

Step 3: Confirm Payment

1. Verify that the payment is processed and the balance owed is updated in QBO.
2. Retain a copy of the payment confirmation for your records.

QBO offers features to automate sales tax tracking and streamline reporting, saving you time and reducing errors.

Enable Automated Sales Tax Tracking:

1. Turn on Automated Sales Tax in Taxes > Sales Tax Settings.
2. Review tax rates regularly to ensure they are up to date.

Schedule Filing Reminders:

1. Set reminders in QBO to notify you of upcoming filing deadlines.
2. Use the Sales Tax dashboard to monitor due dates.

Mistakes in tracking or reporting sales tax can lead to penalties. Here's how to avoid common pitfalls:

Error 1: Missing Transactions

- Cause: Sales not recorded in QBO or miscategorized.
- Solution: Reconcile your accounts regularly and run sales tax reports to catch omissions.

Error 2: Incorrect Tax Rates

- Cause: Outdated or incorrect rates for specific jurisdictions.
- Solution: Verify that your business and customer locations are set up accurately in QBO.

Error 3: Misclassified Exemptions

- Cause: Incorrectly marking a sale as tax-exempt.
- Solution: Double-check exemption status for customers and products.

Error 4: Late Filings

- Cause: Missing filing deadlines.
- Solution: Use QBO's filing reminders and automate your tax filing process if supported.

Sales tax reports aren't just for compliance—they also provide valuable insights into your business operations.

Monitor Revenue Sources:

- Use sales tax data to identify top-performing locations or products.

Analyze Trends:

- Track sales tax liabilities over time to identify seasonal or geographical trends.

Optimize Pricing:

- Factor sales tax into your pricing strategy to maintain profitability.

To ensure accuracy and compliance, follow these best practices:

1. Set Up Sales Tax Correctly:
   » Verify that your business address, tax agencies, and filing schedules are accurate in QBO.
2. Review Regularly:
   » Run sales tax reports monthly to catch discrepancies before filing.
3. Keep Records Organized:
   » Retain copies of filed returns, payment confirmations, and correspondence with tax agencies.

4. Leverage Automation:
   » Use QBO's automated features to reduce manual effort and minimize errors.

QuickBooks Online simplifies the complexities of tracking and reporting sales tax by:

- Automating Calculations: Ensures accurate tax amounts on every transaction.
- Centralizing Records: Keeps all sales tax data in one place for easy access.
- Streamlining Reporting: Generates detailed reports and tax returns with minimal effort.
- Ensuring Compliance: Helps you meet filing deadlines and avoid penalties.

Tracking and reporting sales tax payments in QuickBooks Online is an essential process for maintaining compliance and managing your financial responsibilities. By leveraging QBO's tools and following the steps outlined in this chapter, you can automate tracking, generate accurate reports, and file sales tax returns with confidence. With an efficient system in place, sales tax management becomes a seamless part of your business operations, freeing you to focus on growth and success.

Preparing for Tax Season with Organized Records

Tax season is often a stressful time for business owners, but it doesn't have to be. By staying organized and leveraging the tools provided by QuickBooks Online (QBO), you can simplify the process and ensure accurate tax filings. Organized records not only save you time but also reduce the likelihood of errors, penalties, or audits. Whether you're managing sales tax, income tax, or payroll taxes, having a streamlined system in place is key to a smooth tax season.

This chapter provides a comprehensive guide to preparing for tax season with organized records. You'll learn how to use QBO to track income, expenses, and deductions, generate essential reports, and ensure your business is tax-ready well before the deadline.

Keeping organized records throughout the year is vital for several reasons:

1. Compliance:

- Accurate records ensure your tax filings meet federal, state, and local requirements.

2. Audit Preparedness:

- Organized financial data creates a clear audit trail, reducing stress in the event of an IRS review.

3. Maximizing Deductions:

- Proper documentation of expenses ensures you can claim all eligible tax deductions.

4. Time and Cost Efficiency:

- With everything in order, you'll spend less time scrambling for paperwork and reduce fees for professional tax preparation.

QuickBooks Online simplifies record-keeping by centralizing all financial data in one platform. Here's how to set up an effective system:

Step 1: Customize Your Chart of Accounts

1. Go to Settings > Chart of Accounts.
2. Review existing accounts and add categories that align with your business needs, such as:
   » Office Supplies
   » Marketing Expenses
   » Sales Revenue
   » Taxes Payable
3. Ensure each account is clearly labeled for easy tracking and reporting.

Step 2: Automate Bank Feeds

1. Connect your business bank accounts and credit cards to QBO.
2. Enable automatic transaction imports to reduce manual data entry.
3. Review and categorize transactions weekly to keep your records up-to-date.

Step 3: Organize Receipts and Invoices

1. Use the Receipts feature in QBO to upload and attach receipts to expenses.
2. Regularly reconcile invoices and payments to ensure accuracy.

Accurate income and expense tracking is the foundation of tax preparation. QBO makes this process efficient and transparent.

Step 1: Categorize Income and Expenses

1. Go to Transactions > Banking.
2. Assign categories to each transaction using your Chart of Accounts.
3. Split transactions for items that fall under multiple categories.

Step 2: Identify Tax-Deductible Expenses

- Common deductible expenses include:
   » Rent or lease payments
   » Office supplies and equipment
   » Travel and meals (business-related)

» Marketing and advertising
» Employee wages and benefits

Step 3: Reconcile Accounts Monthly

1. Go to Accounting > Reconcile.
2. Match QBO records with your bank statements to catch discrepancies early.

QuickBooks Online provides a range of reports that are invaluable during tax season. Here's how to use them:

Key Reports for Tax Preparation:

1. Profit and Loss Statement:
   » Summarizes income and expenses to calculate your net profit or loss.
   » Useful for determining taxable income.
2. Balance Sheet:
   » Provides an overview of your business's assets, liabilities, and equity.
3. Sales Tax Liability Report:
   » Tracks sales tax collected and owed to tax agencies.
4. Transaction Detail by Account:
   » Breaks down all transactions within a specific account, offering transparency for deductions and audits.
5. 1099 Transaction Report:
   » Identifies payments to contractors for 1099 preparation.

Generating Reports:

1. Go to Reports in the left-hand menu.
2. Search for the desired report.
3. Customize filters (e.g., date range, accounts) to tailor the report to your needs.

4. Export reports as PDFs or Excel files for sharing with your accountant.

Maximizing deductions is a key part of minimizing your tax liability. Here's how to ensure you capture all eligible deductions:

Step 1: Track Business Expenses

1. Use QBO's Categories to separate deductible expenses from personal or non-deductible items.
2. Attach receipts to expenses in QBO for easy reference.

Step 2: Record Depreciation

1. For assets like office equipment or vehicles, track depreciation to claim it as a deduction.
2. Consult your accountant to ensure correct depreciation methods.

Step 3: Manage Home Office Deductions

• If you operate from a home office, record home-related expenses (e.g., utilities, rent) and allocate a portion based on the percentage of space used for business.

Properly organizing your tax documents ensures a smooth filing process. Here's what to include:

Income Documents:

• Sales invoices
• Receipts for other income streams
• Form 1099s for contractor work

Expense Documentation:

• Receipts and invoices for deductible expenses
• Bank and credit card statements

Tax-Related Forms:

- Previous year's tax return
- W-2s, 1099s, and other relevant tax forms

Storing Documents in QuickBooks Online:

1. Use the Attachments feature to upload and link documents directly to transactions.
2. Create a folder system within your file storage for easy access during tax season.

Once your records are organized, you're ready to file your taxes. QuickBooks Online simplifies this process by integrating with tax preparation tools or allowing you to export data for your accountant.

Step 1: Review Your Financial Data

1. Ensure all transactions for the tax year are recorded and categorized.
2. Reconcile accounts to confirm accuracy.

Step 2: Generate Tax-Specific Reports

1. Use reports like the Profit and Loss Statement and Balance Sheet to calculate taxable income.
2. Provide your accountant with detailed reports to streamline their preparation process.

Step 3: File Your Taxes

1. If using tax software, sync QBO data for seamless integration.
2. For manual filing, export reports and forms as needed.

Even with organized records, tax season can present challenges. Here's how to avoid common mistakes:

Error 1: Missing Deadlines

- Solution: Set reminders in QBO for filing deadlines and estimated tax payments.

Error 2: Misclassified Transactions

- Solution: Regularly review categories to ensure expenses and income are correctly classified.

Error 3: Missing Deductions

- Solution: Use QBO's receipt tracking and expense categorization tools to capture all eligible deductions.

Error 4: Rushing Through Filing

- Solution: Start preparing early to avoid last-minute stress and mistakes.

To make tax season stress-free, follow these best practices:

1. Stay Organized Year-Round:
   - Regularly update your records to avoid a last-minute scramble.
2. Automate Where Possible:
   - Use QBO features like bank feeds and automated sales tax tracking.
3. Work with a Professional:
   - Consult an accountant or tax advisor for complex filings.
4. Retain Records:
   - Keep tax-related documents for at least seven years in case of an audit.

Preparing for tax season with organized records in QuickBooks Online transforms what can be a stressful process into a manageable and efficient task. By leveraging QBO's tools for tracking income, expenses, and deductions, generating reports, and maintaining organized documentation, you'll not only meet your tax obligations but also gain valuable insights into your business's financial health. With a proactive approach to record-keeping, tax season becomes an opportunity to showcase your business's growth and stability rather than a source of stress.

Avoiding Common Tax Filing Errors

Tax filing is an essential yet intricate task for businesses. Even minor mistakes in your tax filings can lead to penalties, delays, or audits, causing unnecessary stress and financial strain. However, with careful planning, accurate record-keeping, and the right tools, you can avoid common tax filing errors and ensure compliance with federal, state, and local regulations.

In this chapter, we'll explore the most common tax filing errors businesses encounter, how to prevent them, and how QuickBooks Online (QBO) can help you streamline your tax process. By implementing the strategies outlined here, you'll reduce the risk of mistakes and gain confidence in managing your business taxes.

Before diving into specific errors, it's essential to understand why accurate tax filings are crucial:

1. Legal Compliance:

- Filing taxes accurately and on time ensures compliance with federal, state, and local tax laws.

2. Avoiding Penalties:

- Mistakes like underreporting income or missing deadlines can result in fines, interest charges, or even legal action.

3. Financial Transparency:

- Correct tax filings provide a clear picture of your business's financial health, helping you make informed decisions.

4. Audit Preparedness:

- Accurate filings reduce the likelihood of audits and make it easier to respond to inquiries from tax authorities.

Error 1: Incorrect Income Reporting

- Cause: Failing to include all income sources or misreporting amounts.
- Solution:
  - » Use QBO's Profit and Loss Report to verify your total income before filing.
  - » Reconcile your accounts monthly to ensure all transactions are accurately recorded.
  - » Cross-check your tax forms with bank statements and invoices.

Error 2: Misclassified Expenses

- Cause: Categorizing personal expenses as business expenses or placing expenses in the wrong category.
- Solution:
  - » Set up a clear Chart of Accounts in QBO with appropriate categories for all expenses.
  - » Regularly review transactions to ensure accurate categorization.
  - » Keep personal and business finances separate by using dedicated accounts for business transactions.

Error 3: Missing or Incorrect Deductions

- Cause: Overlooking eligible deductions or claiming ineligible ones.
- Solution:
  - » Review a list of common business deductions, such as office supplies, travel expenses, and employee wages.
  - » Attach receipts to transactions in QBO using the Receipts feature for proper documentation.
  - » Consult a tax professional for advice on complex deductions like depreciation or home office use.

Error 4: Late Filings

- Cause: Missing tax deadlines due to poor planning or disorganized records.
- Solution:
  - » Set reminders in QBO for key tax deadlines, such as quarterly estimated payments or annual returns.
  - » Use QBO's tax center to track due dates and liabilities.
  - » Start preparing your taxes early to avoid last-minute stress.

Error 5: Incorrect Tax Rates

- Cause: Using outdated or incorrect tax rates for sales or payroll taxes.
- Solution:
  - » Enable Automated Sales Tax in QBO to apply the correct rates for your jurisdiction.
  - » Verify payroll tax rates regularly in the Payroll Settings section.
  - » Review tax rates annually or whenever laws change in your area.

Error 6: Overlooking Tax Credits

- Cause: Failing to claim available credits, such as the Employee Retention Credit or energy-efficient equipment credits.
- Solution:
  - » Stay informed about tax credits applicable to your industry or location.
  - » Consult a tax professional to identify and claim eligible credits.
  - » Use QBO to track expenses that qualify for specific credits.

Error 7: Incorrect Taxpayer Identification Numbers (TINs)

- Cause: Entering incorrect TINs for your business, employees, or contractors.
- Solution:
  - » Double-check your EIN and SSNs before submitting tax forms.
  - » Use QBO to store contractor information securely and generate accurate 1099 forms.

Error 8: Failing to File 1099s for Contractors

- Cause: Neglecting to issue 1099-NEC forms to contractors paid $600 or more during the year.
- Solution:
  - » Use QBO's 1099 Wizard to identify contractors who meet the reporting threshold.
  - » Collect W-9 forms from contractors before issuing payments.
  - » Prepare and file 1099s by January 31 to meet IRS deadlines.

Error 9: Ignoring Estimated Tax Payments

- Cause: Not paying quarterly estimated taxes, leading to underpayment penalties.
- Solution:
  - » Calculate quarterly estimated payments based on your prior year's tax liability.
  - » Set up reminders in QBO for quarterly due dates.
  - » Use QBO's Tax Liability Report to estimate and track payments.

Error 10: Not Keeping Adequate Records

- Cause: Insufficient documentation for income, expenses, or deductions.
- Solution:
  - » Store all financial records, including receipts, invoices, and bank statements, in QBO.
  - » Attach supporting documents to transactions for easy retrieval during audits.
  - » Maintain records for at least seven years to comply with IRS requirements.

QBO offers several tools to help you prevent tax filing errors and stay compliant:

Automated Features:

- Automates sales and payroll tax calculations to ensure accuracy.
- Tracks tax liabilities and reminds you of filing deadlines.

Reports:

- Generate reports like the Profit and Loss Statement, Balance Sheet, and Tax Liability Report for detailed insights into your finances.

Integrations:

- Sync QBO with tax preparation software like TurboTax for seamless filing.
- Share QBO reports with your accountant for professional review.

Customizable Tools:

- Create custom categories in your Chart of Accounts to suit your business's unique needs.
- Use the Receipts feature to attach supporting documentation to transactions.

To minimize the risk of tax mistakes, follow these best practices:

1. Keep Records Updated Year-Round:
   - » Regularly reconcile accounts and categorize transactions in QBO.
   - » Review financial reports monthly to ensure accuracy.

2. Review Before Filing:
   - » Double-check all information on your tax forms, including TINs, income, and deductions.
   - » Use QBO reports to verify data against supporting documents.

3. Consult a Professional:
   - » Work with an accountant or tax advisor for complex filings or significant changes in tax laws.

4. Start Early:
   - » Begin preparing for tax season well before the deadline to avoid last-minute errors.

5. Leverage Technology:
   - » Use QBO's automation and reporting tools to simplify tax preparation and filing.

Avoiding tax filing errors provides several benefits:

- Peace of Mind: Eliminates the stress of potential penalties or audits.
- Financial Savings: Reduces the risk of fines, interest charges, or legal fees.
- Enhanced Reputation: Maintains trust with tax authorities and stakeholders.
- Improved Decision-Making: Accurate records support better financial planning and growth.

Tax filing errors can be costly and time-consuming, but with proactive planning, accurate record-keeping, and the powerful tools in QuickBooks Online, they are entirely avoidable. By understanding common mistakes, implementing best practices, and leveraging QBO's automation features, you can simplify your tax filing process and ensure compliance. With these strategies in place, tax season becomes a manageable part of running your business, allowing you to focus on growth and success.

CHAPTER 8

CASH FLOW AND BUDGETING

Managing your business's cash flow and budgeting effectively is essential for long-term success. Cash flow—the movement of money in and out of your business—directly impacts your ability to pay bills, invest in growth, and navigate unexpected challenges. Likewise, a well-thought-out budget provides a financial roadmap, helping you allocate resources wisely and achieve your goals.

QuickBooks Online (QBO) offers powerful tools like the Cash Flow Planner and budgeting features that make managing your finances more accessible and efficient. These tools provide real-time insights into your financial health, allowing you to anticipate cash shortfalls, optimize spending, and plan for future growth. With automated tracking and reporting, QBO eliminates much of the guesswork, enabling you to make data-driven decisions with confidence.

In this chapter, we'll explore how to use QuickBooks Online to master cash flow and budgeting. You'll learn how to leverage the Cash Flow Planner to stay ahead of your financial needs, create and manage budgets tailored to your business, and analyze cash inflows and outflows for smarter decision-making. Additionally, we'll discuss how to generate financial forecasts, empowering you to anticipate challenges and seize opportunities.

By the end of this chapter, you'll have the knowledge and tools to take control of your

business finances. Whether you're stabilizing your cash flow, preparing for growth, or navigating seasonal fluctuations, these strategies will help you stay financially agile and ready to meet your business's needs. Let's dive into the details and transform how you manage your business's finances!

Using the Cash Flow Planner to Stay Ahead

Effective cash flow management is the lifeblood of any business. Without proper oversight, even profitable businesses can face challenges meeting financial obligations. QuickBooks Online (QBO) offers a powerful tool, the Cash Flow Planner, designed to help business owners predict, analyze, and optimize cash flow. This feature gives you a clear picture of your current and future financial position, helping you make informed decisions and avoid cash shortfalls.

This chapter provides a detailed guide on using the Cash Flow Planner to anticipate your business's financial needs and maintain a healthy cash flow. By the end, you'll understand how to leverage this tool to stay ahead, ensure stability, and seize opportunities for growth.

1. Maintain Financial Stability:

- Monitoring cash flow ensures you have enough liquidity to meet obligations like payroll, rent, and vendor payments.

2. Plan for Growth:

- A clear view of cash flow helps you identify when to invest in inventory, equipment, or new hires.

3. Avoid Financial Crises:

- Anticipating cash shortages allows you to take proactive steps, such as securing funding or deferring expenses.

4. Make Informed Decisions:

- Real-time insights empower you to allocate resources wisely and avoid unnecessary debt.

The Cash Flow Planner in QBO is a forecasting tool that predicts your business's cash position over the coming weeks or months. It uses your historical financial data, scheduled transactions, and connected accounts to provide accurate and actionable insights.

Key Features:

- Real-Time Forecasting: Displays your cash flow status in a user-friendly dashboard.
- Customizable Projections: Allows you to add or adjust income and expense items for more tailored forecasts.
- Scenario Planning: Helps you explore the impact of potential changes, such as delayed payments or unexpected expenses.

Step 1: Connect Your Accounts

1. Go to the Cash Flow tab in the left-hand menu.
2. Link your business bank accounts and credit cards if not already connected.
3. Enable real-time syncing to keep your data up-to-date.

Step 2: Configure Settings

1. Review your financial data to ensure all transactions are categorized correctly in QBO.
2. Confirm that recurring income and expenses, such as rent or subscription payments, are accurately recorded.

Step 3: Understand the Dashboard

- The Cash Flow Planner dashboard provides a snapshot of your current cash position and projected inflows and outflows.
- Key components include:

  » Cash Balance: Displays your current cash available across linked accounts.
  » Upcoming Transactions: Lists scheduled bills, invoices, and other known transactions.
  » Forecast Chart: Visualizes your cash flow trends over time.

To make the most of the Cash Flow Planner, you need to ensure your projections are as accurate as possible. Here's how:

Step 1: Input Known Income and Expenses

1. Add recurring revenue streams, such as subscription fees or monthly invoices, to the planner.
2. Enter fixed expenses, like rent, insurance premiums, or loan repayments.

Step 2: Adjust for Variable Costs

- Include fluctuating expenses, such as utilities, seasonal inventory purchases, or marketing campaigns.
- Use historical data from QBO reports to estimate these costs accurately.

Step 3: Account for Outstanding Invoices

1. Monitor open invoices and their due dates.
2. Add estimated payment dates to the planner to reflect expected cash inflows.

Step 4: Incorporate One-Time Transactions

- Include one-off items, such as equipment purchases or tax payments, to avoid surprises in your cash flow.

The Cash Flow Planner is more than a forecasting tool; it provides insights that can transform your financial management:

Identify Peak and Low Periods

- Use the forecast chart to pinpoint times of surplus or deficit.
- Plan significant expenditures during high-cash periods and conserve resources during lean times.

Monitor Payment Patterns

- Analyze when customers typically pay invoices and adjust your projections accordingly.
- Consider offering incentives for early payments to improve cash flow.

Assess Expense Timing

- Look for opportunities to spread out expenses or negotiate payment terms with vendors to smooth cash flow.

1. Plan for Growth:

- Use surplus periods to fund growth initiatives, such as marketing campaigns, product development, or hiring.

2. Avoid Overdrafts:

- Identify potential cash shortfalls in advance and take action, such as:
  - » Securing a line of credit.
  - » Delaying non-essential purchases.
  - » Accelerating collections on outstanding invoices.

3. Test "What-If" Scenarios:

- Adjust income or expense projections to see how changes impact your cash flow.
- Example: Analyze the impact of investing in new equipment or extending customer payment terms.

4. Schedule Payments Strategically:

- Align vendor payments with incoming cash to avoid unnecessary strain on your cash flow.

QuickBooks Online offers several features that complement the Cash Flow Planner to enhance your cash flow management:

Invoice Automation:

- Automate recurring invoices and send reminders to customers for overdue payments.
- Use QBO's online payment options to encourage faster collections.

Bill Management:

- Schedule bill payments in QBO to ensure they align with your cash flow forecast.

Reports:

- Run the Profit and Loss Statement to compare income and expenses over time.

- Use the Accounts Receivable Aging Report to identify overdue invoices.

Budgeting:

- Combine the Cash Flow Planner with QBO's budgeting tools to align your forecasts with long-term financial goals.

Despite the advantages of the Cash Flow Planner, it's important to avoid common pitfalls:

Mistake 1: Ignoring Small Transactions

- Solution: Track all expenses, no matter how small, to maintain accurate forecasts.

Mistake 2: Overestimating Income

- Solution: Base projections on historical data and conservative estimates.

Mistake 3: Failing to Update Projections

- Solution: Regularly update the planner with new transactions or changes to ensure accuracy.

Mistake 4: Relying Solely on Projections

- Solution: Use the Cash Flow Planner in conjunction with other QBO tools and reports for a complete financial picture.

1. **Review Weekly:**
   » Regularly update and review your cash flow forecast to stay informed.
2. Align with Goals:

» Use the planner to ensure your cash flow supports business objectives, such as expansion or debt reduction.

3. Involve Your Team:
   » Share insights from the planner with key team members to align decision-making across your business.

4. Leverage Professional Advice:
   » Consult an accountant or financial advisor for additional insights and strategies.

Using the Cash Flow Planner in QuickBooks Online provides several benefits:

- Proactive Management: Helps you anticipate and address cash flow issues before they become problems.
- Informed Decisions: Offers data-driven insights to guide spending, investments, and financing.
- Increased Efficiency: Automates calculations and consolidates data, saving time and reducing errors.
- Improved Financial Health: Supports a stable cash flow, ensuring your business can meet obligations and seize opportunities.

The Cash Flow Planner in QuickBooks Online is an indispensable tool for staying ahead of your business's financial needs. By accurately forecasting income and expenses, analyzing trends, and using insights to make informed decisions, you can maintain a healthy cash flow and confidently plan for the future. With regular updates and strategic use of this tool, you'll transform cash flow management from a reactive task into a proactive strategy, ensuring the stability and growth of your business.

Creating and Managing Budgets in QuickBooks Online

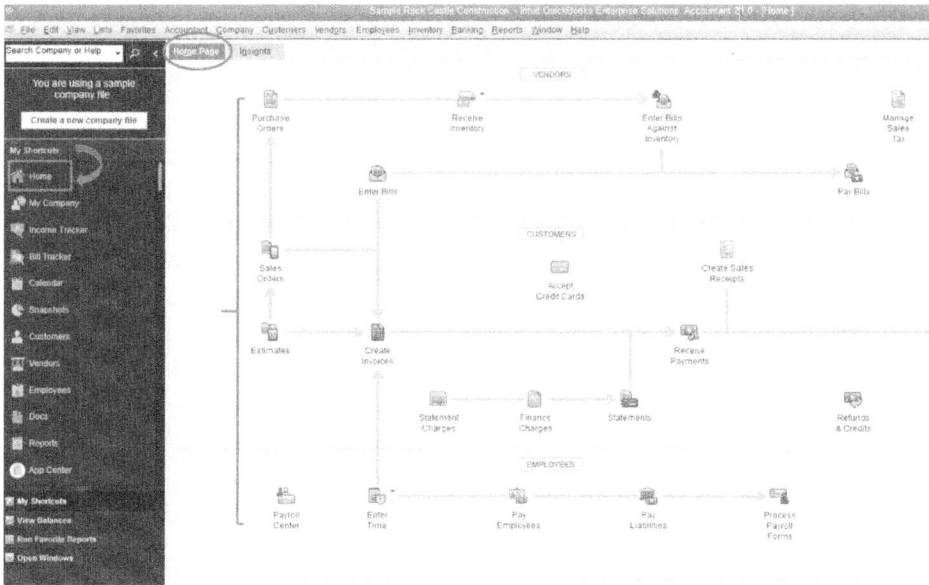

Budgeting is a fundamental aspect of financial management for any business, providing a clear roadmap for spending, saving, and achieving your goals. A well-structured budget helps you allocate resources efficiently, identify opportunities for cost savings, and prepare for unexpected challenges. QuickBooks Online (QBO) simplifies the process of creating and managing budgets, offering tools to track progress and ensure your financial plans stay on course.

In this chapter, we'll explore how to use QBO to create budgets tailored to your business's needs, monitor performance, and adjust as necessary. By the end, you'll have a solid understanding of how to leverage QBO's budgeting features to enhance financial stability and support long-term growth.

Before diving into the practical steps, it's important to understand why budgeting matters:

1. Financial Control:

- Budgets provide a framework for managing income and expenses, preventing overspending.

2. Goal Alignment:

- Helps align financial decisions with short-term and long-term business goals.

3. Improved Decision-Making:

- Offers insights into financial trends, enabling data-driven decisions.

4. Crisis Management:

- Acts as a safety net, helping you identify and address potential financial shortfalls.

QuickBooks Online includes robust budgeting tools designed to simplify the process and enhance accuracy:

Key Features:

- Customizable Budgets: Create budgets by month, quarter, or year, tailored to your business's needs.
- Tracking by Accounts: Allocate income and expenses across specific categories or accounts.
- Comparative Analysis: Compare actual performance to budgeted amounts to track progress.

Accessing the Budgeting Tool:

1. Navigate to Settings > Tools > Budgeting.
2. Click Add Budget to start creating your first budget.

Step 1: Review Historical Data

1. Use QBO reports like the Profit and Loss Statement to analyze past income and expenses.
2. Identify trends and recurring costs to guide your projections.

Step 2: Define Your Goals

- Establish clear objectives for your budget, such as:
  - » Reducing operational costs.
  - » Increasing marketing investment.
  - » Saving for future expansion.

Step 3: Set a Timeframe

- Decide on the period your budget will cover:
  - » Monthly Budgets: Ideal for detailed tracking and short-term planning.
  - » Quarterly Budgets: Balances detail with flexibility.
  - » Annual Budgets: Focused on long-term goals and overall performance.

Step 1: Access the Budgeting Tool

1. Go to Settings > Tools > Budgeting.
2. Click Add Budget.

Step 2: Name and Define the Budget

1. Enter a name that reflects the budget's purpose (e.g., "2024 Marketing Budget").
2. Select the fiscal year and time interval (monthly, quarterly, or yearly).

Step 3: Choose the Data Source

- QBO allows you to:
  - » Start from scratch.
  - » Use actual data from a previous year to prefill budget fields.

Step 4: Allocate Income and Expenses

1. For each account, input budgeted income or expenses based on your projections.
2. Consider seasonal fluctuations or one-time costs.

Step 5: Save and Review

1. Review the completed budget for accuracy and alignment with your goals.
2. Click Save to finalize the budget.

Step 1: Monitor Budget Performance

1. Navigate to Reports > Budget vs. Actuals.
2. Analyze the report to compare your actual income and expenses to your budgeted amounts.

Step 2: Adjust the Budget as Needed

- If performance deviates significantly from the budget, make adjustments to stay on track:
  » Increase budgets for accounts with unexpected expenses.
  » Reallocate funds from underutilized categories.

Step 3: Set Alerts and Reminders

- Use QBO to set alerts for accounts nearing their budget limits.

Step 4: Regular Reviews

- Schedule monthly or quarterly reviews to assess performance and make adjustments.

The budgeting tool in QBO provides insights that go beyond simple tracking. Use these insights to enhance decision-making:

Identify Cost-Saving Opportunities:

- Highlight accounts with consistent overspending and explore ways to reduce costs.

Spot Growth Opportunities:

- Analyze accounts with surplus funds and consider reallocating them to growth initiatives.

Plan for Seasonality:

- Use historical data to adjust budgets for seasonal fluctuations in income or expenses.

Once you're comfortable with the basics, explore advanced strategies to maximize the value of your budgets:

Scenario Planning:

- Create multiple budgets based on different scenarios (e.g., optimistic vs. conservative revenue projections).

Departmental Budgets:

- Break down budgets by department or project to gain deeper insights.

Incorporate Key Performance Indicators (KPIs):

- Link your budget to business KPIs to measure the effectiveness of spending.

Forecast Future Budgets:

- Use insights from current budgets to forecast and plan for future fiscal years.

While QBO makes budgeting easier, it's essential to avoid common pitfalls:

Mistake 1: Overestimating Revenue

- Solution: Use conservative estimates based on historical data.

Mistake 2: Ignoring Small Expenses

- Solution: Track all expenses, no matter how minor, to maintain accuracy.

Mistake 3: Failing to Adjust Budgets

- Solution: Regularly update budgets to reflect changes in business circumstances.

Mistake 4: Lack of Detail

- Solution: Break down income and expenses into specific categories for better tracking.

QBO offers comprehensive reports to help you track and analyze your budget:

Budget vs. Actuals Report:

- Compares actual performance to budgeted amounts, highlighting variances.

Profit and Loss by Budget:

- Shows how budgeted figures align with your overall financial performance.

Custom Reports:

- Create custom reports tailored to specific projects or departments.

Export Options:

- Export reports to Excel or PDF for deeper analysis or sharing with stakeholders.

Using QBO to create and manage budgets provides numerous benefits:

- Efficiency: Automates calculations and reduces manual effort.
- Accuracy: Ensures your budget is based on reliable data and real-time insights.
- Flexibility: Allows you to adjust budgets dynamically as business conditions change.
- Transparency: Provides a clear view of financial performance, aiding communication with stakeholders.

Creating and managing budgets in QuickBooks Online empowers you to take control of your business finances. By leveraging QBO's tools, you can build detailed budgets, monitor performance, and make informed adjustments to stay on track. With regular reviews and a proactive approach, budgeting becomes a powerful tool for achieving financial stability and supporting your business's growth. Whether you're planning for the next month or the next year, QBO ensures your budget aligns with your goals and keeps your business on a path to success.

Analyzing Cash Inflows and Outflows for Smarter Decisions

Cash flow is the heartbeat of any business. Understanding how money flows in and out of your business is crucial for maintaining financial stability, identifying opportunities, and making informed decisions. By analyzing cash inflows and outflows, you can determine where your money is coming from, how it's being spent, and where adjustments may be necessary to achieve your financial goals.

QuickBooks Online (QBO) simplifies the process of cash flow analysis with tools that allow you to track transactions, generate reports, and visualize cash flow trends. This chapter explores the importance of analyzing cash inflows and outflows and how to use QBO effectively to make smarter business decisions.

Cash inflows and outflows represent the movement of money into and out of your business, respectively.

Cash Inflows:

- Sources: Revenue from sales, customer payments, loans, and investment income.
- Significance: Indicates the business's ability to generate income and sustain operations.

Cash Outflows:

- Uses: Payments to vendors, payroll, rent, utilities, taxes, and loan repayments.
- Significance: Reflects the cost of running the business and highlights areas for cost management.

Analyzing these flows helps you assess your cash position, identify inefficiencies, and plan for future financial needs.

1. Maintain Liquidity:

- Ensures you have enough cash on hand to cover immediate obligations, such as payroll and vendor payments.

2. Optimize Resource Allocation:

- Helps prioritize spending on essential operations or growth opportunities.

3. Identify Trends:

- Uncovers patterns in revenue and expenses, allowing you to anticipate seasonal fluctuations or recurring costs.

4. Reduce Risk:

- Highlights potential cash shortfalls, enabling you to take corrective action before problems arise.

5. Improve Decision-Making:

- Provides a clear financial picture to guide strategic decisions, such as expansion or cost-cutting.

Step 1: Connect Financial Accounts

1. Go to Banking > Link Account in QBO.
2. Connect your business bank accounts, credit cards, and payment processors to automatically import transactions.

Step 2: Categorize Transactions

1. Navigate to Transactions > Banking.
2. Review each transaction and assign it to the appropriate category in your Chart of Accounts.
3. Use detailed descriptions to improve accuracy and reporting.

Step 3: Reconcile Accounts Monthly

- Regularly reconcile your accounts to ensure that QBO's records match your bank statements, catching errors or discrepancies early.

1. Monitor Revenue Sources:

- Use the Profit and Loss Statement to break down income by category (e.g., product sales, services, or other revenue streams).
- Identify top-performing revenue sources and focus on maximizing their potential.

2. Track Customer Payments:

- Run the Accounts Receivable Aging Report to identify overdue invoices.
- Implement strategies to accelerate collections, such as offering early payment discounts or sending reminders.

3. Evaluate Recurring Income:

- Use QBO to track subscription-based or recurring revenue, ensuring consistency in cash inflows.

4. Compare Historical Data:

- Analyze cash inflows over time to identify growth trends or seasonal peaks.

1. Review Expense Categories:

- Run the Expense by Vendor Summary report to identify where your money is going.

- Highlight high-cost vendors or categories that may require renegotiation or reduction.

2. Monitor Fixed and Variable Costs:

- Categorize expenses as fixed (e.g., rent) or variable (e.g., raw materials).
- Evaluate whether variable costs align with revenue fluctuations.

3. Identify Inefficiencies:

- Look for redundant expenses, such as unused subscriptions or excess inventory.

4. Assess Payment Timing:

- Analyze payment schedules to ensure they align with cash inflows, avoiding unnecessary strain on cash reserves.

QuickBooks Online provides several reports to help you analyze cash flow and make data-driven decisions.

1. Cash Flow Report:

- Offers a detailed breakdown of cash inflows and outflows for a specific period.
- Helps identify net cash flow (positive or negative).

2. Profit and Loss Statement:

- Summarizes revenue and expenses, providing insights into overall profitability.

3. Balance Sheet:

- Displays your business's assets, liabilities, and equity, offering a snapshot of financial health.

4. Transaction Detail by Account:

- Provides granular details of individual transactions for more in-depth analysis.

5. Custom Reports:

- Create custom reports tailored to your business needs, focusing on specific accounts, categories, or timeframes.

1. Positive Cash Flow:

- Indicates that cash inflows exceed outflows, allowing you to invest in growth or build reserves.

2. Negative Cash Flow:

- Suggests that outflows exceed inflows, potentially requiring corrective actions like cost-cutting or securing financing.

3. Seasonal Variations:

- Identify predictable fluctuations in cash flow, such as increased revenue during holiday seasons or higher expenses during peak production periods.

4. Unexpected Changes:

- Monitor sudden spikes or drops in cash flow to address underlying issues promptly.

1. Optimize Spending:

- Use cash flow analysis to identify non-essential expenses that can be reduced or eliminated.

2. Improve Collections:

- Implement strategies like automated reminders or incentives for early payments to accelerate cash inflows.

3. Plan for Investments:

* Positive cash flow provides opportunities to reinvest in your business, such as upgrading equipment or expanding your product line.

4. Prepare for Shortfalls:

* Use cash flow forecasts to anticipate and address periods of low liquidity, such as securing a line of credit or deferring expenses.

5. Align with Goals:

* Ensure that cash flow aligns with business objectives, such as scaling operations or improving profit margins.

While analyzing cash flow is essential, it's important to avoid common errors:

Mistake 1: Ignoring Small Transactions

* Solution: Record all income and expenses, no matter how minor, to maintain accuracy.

Mistake 2: Overestimating Income

* Solution: Base projections on historical data and realistic assumptions.

Mistake 3: Failing to Monitor Regularly

* Solution: Review cash flow reports weekly or monthly to stay informed.

Mistake 4: Not Adjusting for Seasonal Trends

* Solution: Use historical data to plan for high and low cash flow periods.

1. Regular Reviews:

» Schedule regular cash flow reviews to stay updated on your financial position.

2. Involve Key Stakeholders:

» Share cash flow insights with team members or advisors to align on financial strategies.

3. Leverage Technology:

» Use QBO's automation features to streamline tracking and analysis.

4. Integrate with Forecasting:

» Combine cash flow analysis with financial forecasts to plan for future needs.

Analyzing cash inflows and outflows is critical for making smarter business decisions. With QuickBooks Online, you can gain valuable insights into your financial position, identify trends, and implement strategies to optimize cash flow. By leveraging QBO's tools and reports, you'll not only maintain a healthy cash flow but also position your business for long-term success. Regular analysis and proactive management ensure that every financial decision you make is grounded in accurate, actionable data.

Generating Financial Forecasts

Financial forecasting is a powerful tool for planning your business's future. By predicting revenue, expenses, and cash flow, you can make informed decisions about growth, investments, and risk management. A well-crafted financial forecast provides a roadmap for achieving your goals while preparing for challenges. With QuickBooks Online (QBO), generating accurate financial forecasts becomes a streamlined and efficient process.

This chapter provides a comprehensive guide to generating financial forecasts in QBO. You'll learn the importance of forecasting, how to use QBO tools and data, and strategies to ensure your forecasts are actionable and accurate.

Financial forecasting involves predicting a business's future financial performance based on historical data, market trends, and assumptions.

Types of Financial Forecasts:

- Revenue Forecasts: Estimate future sales and income.
- Expense Forecasts: Predict operational costs and other expenditures.
- Cash Flow Forecasts: Assess future liquidity by projecting cash inflows and outflows.
- Profit Forecasts: Predict net income based on revenue and expenses.

Why Forecasting Matters:

1. Informed Decision-Making: Helps prioritize investments and allocate resources efficiently.
2. Risk Management: Identifies potential financial shortfalls and allows for proactive solutions.
3. Goal Alignment: Ensures financial plans support your business objectives.
4. Stakeholder Confidence: Provides clarity and confidence to investors, lenders, and partners.

Before creating a forecast, ensure your financial data in QBO is accurate and up-to-date.

Step 1: Reconcile Accounts

1. Go to Accounting > Reconcile in QBO.
2. Match transactions in QBO with bank statements to ensure accuracy.

Step 2: Organize Historical Data

1. Use QBO reports like the Profit and Loss Statement and Balance Sheet to review historical performance.
2. Identify trends in revenue, expenses, and cash flow to inform your forecast.

Step 3: Define Your Goals

- Clarify the purpose of your forecast, such as:
  » Planning for growth or expansion.
  » Securing funding.
  » Preparing for seasonal fluctuations.

Step 4: Set a Timeframe

- Choose a forecasting period:
  » Short-Term: Monthly or quarterly forecasts for immediate planning.
  » Long-Term: Annual or multi-year forecasts for strategic planning.

Step 1: Review Historical Revenue Trends

- Use the Sales by Customer Summary or Sales by Product/Service Summary report to analyze revenue sources.
- Identify patterns, such as seasonal peaks or consistent growth.

Step 2: Consider Market Factors

- Incorporate external factors, such as industry trends, economic conditions, or competitor actions, into your forecast.

Step 3: Create Revenue Projections

1. Go to Reports > Profit and Loss.
2. Export historical revenue data to Excel or use QBO's budgeting tool to model future revenue.
3. Apply growth rates or seasonal ad-

justments based on historical trends and market expectations.

Step 1: Analyze Historical Expenses

- Use the Expense by Vendor Summary or Profit and Loss Statement to review past spending.
- Categorize expenses into fixed (e.g., rent, salaries) and variable (e.g., marketing, utilities) costs.

Step 2: Adjust for Inflation and Growth

- Increase expense projections for inflation or planned business growth.
- Consider how new investments, such as hiring or marketing campaigns, will impact costs.

Step 3: Include One-Time Costs

- Factor in one-off expenses, such as equipment purchases, software upgrades, or event sponsorships.

Step 1: Review Current Cash Flow

- Use the Cash Flow Report in QBO to analyze past cash inflows and outflows.

Step 2: Predict Cash Inflows

- Base inflow projections on your revenue forecast.
- Account for payment terms and typical collection times from customers.

Step 3: Predict Cash Outflows

- Base outflow projections on your expense forecast.
- Include loan repayments, tax payments, and other obligations.

Step 4: Build the Forecast

1. Navigate to the Cash Flow Planner in QBO.

2. Input expected income and expenses.
3. Adjust for timing differences, such as delayed customer payments or staggered vendor payments.

QBO offers several tools to simplify financial forecasting:

1. Budgeting Tool

- Create detailed budgets to forecast income and expenses.
- Access via Settings > Tools > Budgeting.

2. Reports

- Use historical reports like the Profit and Loss Statement, Balance Sheet, and Cash Flow Report to gather data for forecasting.

3. Cash Flow Planner

- Provides a visual representation of projected cash flow.
- Integrates with connected accounts for real-time updates.

4. Custom Reports

- Create custom reports to focus on specific accounts, periods, or categories relevant to your forecast.

Step 1: Base Forecasts on Reliable Data

- Use verified historical data from QBO to ensure accurate projections.

Step 2: Use Conservative Estimates

- Avoid overly optimistic assumptions about revenue growth or cost reductions.

Step 3: Regularly Update Forecasts

- Revise forecasts as new data becomes available or business conditions change.

Step 4: Involve Stakeholders

- Collaborate with team members, accountants, or financial advisors to validate assumptions and ensure alignment.

1. Plan for Growth:

- Use revenue forecasts to identify when to invest in expansion, hiring, or marketing.

2. Manage Risks:

- Use cash flow forecasts to anticipate and address potential liquidity issues.

3. Optimize Spending:

- Compare expense forecasts to budgets and identify areas for cost savings.

4. Secure Funding:

- Present detailed forecasts to lenders or investors to demonstrate financial viability.

Mistake 1: Overestimating Revenue

- Solution: Base projections on realistic growth rates and historical data.

Mistake 2: Ignoring Seasonal Trends

- Solution: Adjust forecasts for predictable fluctuations in sales or expenses.

Mistake 3: Underestimating Costs

- Solution: Account for inflation, unexpected repairs, or other unforeseen expenses.

Mistake 4: Failing to Monitor Progress

- Solution: Compare forecasts to actual performance regularly and make adjustments as needed.

Using QBO for financial forecasting provides numerous benefits:

- Time Efficiency: Automates data collection and calculations.
- Accuracy: Reduces errors by leveraging real-time and historical data.
- Flexibility: Allows for quick adjustments as new information becomes available.
- Insights: Offers actionable insights into financial trends and opportunities.
- Confidence: Empowers you to make informed decisions with a clear understanding of your financial position.

Generating financial forecasts in QuickBooks Online is an invaluable practice for business owners seeking to plan for the future with confidence. By using QBO's tools to analyze historical data, predict income and expenses, and assess cash flow, you can create actionable and reliable forecasts. Regularly updating and monitoring these forecasts ensures your financial plans remain aligned with your goals and adaptable to changes in your business environment. With QBO as your partner, financial forecasting becomes a strategic advantage, enabling you to grow, adapt, and thrive.

CHAPTER 9

REPORTS AND FINANCIAL INSIGHTS

Accurate and insightful financial reporting is the cornerstone of sound business management. QuickBooks Online (QBO) offers a comprehensive suite of reporting tools that transform raw financial data into actionable insights, helping you make informed decisions and track your business's financial health. From understanding your profitability to monitoring assets and liabilities, QBO's reports provide clarity and control over your finances.

In this chapter, we'll explore the various financial reports available in QuickBooks Online and how to customize them to meet your specific business needs. We'll delve into two of the most critical reports—Profit and Loss Statements and Balance Sheets—to understand how they provide a snapshot of your financial performance and overall stability. These reports are essential not only for internal decision-making but also for presenting your financial position to stakeholders, such as investors or lenders.

Additionally, you'll learn how to export these reports into formats like Excel and PDF for further analysis, sharing, or archiving. This capability allows you to collaborate with your accountant or team and integrate data into other tools for deeper insights.

Whether you're tracking income and ex-

penses, evaluating profitability, or planning for growth, mastering financial reporting in QBO will empower you to take control of your business's finances. By the end of this chapter, you'll understand how to customize, analyze, and leverage reports to gain a clear and comprehensive view of your business's financial health. Let's unlock the full potential of QuickBooks Online's reporting features to drive smarter decisions and achieve your financial goals!

Customizing Financial Reports for Your Business Needs

Financial reports are powerful tools for understanding your business's performance and planning its future. Standard reports provide valuable insights, but customizing them ensures they align with your specific goals and needs. QuickBooks Online (QBO) allows you to tailor financial reports by adding filters, grouping data, and adjusting formatting, helping you create reports that are both actionable and relevant.

This chapter explores how to customize financial reports in QuickBooks Online to suit your unique business requirements. By mastering customization, you can track key performance indicators (KPIs), identify trends, and make informed decisions to improve profitability and efficiency.

Customized financial reports provide several advantages over generic templates:

1. Relevance:

- Focus on metrics and data points that are critical to your business's operations.

2. Clarity:

- Organize and present data in a way that's easy to interpret for you and your stakeholders.

3. Decision-Making:

- Highlight actionable insights to guide strategic planning.

4. Efficiency:

- Save time by creating templates for recurring reports tailored to your needs.

To begin customizing, navigate to the Reports section in QBO:

1. Click on Reports in the left-hand menu.
2. Browse the available standard reports, such as:

   » Profit and Loss Statement
   » Balance Sheet
   » Cash Flow Report
   » Sales by Product/Service
   » Expense by Vendor

3. Select a report to open it and access customization options.

Step 1: Adjusting Report Dates

- Choose a date range that aligns with your analysis goals:

   » Year-to-Date (YTD): Review performance for the current fiscal year.

   » Monthly or Quarterly: Track shorter-term trends.
   » Custom Dates: Focus on specific periods, such as seasonal sales peaks.

Step 2: Adding and Removing Columns

1. Click the Customize button at the top of the report.
2. Select the Rows/Columns section to modify displayed data.
3. Add columns such as:

   » Customer or vendor names.
   » Products or services.
   » Transaction types.

4. Remove irrelevant columns to simplify the report.

Step 3: Filtering Data

Filters help you narrow the focus of your report to specific criteria:

1. Go to the Filter section in the customization menu.
2. Apply filters such as:

   » Customer: Show data for a specific client.
   » Vendor: Focus on a single supplier.
   » Account: Limit results to a specific account, such as Sales or Utilities.

3. Click Run Report to apply the filters.

Step 4: Grouping Data

1. Use the Group by feature to organize data into meaningful categories.
2. Examples of grouping options:

   » Group expenses by vendor to identify high-cost suppliers.
   » Group sales by product or service to see which offerings drive revenue.

Step 5: Customizing Headers and Footers

1. Navigate to the Header/Footer section in the customization menu.
2. Modify the report title, add subtitles, or include notes for additional context.

Step 6: Applying Comparative Data

1. Add comparison columns to see changes over time:
   » Compare performance year-over-year (YOY) or month-over-month (MOM).
   » Add percentage changes to highlight trends.
2. Example: Compare Q1 sales in 2023 vs. 2022 to assess growth.

Customizing reports takes time, but QBO lets you save your settings for future use:

Step 1: Save Customizations

1. After customizing a report, click Save Customization at the top of the page.
2. Assign a unique name to your customized report.

Step 2: Access Saved Reports

1. Navigate to Reports > Custom Reports to find your saved templates.
2. Open, update, or share the saved report as needed.

Step 3: Schedule Automatic Reports

1. Use QBO to schedule automatic emails of customized reports.
2. Example: Send a weekly Profit and Loss report to stakeholders.

1. Sales Analysis Report

- Purpose: Track revenue trends by product, service, or region.
- Customizations:
  » Group sales by product or service.
  » Filter by date to focus on a specific period.
  » Add a comparison column for YOY sales.

2. Expense Report by Vendor

- Purpose: Identify top vendors and manage spending.
- Customizations:
  » Group expenses by vendor.
  » Filter to exclude minor accounts.
  » Highlight trends by adding monthly comparisons.

3. Cash Flow Forecast

- Purpose: Predict future cash needs and surpluses.
- Customizations:
  » Focus on cash inflows and outflows.
  » Group by category (e.g., operational, investment, financing).
  » Include custom date ranges for short- or long-term forecasts.

4. Budget vs. Actual Report

- Purpose: Assess financial performance against budgeted goals.
- Customizations:
  » Add columns for budgeted vs. actual amounts.
  » Highlight variances with percentage differences.
  » Group data by account for a detailed view.

QuickBooks Online allows you to export reports for further analysis or sharing:

Step 1: Export to Excel

1. Click Export > Export to Excel at the top of the report.
2. Open the file in Excel to:
   » Apply advanced formulas or pivot tables.
   » Combine data with other financial records.

Step 2: Export to PDF

1. Click Export > Export to PDF.
2. Use the PDF format for:
   » Sharing reports with stakeholders.
   » Printing hard copies for presentations or meetings.

Customized reports empower you to:

1. Monitor KPIs:

- Track metrics like gross profit margin, customer acquisition costs, or inventory turnover.

2. Optimize Spending:

- Identify inefficiencies and reduce unnecessary expenses.

3. Plan for Growth:

- Use sales reports to evaluate potential markets or products.

4. Improve Cash Flow:

- Analyze payment patterns and adjust billing strategies to accelerate collections.

5. Communicate with Stakeholders:

- Share clear, relevant reports to keep stakeholders informed and aligned.

While customizing reports, avoid these pitfalls:

Mistake 1: Including Too Much Data

- Solution: Focus on key metrics to maintain clarity and relevance.

Mistake 2: Ignoring Trends

- Solution: Use comparative data to identify and act on trends.

Mistake 3: Failing to Update Reports

- Solution: Regularly refresh and review reports to keep them accurate and actionable.

Mistake 4: Overcomplicating Customizations

- Solution: Start with simple adjustments and expand as needed.

1. **Define Your Objectives:**
   » Know the purpose of each report before customizing it.
2. Regularly Review Reports:
   » Schedule monthly or quarterly reviews to stay updated.
3. Collaborate with Your Team:
   » Share customized reports with accountants or team members for feedback.
4. Leverage Automation:
   » Use saved reports and scheduling features to streamline workflows.

Using customized reports in QBO provides several benefits:

- Improved Decision-Making: Access focused insights tailored to your business.
- Efficiency: Save time with reusable templates and automated scheduling.
- Transparency: Provide clear, concise data to stakeholders or team members.
- Scalability: Adapt reports as your business grows or changes.

Customizing financial reports in Quick-Books Online transforms raw data into actionable insights. By tailoring reports to your business's unique needs, you gain clarity, focus, and control over your finances. With tools for filtering, grouping, and exporting data, QBO empowers you to create professional-grade reports that drive smarter decisions. By implementing the strategies in this chapter, you'll master the art of financial reporting and position your business for sustained success.

Understanding Profit and Loss Statements

A Profit and Loss Statement (P&L), also known as an Income Statement, is one of the most critical financial reports for any business. It provides a snapshot of your company's revenues, expenses, and profits over a specific period, helping you gauge your financial performance. Understanding your P&L statement allows you to make informed decisions, identify trends, and plan for growth.

In this chapter, we'll explore the components of a Profit and Loss Statement, how to interpret the data, and how QuickBooks Online (QBO) simplifies generating and analyzing this report. By the end, you'll be equipped to use your P&L statement as a powerful tool for managing your business finances.

A Profit and Loss Statement is a financial report summarizing your business's income and expenses over a specific period, such as a month, quarter, or year. It shows whether your business made a profit (positive net income) or incurred a loss (negative net income).

Purpose of a P&L Statement:

- Assess Profitability: Determines whether your business is making money after covering expenses.
- Track Performance: Compares financial performance across different periods.
- Support Decision-Making: Guides budgeting, cost-cutting, and investment strategies.
- Compliance: Provides essential data for tax filings and financial disclosures.

1. Revenue (Income):

This section lists all the income your business earns from sales, services, or other sources.

- Sales Revenue: Income from selling goods or services.
- Other Income: Earnings from non-operational sources, such as interest or asset sales.

2. Cost of Goods Sold (COGS):

COGS represents the direct costs of producing goods or services, such as materials, labor, and manufacturing expenses.

- Formula: Gross Profit=Revenue−COGS\text{Gross Profit} = \text{Revenue} - \text{COGS}Gross Profit=Revenue−COGS

3. Operating Expenses:

Operating expenses are costs incurred to run your business, excluding COGS.

- Common categories include:
  - » Rent and utilities.
  - » Marketing and advertising.
  - » Salaries and wages.
  - » Office supplies.

4. Operating Income:

Operating income reflects your profit after deducting operating expenses from gross profit.

- Formula: Operating Income=Gross Profit−Operating Expenses\text{Operating Income} = \text{Gross Profit} - \text{Operating Expenses}Operating Income=Gross Profit−Operating Expenses

5. Other Income and Expenses:

This section includes non-operating financial activities, such as:

- Loan interest.
- Gains or losses from investments.

6. Net Income:

Net income is the bottom line of your P&L statement, showing your total profit or loss.

- Formula: Net Income=Operating Income+(Other Income−Other Expenses)\text{Net Income} = \text{Operating Income} + (\text{Other Income} - \text{Other Expenses})Net Income=Operating Income+(Other Income−Other Expenses)

1. Evaluate Profitability:

- Determines whether your business is financially viable.

2. Identify Trends:

- Tracks changes in revenue and expenses over time, helping you identify growth opportunities or potential issues.

3. Inform Decision-Making:

- Provides data to guide strategic choices, such as reducing costs or increasing investment.

4. Monitor Tax Obligations:

- Ensures accurate reporting of taxable income.

5. Secure Funding:

- Lenders and investors often review P&L statements to assess your financial health.

QuickBooks Online simplifies creating and analyzing your P&L statement:

Step 1: Navigate to Reports

1. Log in to QBO and click Reports in the left-hand menu.
2. Search for Profit and Loss Statement in the report library.

Step 2: Select a Date Range

1. Choose the reporting period (e.g., monthly, quarterly, yearly).
2. Use custom date ranges to focus on specific periods.

Step 3: Customize the Report

1. Click Customize at the top of the report.
2. Adjust filters, such as:
   » Accounts to include or exclude.
   » Display format (e.g., percentage of revenue).
3. Save customizations for future use.

Step 4: Run the Report

1. Click Run Report to generate the statement.

2. Review the data for accuracy and insights.

Step 5: Export or Share

- Export the report to Excel or PDF for further analysis or sharing with stakeholders.

1. Analyze Revenue:

- Look for trends in sales over time.
- Identify high-performing products or services.

2. Assess Gross Profit Margin:

- Gross Profit Margin = (Gross Profit ÷ Revenue) × 100
- A high margin indicates efficient cost management in production.

3. Review Operating Expenses:

- Examine categories with significant costs, such as salaries or rent.
- Identify areas where expenses can be reduced without compromising operations.

4. Evaluate Operating Income:

- Positive operating income indicates your business generates profit from core activities.

5. Monitor Net Income:

- Track net income trends to assess overall profitability.
- Negative net income signals a need to cut costs, increase revenue, or both.

1. Set Financial Goals:

- Use historical data to establish revenue and expense targets.

2. Plan for Growth:

- Identify profitable areas to invest in or expand.

3. Manage Costs:

- Monitor expenses and adjust budgets to maximize profitability.

4. Evaluate Pricing Strategies:

- Assess whether current pricing covers costs and generates a healthy profit margin.

5. Present to Stakeholders:

- Share P&L insights with investors or lenders to demonstrate financial stability.

1. Misclassifying Transactions:

- Ensure income and expenses are recorded in the correct accounts.

2. Ignoring Trends:

- Compare P&L data across periods to identify patterns or anomalies.

3. Overlooking COGS:

- Include all direct costs to calculate an accurate gross profit.

4. Focusing Only on Net Income:

- Analyze all components, including operating income and margins, for a complete picture.

5. Neglecting Regular Reviews:

- Generate and review P&L statements monthly or quarterly to stay informed.

1. Customize for Clarity:

- Tailor the report to include only relevant data, making it easier to interpret.

2. Regular Updates:

- Keep your QBO data current to ensure accurate P&L reports.

3. Combine with Other Reports:

- Use alongside Balance Sheets and Cash Flow Statements for a comprehensive financial analysis.

4. Seek Professional Advice:

- Consult an accountant for deeper insights or to address complex financial issues.

QuickBooks Online offers features that enhance your ability to analyze and act on P&L insights:

Comparative Analysis:

- Add comparison columns to view performance across different periods.

Percentage Columns:

- Display revenue, expenses, and profit as percentages to identify high-impact areas.

Custom Reports:

- Save customized P&L reports tailored to your business's specific needs.

A Profit and Loss Statement is more than just a financial report—it's a roadmap to your business's success. By understanding its components and leveraging QuickBooks Online to generate and analyze P&L statements, you can make informed decisions, optimize profitability, and plan for the future. Regularly reviewing this essential report keeps you in control of your finances, ensuring your business remains resilient and poised for growth.

Using Balance Sheets to Monitor Financial Health

A Balance Sheet is a cornerstone financial statement that provides a snapshot of your business's financial position at a specific point in time. It outlines what your business owns (assets), what it owes (liabilities), and the net value of your business (equity). Unlike a Profit and Loss Statement, which tracks performance over a period, the Balance Sheet focuses on a single moment, making it an essential tool for assessing your company's stability and long-term viability.

In this chapter, we'll delve into the components of a Balance Sheet, how to interpret it, and how QuickBooks Online (QBO) makes generating and analyzing this critical report simple and effective. By mastering Balance Sheets, you'll be equipped to make informed financial decisions, ensure compliance, and showcase your business's health to stakeholders.

A Balance Sheet is a financial report that summarizes your business's assets, liabilities, and equity at a given point. It follows the fundamental accounting equation:

$$\text{Assets} = \text{Liabilities} + \text{Equity}$$

Purpose of a Balance Sheet:

- Assess Financial Health: Provides a clear view of your business's stability.
- Inform Decision-Making: Guides strategic planning and risk management.
- Demonstrate Solvency: Shows your ability to meet short- and long-term obligations.
- Support Financing: Used by lenders and investors to evaluate your business.

A Balance Sheet is divided into three main sections:

1. Assets:

Assets represent everything your business owns that has monetary value.

- Current Assets: Items expected to be converted into cash within a year.
  - » Examples: Cash, accounts receivable, inventory, and short-term investments.
- Fixed (Non-Current) Assets: Long-term resources used in your business.
  - » Examples: Equipment, vehicles, real estate, and intangible assets (e.g., patents).

2. Liabilities:

Liabilities are what your business owes to creditors, suppliers, or lenders.

- Current Liabilities: Obligations due within one year.
  - » Examples: Accounts payable, short-term loans, and taxes payable.
- Long-Term Liabilities: Debts due beyond one year.
  - » Examples: Mortgages, bonds payable, and long-term leases.

3. Equity:

Equity represents the owner's stake in the business after liabilities are subtracted from assets.

- Owner's Equity: Includes initial capital, retained earnings, and net income.
- Formula: $\text{Equity} = \text{Assets} - \text{Liabilities}$

A Balance Sheet provides crucial insights into your business's financial health:

1. Measure Solvency:

- Demonstrates your ability to meet long-term obligations and stay operational.

2. Assess Liquidity:

- Evaluates your ability to cover short-term debts with current assets.

3. Monitor Growth:

- Tracks changes in assets, liabilities, and equity over time.

4. Plan Strategically:

- Guides decisions about financing, investments, and cost management.

5. Showcase Stability:

- Provides a clear financial picture for investors, lenders, or potential buyers.

QuickBooks Online simplifies the process of creating and customizing a Balance Sheet.

Step 1: Navigate to Reports

1. Log in to QBO and click Reports in the left-hand menu.
2. Search for Balance Sheet in the report library.

Step 2: Select a Date

- Choose a specific date to generate the Balance Sheet for a particular point in time.

Step 3: Customize the Report

1. Click Customize at the top of the report.
2. Adjust filters for:

- » Accounts: Include or exclude specific accounts.
- » Grouping: Organize data by type (e.g., current vs. non-current assets).
- » Comparisons: Add columns to compare balances across dates.

3. Save your customizations for future use.

Step 4: Export or Share

- Export the report as a PDF or Excel file for sharing or further analysis.

Understanding the data on your Balance Sheet is key to using it effectively:

1. Analyze Assets:

- Assess whether your current assets are sufficient to cover short-term liabilities.
- Identify trends in fixed assets, such as depreciation or new acquisitions.

2. Evaluate Liabilities:

- Monitor debt levels to ensure they remain manageable relative to assets.
- Compare current liabilities with current assets to assess liquidity.

3. Review Equity:

- Track retained earnings and net income to evaluate profitability and reinvestment.

4. Use Ratios for Deeper Insights:

- Current Ratio:

$$\text{Current Ratio} = \frac{\text{Current Assets}}{\text{Current Liabilities}}$$ Indicates liquidity; a ratio above 1 suggests sufficient coverage of short-term obligations.

- Debt-to-Equity Ratio:

Debt-to-Equity Ratio=Total LiabilitiesTotal Equity\text{Debt-to-Equity Ratio} = \frac{\text{Total Liabilities}}{\text{Total Equity}} Debt-to-Equity Ratio=Total EquityTotal Liabilities Measures leverage; a lower ratio indicates less reliance on debt.

A Balance Sheet is a versatile tool for guiding business strategies:

1. Plan Investments:

- Use asset data to determine whether you can afford new purchases or upgrades.

2. Manage Debt:

- Monitor liabilities to ensure you're not over-leveraged.

3. Evaluate Funding Needs:

- Assess equity and cash reserves to decide whether external financing is necessary.

4. Optimize Working Capital:

- Balance current assets and liabilities to maintain liquidity.

5. Prepare for Growth:

- Analyze equity trends to gauge your capacity for expansion.

While Balance Sheets are straightforward, errors can distort your financial picture:

1. Misclassified Assets or Liabilities

- Solution: Review account categorization regularly to ensure accuracy.

2. Missing Entries

- Solution: Reconcile accounts monthly to capture all transactions.

3. Overlooking Depreciation

- Solution: Record depreciation to reflect the true value of fixed assets.

4. Failing to Update Data

- Solution: Ensure QBO records are current before generating reports.

1. **Regular Reviews:**
   - » Generate and analyze Balance Sheets monthly or quarterly.
2. Use Comparative Data:
   - » Compare Balance Sheets over time to track trends and changes.
3. Collaborate with Advisors:
   - » Share Balance Sheets with accountants or financial consultants for deeper insights.
4. Integrate with Other Reports:
   - » Combine Balance Sheet data with Profit and Loss Statements and Cash Flow Reports for a comprehensive analysis.

QuickBooks Online offers several advantages for generating and analyzing Balance Sheets:

- Automation: Syncs with bank accounts and categorizes transactions automatically.
- Customization: Tailor reports to focus on specific accounts or metrics.
- Real-Time Data: Reflects the most current financial information.
- Export Options: Provides easy sharing with stakeholders in Excel or PDF formats.

The Balance Sheet is a critical tool for understanding your business's financial health and planning its future. By using Quick-Books Online to generate and analyze this report, you gain a clear picture of your assets, liabilities, and equity, empowering you to make data-driven decisions. Regularly reviewing your Balance Sheet ensures your business remains stable, solvent, and poised for growth. With QBO's user-friendly tools and customizable options, monitoring your financial health has never been easier.

Exporting Reports to Excel and PDF for Analysis

Financial reports are essential for understanding your business's performance, making informed decisions, and communicating with stakeholders. While Quick-Books Online (QBO) provides robust tools for generating and customizing reports, exporting them to external formats like Excel or PDF is often necessary for deeper analysis, sharing, or archiving. Exporting allows you to enhance your reports with additional calculations, integrate data with other tools, or create polished documents for presentations.

In this chapter, we'll explore how to export reports from QBO to Excel and PDF, the advantages of each format, and tips for effectively using these exports to gain deeper insights into your financial data.

Exporting reports from QBO offers several benefits:

1. Advanced Analysis:

- Excel provides flexibility for customizing data, applying formulas, and creating charts or pivot tables.

2. Integration:

- Exported reports can be integrated with other tools, such as budgeting software or financial dashboards.

3. Presentation:

- PDF exports are professional, easy to share, and ideal for stakeholders who don't require editable data.

4. Record-Keeping:

- Exporting ensures that you maintain offline records for audits, tax filings, or historical comparisons.

Excel is a versatile tool for analyzing financial data. Here's how to export reports to Excel from QuickBooks Online:

Step 1: Generate a Report in QBO

1. Log in to QBO and go to Reports in the left-hand menu.
2. Select the desired report (e.g., Profit and Loss, Balance Sheet, or Custom Report).
3. Customize the report as needed:

   » Adjust date ranges.
   » Apply filters for specific accounts, customers, or vendors.
   » Add comparison columns or percentages.

Step 2: Export the Report

1. Click the Export button at the top-right corner of the report.
2. Select Export to Excel.
3. The file will download as an Excel workbook (.xlsx).

Step 3: Open the File

- Open the exported Excel file using Microsoft Excel, Google Sheets, or another spreadsheet application.

- Review the data to ensure it matches your expectations.

Step 4: Enhance the Data in Excel

- Apply Formulas: Use Excel's built-in formulas to calculate additional metrics, such as ratios or variances.
- Create Charts: Visualize data with charts to identify trends or patterns.
- Build Pivot Tables: Summarize large datasets quickly for deeper analysis.

PDF is the ideal format for sharing reports with stakeholders or creating professional, non-editable documents. Here's how to export to PDF from QuickBooks Online:

Step 1: Generate a Report in QBO

1. Follow the same steps as above to generate and customize the desired report.
2. Ensure the report includes all relevant details, such as headers, footers, and notes.

Step 2: Export the Report

1. Click the Export button at the top-right corner of the report.
2. Select Export to PDF.
3. The file will download as a PDF document.

Step 3: Review and Share

- Open the PDF to verify its format and content.
- Share the file via email, attach it to presentations, or save it for offline record-keeping.

Each format has unique advantages depending on your needs:

Advantages of Excel:

- Editable: Allows for further customization and analysis.
- Flexible: Supports formulas, charts, and additional data integration.
- Interactive: Ideal for collaborating with teams or advisors.

Advantages of PDF:

- Professional: Provides a clean, polished format for presentations or reports.
- Secure: Non-editable, ensuring data integrity.
- Shareable: Easy to distribute to stakeholders who don't need to edit the data.

When to Use Each Format:

- Excel: For in-depth analysis, financial modeling, or integration with other tools.
- PDF: For official reports, presentations, or sharing with stakeholders who need a final version.

1. Clean the Data:

- Remove unnecessary rows or columns to focus on the most relevant information.

2. Add Calculations:

- Use formulas to calculate metrics such as:
  - » Revenue growth rate.
  - » Profit margins.
  - » Variances between budgeted and actual amounts.

3. Use Conditional Formatting:

- Highlight key metrics, such as expenses exceeding budgeted limits or accounts with overdue balances.

4. Create Visualizations:

- Insert charts or graphs to make trends more accessible and actionable.

5. Combine Multiple Reports:

- Merge data from different QBO reports to create a comprehensive analysis, such as combining sales data with expense reports for a profitability analysis.

1. Review Formatting:

- Ensure the report is clean and professional, with no unnecessary data or clutter.

2. Add Notes:

- Use the customization options in QBO to add headers, footers, or notes explaining the report's context or findings.

3. Use for Presentations:

- Include exported PDFs in stakeholder meetings, presentations, or pitches to provide a clear and concise summary of financial data.

4. Archive Reports:

- Save PDFs for tax purposes, audits, or historical reference.

QuickBooks Online allows you to automate report generation and delivery:

Step 1: Save Custom Reports

1. Customize your report as needed.

2. Click Save Customization to create a reusable template.

Step 2: Schedule Report Emails

1. Navigate to Reports > Custom Reports.
2. Select the report you want to schedule.
3. Set a delivery frequency (e.g., weekly, monthly).
4. Specify recipients and delivery format (Excel or PDF).

While exporting reports is straightforward, these tips will help you avoid common pitfalls:

1. Verify Data Accuracy:

- Ensure all transactions are recorded and categorized correctly in QBO before exporting.

2. Double-Check Filters:

- Confirm that filters applied in QBO are appropriate and do not exclude relevant data.

3. Review Exported Formats:

- Open the exported file to verify its formatting and content before sharing.

4. Use Secure Sharing Methods:

- For sensitive financial data, use secure email services or password-protected files when sharing.

Exporting reports from QBO to Excel or PDF enhances your ability to analyze, share, and act on financial data:

1. Enhanced Insights:

- Perform deeper analysis with Excel's advanced features.

- Highlight trends and anomalies that may not be evident in QBO.

2. Better Collaboration:

- Share editable Excel files with accountants or team members for joint analysis.
- Provide polished PDFs to stakeholders for clarity and professionalism.

3. Improved Decision-Making:

- Combine data from multiple sources in Excel for comprehensive financial models.
- Use insights from exports to make informed strategic decisions.

4. Efficient Record-Keeping:

- Maintain offline records in PDF format for tax filings, audits, or future reference.

Exporting financial reports to Excel and PDF is an essential feature of QuickBooks Online that enables deeper analysis, effective collaboration, and professional presentation of your data. By leveraging the unique benefits of each format, you can tailor reports to your specific needs, whether for advanced financial modeling in Excel or polished stakeholder presentations in PDF. With these tools, your financial reporting becomes more versatile, actionable, and impactful, empowering you to make smarter decisions and drive business success.

CHAPTER 10

ADVANCED FEATURES FOR INTERMEDIATE USERS

As your business grows, so do the complexities of managing its financial operations. While the foundational features of QuickBooks Online (QBO) are excellent for everyday tasks, the platform also offers advanced tools designed to optimize workflows, enhance data management, and empower strategic decision-making. Mastering these features is the next step for intermediate users looking to streamline processes and gain deeper insights into their business's performance.

In this chapter, we'll explore advanced functionalities in QBO, starting with workflow automation. Recurring entries and automated tasks can save time and reduce errors, allowing you to focus on strategic growth rather than repetitive data entry. We'll also dive into tags and custom fields, which provide a powerful way to organize and analyze data beyond standard categories, giving you greater control over tracking specific metrics.

For users who rely on data-driven decisions, advanced reporting features offer customizable options to generate insights tailored to your business needs. From forecasting to trend analysis, these tools enable you to make informed choices with confidence. Lastly, we'll look at integrations with AI tools, which are revolutionizing how businesses use QuickBooks. From predictive analytics to automated invoice processing, these integrations can significantly enhance efficiency and accuracy.

By leveraging these advanced features, you'll unlock the full potential of QuickBooks Online, transforming it into a robust financial management system that evolves with your business. Whether you aim to save time, improve data organization, or gain a competitive edge through smarter decisions, this chapter provides the tools and strategies you need to take your QBO skills to the next level.

Workflow Automation: Save Time with Recurring Entries

In any business, time is a precious resource. Repetitive tasks like creating invoices, scheduling payments, and recording transactions can eat away at your day, leaving less time for strategic planning and growth. Workflow automation, especially through recurring entries in QuickBooks Online (QBO), provides a powerful solution to streamline these processes, reduce errors, and increase efficiency.

This chapter explores how to use recurring entries in QBO to automate repetitive tasks. You'll learn how to set up recurring transactions for invoices, bills, journal entries, and more. By mastering this feature, you can ensure consistency in your financial records, save time, and focus on high-value activities that drive your business forward.

Recurring entries are templates for transactions that happen on a regular basis, such as:

- Invoices: For customers who pay on a subscription basis or have ongoing services.
- Bills: For recurring expenses like rent, utilities, or loan payments.
- Journal Entries: For regular adjustments, such as depreciation or interdepartmental allocations.

Benefits of Recurring Entries:

1. Time-Saving: Reduces the need for manual data entry.
2. Consistency: Ensures accuracy by automating repetitive tasks.
3. Timeliness: Avoids delays in invoicing customers or paying bills.
4. Error Reduction: Minimizes the risk of overlooking critical transactions.

Step 1: Create a Recurring Template

1. Go to the Gear Icon in QBO and select Recurring Transactions under the "Lists" section.
2. Click New to create a new template.

Step 2: Choose the Transaction Type

- Select the type of transaction you want to automate:
  - » Invoice
  - » Bill
  - » Check
  - » Journal Entry
  - » Estimate

Step 3: Define the Recurrence Details

1. Template Name: Assign a clear and descriptive name to the template (e.g., "Monthly Rent Payment").

2. Type: Choose from the following options:
  - » Scheduled: Automatically creates the transaction on a set schedule.
  - » Reminder: Sends a notification to create the transaction manually.
  - » Unscheduled: Saves the template for use as needed.
3. Interval: Set how often the transaction occurs (e.g., daily, weekly, monthly).
4. Start and End Dates: Specify the date range for the recurring transaction.

Step 4: Enter the Transaction Details

- Fill in all necessary fields for the transaction, such as:
  - » Customer or vendor name.
  - » Accounts and amounts.
  - » Payment terms or due dates.
  - » Notes or descriptions.

Step 5: Save and Activate the Template

- Review the template for accuracy and click Save Template to activate it.

1. Use Case: Subscription-Based Services

- If your business offers monthly or annual subscriptions, set up recurring invoices to bill customers automatically.

Step-by-Step Guide:

1. Go to Sales > Invoices and click New Invoice.
2. Enter the details of the recurring invoice, including the customer's name, the product or service, and the amount.
3. Save the invoice as a recurring template by selecting Make Recurring before finalizing.

Benefits:

- Ensures timely invoicing and reduces the risk of late payments.
- Streamlines revenue tracking for predictable cash flow.

1. Use Case: Fixed Monthly Expenses

- For regular expenses like rent, utilities, or insurance premiums, recurring entries automate bill creation and payment scheduling.

Step-by-Step Guide:

1. Go to Expenses > Bills and click New Bill.
2. Enter the vendor, account, and expense details.
3. Save the bill as a recurring template by selecting Make Recurring.

Benefits:

- Prevents missed payments and late fees.
- Simplifies accounts payable tracking.

1. Use Case: Regular Adjustments

- Automate journal entries for transactions like depreciation, recurring accruals, or interdepartmental charges.

Step-by-Step Guide:

1. Go to + New > Journal Entry.
2. Enter the debit and credit accounts and amounts.
3. Save the journal entry as a recurring template.

Benefits:

- Ensures consistent accounting for complex transactions.
- Reduces the risk of errors in manual adjustments.

Step 1: View Recurring Templates

1. Navigate to the Gear Icon > Recurring Transactions.
2. Review the list of active templates.

Step 2: Edit Templates

- Click on the template you want to update, make changes, and save.

Step 3: Delete or Pause Templates

- Delete templates for transactions you no longer need or pause them temporarily by setting the end date.

Step 4: Monitor Performance

- Use the Recurring Transactions List to track scheduled transactions and ensure they're functioning as intended.

1. **Start Small:**
   - » Begin with a few recurring transactions and expand as you grow comfortable with the feature.
2. Set Accurate Intervals:
   - » Choose realistic schedules to avoid duplicate or missed transactions.
3. Review Regularly:
   - » Periodically check recurring templates to ensure they reflect current amounts, accounts, and terms.
4. Test Before Activating:
   - » Run a trial transaction to confirm accuracy before automating it.
5. Use Descriptive Names:
   - » Assign clear names to templates for easy identification.

1. Combine with Payment Processing

- Use QBO's online payment options to link recurring invoices with automatic payment collection.

2. Set Up Notifications

- Enable reminders for recurring entries that require manual approval or review.

3. Leverage Custom Fields

- Add custom fields to recurring transactions for tracking additional data, such as project codes or job numbers.

4. Integrate with Third-Party Tools

- Combine QBO's recurring features with external apps for project management or customer relationship management (CRM).

1. Overlapping Templates

- Solution: Check existing templates to avoid duplicating entries for the same transaction.

2. Incorrect Data

- Solution: Verify amounts, accounts, and other details before saving templates.

3. Forgetting to Update Templates

- Solution: Review templates regularly to account for changes in terms, amounts, or schedules.

Automating workflows with recurring entries offers significant advantages:

- Time Efficiency: Frees up time spent on manual data entry.
- Accuracy: Reduces errors by automating repetitive tasks.
- Consistency: Ensures regular transactions are processed on time.
- Scalability: Supports growth by managing increasing transaction volumes efficiently.

Workflow automation through recurring entries in QuickBooks Online is a game-changer for businesses looking to save time and enhance accuracy. By automating tasks like invoicing, bill payments, and journal entries, you can streamline your operations and focus on strategic growth. With the step-by-step guidance in this chapter, you'll be ready to unlock the full potential of QBO's recurring features and take your financial management to the next level. Regular reviews and best practices will ensure your automated workflows remain accurate, efficient, and aligned with your business goals.

Using Tags and Custom Fields for Enhanced Data Management

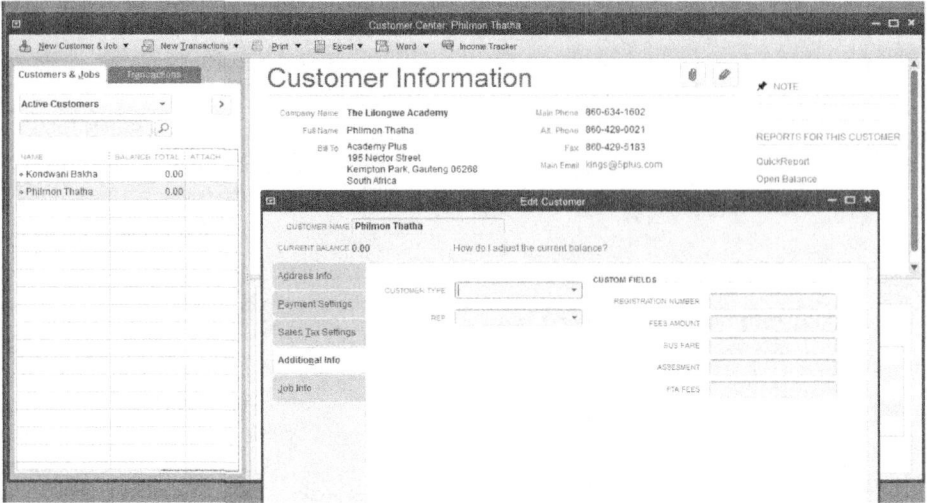

Managing financial data effectively is crucial for running a successful business. While QuickBooks Online (QBO) provides standard categories for organizing transactions, the use of tags and custom fields takes data management to the next level. These tools allow you to organize, track, and analyze data in ways that align perfectly with your unique business needs. Whether it's tracking project-specific expenses, categorizing customer transactions, or analyzing product performance, tags and custom fields provide the flexibility to capture the details that matter most.

In this chapter, we'll explore how to use tags and custom fields in QBO, the benefits they offer, and practical examples of how they can enhance your data management processes. By mastering these tools, you'll gain more control over your financial data and unlock valuable insights to guide business decisions.

Tags:

- Tags are customizable labels that you can assign to transactions for tracking and reporting purposes.
- They provide an additional layer of categorization beyond the standard accounts or classes in QBO.

Custom Fields:

- Custom fields allow you to add personalized data fields to invoices, sales forms, and other transactions.
- These fields can capture information specific to your business, such as job codes, order numbers, or customer preferences.

1. Enhanced Organization:

- Categorize transactions based on unique criteria, such as marketing campaigns, regions, or events.

2. Improved Reporting:

- Generate reports that include tag and custom field data to analyze performance and trends.

3. Flexibility:

- Adapt tags and fields to fit your specific needs, providing a level of customization not available with standard categories.

4. Better Decision-Making:

- Gain deeper insights into your finances by tracking and analyzing custom data points.

Tags are an intuitive way to track transactions across different categories or projects. Here's how to set them up:

Step 1: Access the Tag Feature

1. Navigate to Banking > Tags in the left-hand menu.
2. Click New Tag Group to create a group that will organize related tags.

Step 2: Create a Tag Group

- Name the group (e.g., "Projects," "Departments," "Campaigns").
- Add tags to the group that represent specific items or categories (e.g., "Website Redesign," "North Region," or "Spring Sale").

Step 3: Assign Tags to Transactions

1. When creating or editing a transaction (e.g., invoice, expense, or bill), locate the Tags section.
2. Select the relevant tag(s) from the drop-down menu.
3. Save the transaction.

Step 4: Use Tags for Reporting

- Run the Tags Summary Report to analyze transactions grouped by tags, providing insights into expenses, income, or profitability by category.

Custom fields allow you to collect and display additional information on your forms and reports. Here's how to create and use them:

Step 1: Enable Custom Fields

1. Go to the Gear Icon > Custom Fields.
2. Click Add Field to create a new custom field.

Step 2: Define Field Settings

- Name the field (e.g., "Order Number," "Job Code").
- Choose where the field will appear:
  - » All Sales Forms: Invoices, estimates, and sales receipts.
  - » Purchase Transactions: Bills and expenses.

Step 3: Apply Custom Fields

1. When creating or editing a transaction, locate the Custom Fields section.
2. Fill in the relevant data (e.g., entering an order number or project code).

Step 4: Use Custom Fields for Reporting

- Include custom field data in your reports by customizing the report and selecting the relevant fields to display.

1. Project Management:

- Tags: Assign tags to expenses and invoices related to specific projects (e.g., "Building Renovation").
- Custom Fields: Add a project code or name to track transactions at a detailed level.

2. Marketing Campaigns:

- Tags: Track expenses and revenue associated with different campaigns (e.g., "Holiday Sale" or "Social Media Ads").

- Custom Fields: Include campaign-specific identifiers, such as "Ad Set Name" or "Target Audience."

3. Regional Tracking:

- Tags: Use tags to categorize transactions by geographic regions (e.g., "East Coast" or "International").
- Custom Fields: Add a region field to sales forms to analyze performance across locations.

4. Vendor Management:

- Tags: Track purchases by vendor or vendor type (e.g., "Raw Materials" or "Consultants").
- Custom Fields: Include vendor-specific details, such as "Preferred Payment Method."

5. Event Management:

- Tags: Assign tags to transactions for events, such as "Annual Conference" or "Trade Show."
- Custom Fields: Add event codes or participant numbers for detailed tracking.

Using tags and custom fields in reports provides a deeper understanding of your financial data:

Step 1: Run a Tags Summary Report

1. Navigate to Reports > Tags Summary Report.
2. Filter the report by tag group or date range to analyze specific data.

Step 2: Customize Reports with Custom Fields

1. Open the report you want to customize (e.g., Profit and Loss, Sales by Product/Service).
2. Click Customize Report.

3. Add custom fields to the report layout to display the additional data.

Step 3: Export Reports

- Export reports with tags or custom fields to Excel for further analysis or to create presentations for stakeholders.

1. Define Clear Naming Conventions:

» Use consistent and descriptive names for tags and custom fields to avoid confusion.

2. Limit Tag and Field Usage:

» Avoid creating too many tags or fields, which can make data management cumbersome.

3. Review Regularly:

» Periodically review and update tags and fields to ensure they remain relevant.

4. Train Your Team:

» Ensure all users understand how to use tags and custom fields consistently.

5. Combine Tags and Fields Strategically:

» Use tags for broad categories and custom fields for more specific details.

1. Overloading Transactions:

- Assigning too many tags or custom fields to a single transaction can make reporting complex.

2. Inconsistent Usage:

- Inconsistent application of tags or fields reduces their effectiveness in tracking and reporting.

3. Ignoring Unused Tags or Fields:

- Regularly archive or delete irrelevant tags and fields to maintain clean data.

Tags and custom fields provide significant advantages for managing your financial data:

- Greater Flexibility: Tailor data organization to your specific business needs.
- Improved Insights: Gain deeper understanding through detailed tracking and reporting.
- Streamlined Processes: Simplify complex workflows with targeted data fields.
- Enhanced Decision-Making: Use detailed analysis to guide strategic choices.

Tags and custom fields are powerful tools in QuickBooks Online that go beyond standard categorization, allowing you to organize and analyze your financial data in ways that matter most to your business. By implementing these features, you'll gain greater control over your transactions, unlock actionable insights, and streamline your reporting processes. With the practical applications and best practices outlined in this chapter, you can transform how you manage your data and make more informed decisions to drive your business forward.

Advanced Reporting Features for Strategic Decisions

In today's data-driven business environment, strategic decision-making hinges on the ability to analyze accurate and detailed financial information. While standard reports in QuickBooks Online (QBO) offer valuable insights, its advanced reporting features allow you to take financial analysis to a higher level. With the ability to customize, compare, and drill down into data,

QBO's advanced reporting tools empower you to gain a clearer understanding of your business performance and make informed decisions.

This chapter explores the advanced reporting capabilities of QuickBooks Online, including custom reports, comparative analyses, and key metrics tracking. By mastering these features, you'll be able to generate actionable insights tailored to your business needs, helping you navigate challenges, identify opportunities, and strategize for long-term success.

Advanced reporting is essential for businesses looking to grow and remain competitive. It allows you to:

1. Track Key Performance Indicators (KPIs):

- Monitor metrics like profit margins, customer acquisition costs, and return on investment (ROI).

2. Uncover Trends:

- Identify patterns in revenue, expenses, and cash flow to optimize operations.

3. Optimize Resource Allocation:

- Determine which products, services, or departments generate the most profit and allocate resources accordingly.

4. Mitigate Risks:

- Spot potential issues, such as declining sales or rising costs, before they impact profitability.

5. Plan Strategically:

- Use insights to guide budgeting, forecasting, and growth strategies.

Customization is at the heart of advanced reporting in QBO. Tailored reports provide data that aligns with your business priorities.

Step 1: Select a Report to Customize

1. Go to Reports in QBO.
2. Choose a standard report, such as:
   - » Profit and Loss Statement
   - » Balance Sheet
   - » Sales by Customer Summary

Step 2: Access the Customization Options

1. Click Customize at the top of the report.
2. Adjust settings to match your needs:
   - » Date ranges (e.g., monthly, quarterly, or year-to-date).
   - » Filters to focus on specific accounts, customers, or vendors.
   - » Display options, such as percentages or comparison columns.

Step 3: Save Custom Reports

1. After customizing, click Save Customization.
2. Name the report and organize it in a group (e.g., "Management Reports" or "Sales Reports").
3. Access saved reports anytime under Reports > Custom Reports.

Comparative analysis is critical for identifying trends and evaluating performance over time. QBO's advanced features make it easy to compare data across periods or categories.

1. Adding Comparison Columns:

1. Open a report (e.g., Profit and Loss Statement).
2. Click Customize and go to the Rows/Columns section.
3. Add comparison columns, such as:
   - » Year-over-Year (YOY)
   - » Month-over-Month (MOM)
   - » Budget vs. Actual

2. Analyzing Trends with Percentages:

1. Enable percentage columns to see the relative impact of each category on total income or expenses.
2. Use this feature to identify high-impact areas that need attention or optimization.

3. Highlighting Variances:

- Use variance analysis to identify deviations from budgets or previous periods, helping you investigate the root causes and take corrective action.

QBO allows you to monitor KPIs directly through reports and dashboards, offering insights into your business's performance.

Common KPIs to Track:

1. Gross Profit Margin:
   - » Formula: $\text{Gross Profit Margin} = \frac{\text{Gross Profit}}{\text{Revenue}} \times 100$
   - » Use the Profit and Loss report to calculate this metric.

2. Current Ratio:
   - » Formula: $\text{Current Ratio} = \frac{\text{Current Assets}}{\text{Current Liabilities}}$
   - » Use the Balance Sheet report to assess liquidity.

3. Customer Lifetime Value (CLV):
   - » Use sales and customer reports to analyze how much revenue

a customer generates over their relationship with your business.

4. Net Profit Margin:
   » Formula: Net Profit Margin=Net IncomeRevenue×100\text{Net Profit Margin} = \frac{\text{Net Income}}{\text{Revenue}} \times 100Net Profit Margin=RevenueNet Income×100
   » Assess overall profitability using the Profit and Loss report.

Drill-down features in QBO allow you to investigate specific transactions or categories within reports, providing granular insights.

Step 1: Access Drill-Down Data

- Click on any value in a report (e.g., total expenses in the Profit and Loss report) to view the underlying transactions.

Step 2: Analyze Transaction Details

- Review individual entries to identify anomalies, errors, or trends.

Step 3: Take Action

- Use drill-down insights to adjust budgets, refine operations, or address discrepancies.

Dashboards provide a visual overview of your business's financial performance, making it easier to track metrics at a glance.

1. Use QBO's Built-In Dashboards:

- Access the Business Overview tab for charts and graphs summarizing income, expenses, and cash flow.

2. Integrate with Third-Party Tools:

- Use apps like Fathom, Spotlight Reporting, or Microsoft Power BI to create advanced dashboards tailored to your business needs.

Exporting reports to Excel or PDF allows you to enhance your analysis and share insights with stakeholders.

1. Export to Excel:

- Add advanced calculations, create pivot tables, or combine data from multiple reports for comprehensive analysis.

2. Export to PDF:

- Share professional, non-editable reports with investors, lenders, or management.

3. Automate Report Delivery:

- Schedule recurring email reports to keep your team informed of key metrics.

Integrating QBO with external tools can extend its reporting capabilities:

1. AI-Powered Tools:

- Use AI tools like Syft or Fathom to automate data analysis and generate predictive insights.

2. Industry-Specific Software:

- Integrate QBO with tools designed for your industry (e.g., Shopify for e-commerce, Buildertrend for construction) to enhance reporting.

3. Excel and Google Sheets:

- Sync QBO data with spreadsheets for advanced modeling or scenario planning.

Even with advanced tools, mistakes can limit the effectiveness of your reports. Here's how to avoid them:

1. Inconsistent Data Entry:

- Ensure transactions are categorized correctly to avoid skewed results.

2. Overcomplicating Reports:

- Focus on key metrics and avoid overwhelming reports with unnecessary details.

3. Neglecting Regular Reviews:

- Schedule monthly or quarterly reviews of key reports to stay informed.

4. Ignoring Customization:

- Customize reports to align with your business's unique goals and needs.

1. **Set Clear Objectives:**
   » Define what you want to achieve with your reports before generating them.

2. Use Comparison Tools:
   » Regularly compare data across periods or budgets to identify trends.

3. Collaborate with Stakeholders:
   » Share customized reports with team members or advisors for feedback and action planning.

4. Leverage Automation:
   » Automate report generation and delivery to save time and ensure consistency.

5. Integrate with Strategic Planning:
   » Use insights from reports to inform business strategies, such as expansion, cost-cutting, or new product launches.

Advanced reporting features in QuickBooks Online empower you to transform raw data into actionable insights, making it an invaluable tool for strategic decision-making. By customizing reports, tracking KPIs, leveraging comparative analyses, and integrating with external tools, you can gain a deeper understanding of your business's performance. With regular use and best practices, QBO's advanced reporting capabilities will help you navigate challenges, seize opportunities, and drive long-term success.

Exploring Integrations: QuickBooks and AI Tools

QuickBooks Online (QBO) is an industry-leading platform for managing business finances, but its true potential lies in its ability to integrate seamlessly with advanced tools, including those powered by artificial intelligence (AI). These integrations allow you to enhance functionality, streamline workflows, and make smarter decisions using predictive insights and automation. Whether it's automating routine tasks, forecasting financial trends, or improving customer service, AI-powered tools complement QBO's capabilities and help you take your financial management to the next level.

In this chapter, we'll explore the benefits of integrating AI tools with QuickBooks, highlight some of the most impactful integrations available, and discuss how these tools can transform your financial operations. By leveraging these technologies, you'll unlock efficiencies, gain deeper insights, and position your business for sustained growth.

AI integrations enhance the functionality of QuickBooks by automating repetitive tasks, providing advanced analytics, and simplifying decision-making. Key benefits include:

1. Increased Efficiency:

- Automates data entry, invoice processing, and reconciliation tasks, saving time and reducing errors.

2. Predictive Insights:

- Uses AI algorithms to forecast cash flow, predict sales trends, and identify potential risks.

3. Enhanced Decision-Making:

- Provides actionable recommendations based on real-time data analysis.

4. Improved Accuracy:

- Minimizes human errors in financial operations through intelligent automation.

5. Scalability:

- Supports growing businesses by handling large volumes of transactions and data effortlessly.

There are numerous AI-powered tools that integrate seamlessly with QuickBooks Online. Here are some of the most popular and impactful:

1. Syft Analytics:

- Provides advanced financial reporting and analysis tools.
- Features:
  » Automated creation of detailed financial reports and dashboards.
  » Predictive analytics for revenue, expenses, and profitability.
- Use Case: Ideal for businesses seeking enhanced reporting capabilities and strategic insights.

2. HubSpot:

- AI-powered customer relationship management (CRM) software.
- Features:
  » Synchronizes customer data with QuickBooks to streamline invoicing and sales tracking.
  » Provides sales forecasts based on historical trends.
- Use Case: Perfect for managing customer data and improving sales pipeline visibility.

3. Bill.com:

- Streamlines accounts payable and receivable processes with AI-driven automation.
- Features:
  » Automates invoice approvals and payments.
  » Uses AI to detect duplicate bills and flag errors.
- Use Case: Reduces manual effort in managing vendor and client payments.

4. Expensify:

- Simplifies expense reporting and management using AI.
- Features:
  » Automatically categorizes expenses based on receipts.
  » Syncs expense data directly to QuickBooks for seamless accounting.
- Use Case: Ideal for businesses with frequent travel or expense reporting needs.

5. Fathom:

- Offers advanced analytics and performance monitoring.
- Features:
  - » AI-driven financial KPIs and benchmarking tools.
  - » Scenario modeling for strategic decision-making.
- Use Case: Helps businesses track performance and plan for growth.

One of the primary benefits of integrating AI tools with QuickBooks is task automation. Here are key tasks that AI integrations can handle:

1. Data Entry:

- AI tools like Hubdoc and AutoEntry extract data from receipts, invoices, and bank statements, automatically syncing it with QBO.
- Benefit: Eliminates manual entry, reducing errors and saving time.

2. Invoice Management:

- Tools like Bill.com automate the creation, approval, and tracking of invoices.
- Benefit: Ensures timely payments and reduces the risk of missed deadlines.

3. Reconciliation:

- AI-powered tools match transactions from your bank statements with QuickBooks records.
- Benefit: Simplifies reconciliation and ensures accuracy.

4. Expense Categorization:

- Apps like Expensify use AI to categorize expenses based on historical data.
- Benefit: Streamlines expense reporting and improves record accuracy.

AI integrations provide advanced analytics capabilities, offering insights that go beyond standard QuickBooks reports:

1. Predictive Analytics:

- Tools like Syft Analytics and Fathom use historical data to predict future trends in revenue, expenses, and cash flow.
- Example: Forecasting seasonal sales trends to plan inventory or marketing budgets.

2. Real-Time Insights:

- AI-powered dashboards display up-to-date metrics, enabling quicker responses to changes in financial performance.
- Example: Monitoring cash flow in real-time to avoid potential shortfalls.

3. Scenario Modeling:

- Simulate different business scenarios (e.g., adding a new product line or expanding to a new market) to evaluate financial impact.
- Example: Using Fathom to model the effects of hiring additional staff on profitability.

4. Benchmarking:

- Compare your business performance to industry standards or competitors using AI-powered benchmarks.
- Example: Evaluating your gross profit margin against similar businesses to identify areas for improvement.

Integrations with AI-powered CRM tools improve customer interactions and financial processes:

1. HubSpot Integration:

- Syncs customer data from QBO to the CRM platform, ensuring accurate invoicing and payment tracking.
- Uses AI to provide customer insights, such as purchasing patterns and payment history.

2. Zendesk Integration:

- Connects customer service software with QuickBooks to track customer support tickets alongside financial data.
- Provides a holistic view of customer interactions, enabling personalized service.

3. AI-Driven Customer Insights:

- Tools analyze customer behavior to recommend upselling or cross-selling opportunities.
- Example: Identifying frequent buyers and offering them tailored promotions.

AI tools integrated with QuickBooks can transform financial planning through accurate forecasting:

1. Cash Flow Forecasting:

- Predict cash inflows and outflows using AI-based tools like Syft Analytics.
- Helps anticipate periods of surplus or shortfall, enabling proactive decision-making.

2. Budget Planning:

- AI-powered tools analyze historical data to suggest realistic budget allocations.

- Example: Creating department-level budgets based on past spending trends.

3. Long-Term Projections:

- Generate 3- to 5-year financial forecasts using AI algorithms.
- Example: Modeling the impact of market expansion on long-term profitability.

AI tools also help businesses stay compliant and manage financial risks:

1. Audit Preparation:

- Tools like AuditFile automate audit trails and ensure transactions are properly documented.
- Benefit: Simplifies tax filings and reduces audit-related stress.

2. Fraud Detection:

- AI-powered systems identify unusual patterns in financial transactions, flagging potential fraud.
- Example: Detecting duplicate invoices or unexpected vendor payments.

3. Tax Compliance:

- Tools like Avalara automate sales tax calculations and filings, ensuring compliance with local regulations.
- Benefit: Minimizes errors in tax reporting.

When choosing AI tools to integrate with QuickBooks, consider the following:

1. Business Needs:

- Identify pain points, such as time-consuming tasks or areas where insights are lacking.

2. Scalability:

- Choose tools that can grow with your business, handling larger transaction volumes as needed.

3. Compatibility:

- Ensure the tool integrates seamlessly with QuickBooks Online and other software you use.

4. Usability:

- Look for user-friendly interfaces and tools that don't require extensive training.

5. Cost:

- Evaluate pricing plans to ensure the tool fits within your budget.

1. Over-Automating:

- Avoid automating tasks that require human oversight, such as strategic decisions.

2. Ignoring Data Accuracy:

- Ensure your QuickBooks data is clean and accurate before integrating AI tools.

3. Failing to Train Staff:

- Provide training to ensure your team understands how to use the tools effectively.

Integrating AI tools with QuickBooks Online is a game-changer for businesses looking to optimize workflows, enhance data management, and make smarter decisions. From automating repetitive tasks to providing predictive insights and ensuring compliance, AI-powered integrations unlock new possibilities for efficiency and growth.

CHAPTER 11

QUICKBOOKS ONLINE MOBILE APP AND ON-THE-GO FEATURES

In today's fast-paced business world, the ability to manage your finances on the go is essential. The QuickBooks Online Mobile App offers a powerful, convenient solution for staying connected to your business anytime, anywhere. With this app, you can seamlessly handle key accounting tasks, from tracking expenses to sending invoices, without being tied to a desk.

The QuickBooks Online Mobile App is designed to bring the core features of the desktop version to your fingertips, optimized for smartphones and tablets. Its intuitive interface makes it easy to navigate, allowing you to perform essential tasks efficiently while on the move. Whether you're meeting clients, traveling for business, or managing operations from home, this app ensures you stay in control of your business finances.

In this chapter, we'll explore the app's interface and key on-the-go features. You'll learn how to capture receipts and track expenses in real-time, saving you hours of data entry later. We'll also discuss how to create and send professional invoices directly from your mobile device, ensuring faster payments. Additionally, the app provides access to critical financial insights, allowing you to review cash flow and reports wherever you are.

By mastering the QuickBooks Online Mobile App, you'll gain the flexibility and con-fidence to manage your business with ease, no matter where your day takes you. Let's dive into the features that make this app a must-have for modern business owners.

Navigating the QuickBooks Online Mobile App Interface

The QuickBooks Online Mobile App is a powerful tool that puts your business finances at your fingertips. Designed for busy professionals, it offers an intuitive and user-friendly interface, allowing you to perform critical accounting tasks anytime, anywhere. Whether you're sending invoices, tracking expenses, or reviewing reports, the app ensures you remain in control of your business on the go.

In this chapter, we'll guide you through the app's interface, explain its key features, and help you maximize its functionality. By understanding how to navigate the Quick-Books Online Mobile App effectively, you can streamline your workflow and save valuable time.

The QuickBooks Online Mobile App is available for iOS and Android devices, offering a scaled-down but powerful version of the desktop platform. The app is designed to balance simplicity with functionality, making it accessible to users of all experience levels.

Key Benefits:

- Convenience: Access your financial data and perform tasks from anywhere.
- Real-Time Updates: Syncs seamlessly with your QuickBooks Online account, ensuring data accuracy.
- Efficiency: Reduces reliance on desktop access, enabling quick responses to business needs.

Step 1: Download and Install

1. Visit the App Store (iOS) or Google Play Store (Android).
2. Search for "QuickBooks Online Accounting" and download the app.

Step 2: Log In

1. Open the app and log in using your QuickBooks Online credentials.
2. Ensure the login details match your desktop account to sync data seamlessly.

Step 3: Enable Notifications

- Allow the app to send notifications for reminders, updates, and alerts about invoices, payments, and more.

Step 4: Customize Settings

- Adjust app settings to match your preferences, such as:
  - » Default currency.
  - » Tax settings.
  - » Notifications and alerts.

Upon logging in, the Dashboard is the first screen you'll see. It provides a snapshot of your business's financial health.

Key Sections of the Dashboard:

1. Profit and Loss:
   - » View a quick summary of income, expenses, and net profit for the current period.

2. Invoices:
   - » Check the status of sent invoices (e.g., unpaid, overdue, paid).
   - » Send reminders or create new invoices directly from this section.

3. Expenses:
   - » Monitor recent expense transactions.
   - » Categorize and edit expenses as needed.

4. Bank Accounts:
   - » Review balances for connected bank accounts and credit cards.
   - » Identify any discrepancies or transactions needing review.

5. Notifications:
   - » Access alerts for overdue invoices, bill reminders, and other important updates.

Navigation Tips:

- Swipe Gestures: Use swipes to navigate between sections.
- Icons and Menus: Tap icons for quick access to specific features like reports, invoicing, and expenses.

1. Navigation Menu:

- Accessible via the hamburger icon (three horizontal lines) in the top-left corner.
- Provides quick links to all major sections:
  - » Dashboard
  - » Sales (Invoices and Customers)
  - » Expenses
  - » Banking
  - » Reports
  - » Settings

2. Quick Actions Button:

- A floating + Button at the bottom of the screen offers one-tap access to frequently used functions:
  » Create an invoice.
  » Record an expense.
  » Capture a receipt.
  » Add a customer or vendor.

3. Search Bar:

- Located at the top of the screen, allowing you to search for specific transactions, customers, or reports quickly.

4. Reports Tab:

- Provides access to essential financial reports, such as:
  » Profit and Loss
  » Balance Sheet
  » Cash Flow Statement
- Customize reports directly within the app for specific timeframes or categories.

5. Notifications Tab:

- Keeps you updated on critical tasks, such as overdue invoices or reconciliation issues.

1. Creating and Sending Invoices

1. Tap the + Button and select Invoice.
2. Choose a customer or add a new one.
3. Fill in invoice details:
   » Products or services.
   » Quantity and price.
   » Payment terms and due date.
4. Tap Send to email the invoice directly to the customer.

2. Recording Expenses

1. Tap the + Button and select Expense.
2. Enter details, including:

» Vendor name.
» Expense category.
» Amount and payment method.

3. Attach a receipt by capturing an image or uploading a file.
4. Save the transaction for automatic syncing with your desktop account.

3. Capturing Receipts

1. Tap the + Button and select Receipt.
2. Use your device's camera to take a picture of the receipt.
3. The app automatically extracts data using OCR (Optical Character Recognition) and categorizes the expense.

4. Reviewing Reports

1. Go to the Reports tab from the navigation menu.
2. Select the desired report and customize it by date range or account.
3. View, share, or download the report as needed.

5. Managing Bank Transactions

1. Access the Banking tab to review connected accounts.
2. Categorize and match transactions to ensure accurate records.
3. Mark reconciled transactions for better financial tracking.

1. Use Favorites:

- Mark frequently accessed features as favorites for quick navigation.

2. Enable Offline Mode:

- Work offline and sync changes automatically once reconnected to the internet.

3. Regular Updates:

- Keep the app updated to ensure access to the latest features and security improvements.

4. Sync Across Devices:

- Ensure that changes made on mobile are reflected on your desktop account by syncing data regularly.

The QuickBooks Online Mobile App offers several advantages for business owners on the move:

1. Time Savings:

- Perform essential tasks quickly without needing a computer.

2. Real-Time Updates:

- Access up-to-date financial data, ensuring informed decision-making.

3. Flexibility:

- Manage finances anytime and anywhere, enhancing productivity.

4. Enhanced Accuracy:

- Record transactions in real time, reducing the risk of forgetting details or losing receipts.

While the mobile app is robust, it has some limitations compared to the desktop version:

1. Limited Customization:

- Advanced customizations for reports or invoices are best handled on a desktop.

2. Restricted Integrations:

- Some third-party app integrations may not be accessible via mobile.

Workaround:

- Use the mobile app for on-the-go tasks and switch to the desktop version for advanced features.

1. **Daily Check-Ins:**

   » Use the app to review finances each day and stay on top of tasks.

2. Capture Receipts Immediately:

   » Photograph and upload receipts as soon as purchases are made to avoid losing them.

3. Keep Notifications Enabled:

   » Stay informed about important updates, such as overdue invoices or reconciliation alerts.

4. Secure Your Device:

   » Enable biometric authentication (e.g., fingerprint or face recognition) for added security.

The QuickBooks Online Mobile App is a game-changer for managing your business finances on the go. Its intuitive interface, coupled with powerful features like receipt capture, invoice creation, and real-time reporting, ensures you stay productive and informed, no matter where you are. By mastering the navigation and functionality of the app, you'll unlock new levels of efficiency and control, empowering you to focus on growing your business while staying connected to its financial health.

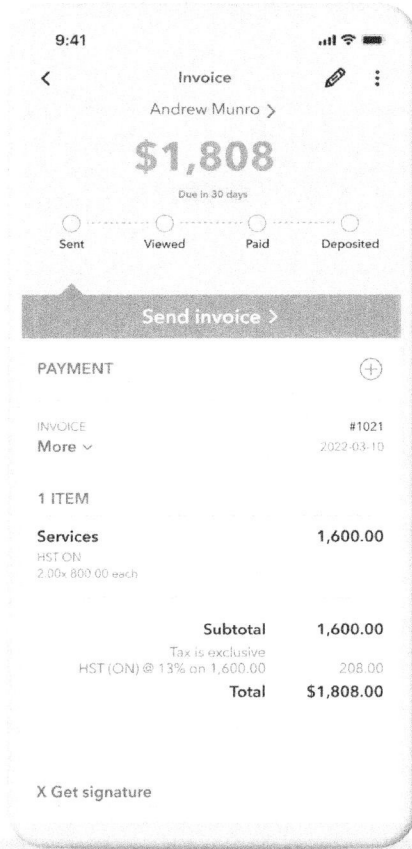

Efficiently managing expenses and keeping track of receipts is a critical part of maintaining accurate financial records. With the QuickBooks Online Mobile App, capturing receipts and managing expenses becomes an effortless task, enabling business owners to stay organized while on the go. By leveraging the app's powerful features, you can digitize receipts, automatically categorize expenses, and maintain real-time control over your spending.

In this chapter, we'll explore how to use the mobile app to streamline expense tracking and receipt management. From photographing receipts to syncing expense data with your QuickBooks Online account, these tools will save you time, reduce errors, and help you maintain compliance.

1. Accuracy in Financial Records:

- Properly categorizing expenses ensures accurate financial reporting and helps you understand your spending patterns.

2. Tax Compliance:

- Digital copies of receipts serve as proof for tax deductions and audits, reducing the risk of penalties.

3. Time Efficiency:

- Automating expense tracking and receipt capture saves hours of manual data entry.

4. Cost Control:

- Real-time expense tracking allows you to monitor spending and identify areas for cost savings.

Step 1: Enable Receipt Capture

1. Download the QuickBooks Online Mobile App and log in with your credentials.
2. Go to Settings > Expense Management and enable the receipt capture feature.

Step 2: Connect Bank Accounts and Credit Cards

1. Access the Banking tab in the app.
2. Link your business bank accounts and credit cards to automatically import transactions.
3. Syncing these accounts ensures real-time expense tracking.

Step 3: Customize Expense Categories

1. Navigate to Settings > Chart of Accounts.
2. Add or edit categories to match your business needs (e.g., travel, utilities, office supplies).

Step 1: Capture Receipts Using the Camera

1. Tap the + Button in the app and select Receipt.

2. Use your smartphone's camera to take a clear photo of the receipt.
3. Confirm the image quality and save it to the app.

Step 2: Upload Existing Receipts

1. If you have digital receipts, tap the Upload Receipt option.
2. Select images or PDF files stored on your device and upload them to the app.

Step 3: Automatic Data Extraction

- The app uses Optical Character Recognition (OCR) technology to extract key details from receipts, including:
  » Vendor name.
  » Date of purchase.
  » Total amount.
  » Payment method.

Step 4: Match Receipts to Transactions

- The app automatically matches uploaded receipts with transactions imported from linked bank accounts or credit cards.
- If no match is found, you can manually link the receipt to the correct transaction.

Step 1: Record an Expense

1. Tap the + Button and select Expense.
2. Fill in the following details:
   » Vendor name.
   » Expense category (e.g., travel, utilities).
   » Payment method (e.g., credit card, cash).
   » Amount and date.
3. Attach a receipt to the expense record for documentation.

Step 2: Categorize Expenses

- The app automatically suggests categories based on the vendor or transaction details.
- Review and confirm or update the category to ensure accuracy.

Step 3: Split Expenses

- If an expense applies to multiple categories, use the Split Expense feature to divide it proportionally.

Step 4: Track Reimbursable Expenses

1. Mark expenses that need reimbursement (e.g., employee travel costs).
2. Add notes or tags to track reimbursement status.

Step 5: Monitor Real-Time Expense Tracking

- Access the Expenses tab to review all recorded expenses.
- Use filters to sort expenses by category, vendor, or date.

The mobile app automatically syncs expense data with your QuickBooks Online account, ensuring consistency across devices.

1. Real-Time Syncing:

- Expenses recorded via the mobile app appear instantly on the desktop version.

2. Multi-User Updates:

- If multiple team members use the app, syncing ensures all data is centralized and up to date.

3. Audit Trails:

- Every expense recorded includes a digital audit trail, making it easy to verify transactions during reviews or audits.

The app provides access to key expense reports, offering insights into your spending patterns:

1. Expense Summary Report:

- Provides a breakdown of expenses by category.
- Useful for identifying high-cost areas and optimizing budgets.

2. Vendor Expense Report:

- Lists expenses by vendor, helping you track supplier costs and negotiate better terms.

3. Reimbursable Expense Report:

- Tracks reimbursable expenses for employees or clients.
- Ensures timely processing and transparency.

1. Real-Time Tracking:

- Allows you to record expenses immediately, reducing the risk of forgetting details or losing receipts.

2. Improved Accuracy:

- Automates data entry and categorization, minimizing errors.

3. Enhanced Organization:

- Centralizes all expense records and receipts in a single platform.

4. Compliance Ready:

- Maintains a digital archive of receipts and expenses, ensuring preparedness for audits or tax filings.

5. Time Savings:

- Automates processes like matching receipts to transactions, freeing up time for other tasks.

1. Capture Receipts Immediately:

- Take a photo of the receipt as soon as you make a purchase to avoid losing it.

2. Regularly Categorize Expenses:

- Review and categorize expenses weekly to keep your records organized.

3. Set Spending Alerts:

- Use the app's notification feature to alert you when spending exceeds set thresholds.

4. Train Your Team:

- If employees handle expenses, ensure they know how to use the app for accurate tracking and documentation.

5. Monitor Trends:

- Analyze expense reports regularly to identify trends and adjust budgets as needed.

1. Neglecting Receipt Capture:

- Solution: Make it a habit to capture receipts immediately after a purchase.

2. Misclassifying Expenses:

- Solution: Review categories regularly and ensure they align with your chart of accounts.

3. Failing to Match Receipts to Transactions:

- Solution: Use the app's automatic matching feature and manually match any unlinked receipts.

4. Ignoring Reimbursable Expenses:

- Solution: Tag reimbursable expenses and track their status to ensure timely reimbursements.

The QuickBooks Online Mobile App revolutionizes expense tracking and receipt management by providing a seamless, real-time solution for business owners and their teams. From capturing receipts with a single tap to categorizing and syncing expenses automatically, the app simplifies financial management and enhances accuracy. By mastering these features and following best practices, you'll gain complete control over your expenses, streamline your workflows, and focus on growing your business with confidence.

Creating and Sending Invoices on the Go

Invoicing is a critical component of running a business, and the faster you can create and send invoices, the sooner you can get paid. The QuickBooks Online Mobile App simplifies this process, enabling you to create, customize, and send invoices directly from your mobile device. Whether you're at a client meeting, traveling, or managing operations remotely, the app ensures you can handle invoicing efficiently and professionally.

This chapter explores how to create and send invoices on the go using the QuickBooks Online Mobile App. You'll learn how to set up invoice templates, add customer details, include products or services, and send invoices via email or messaging platforms. Additionally, we'll discuss how to track invoice statuses, accept payments, and resolve common invoicing issues.

1. Faster Payment Cycles:

- The quicker you send invoices, the sooner clients can process payments.

2. Improved Efficiency:

- Streamlines the invoicing process, reducing delays caused by waiting to return to your desk.

3. Professionalism:

- Allows you to deliver polished invoices immediately after a job or meeting, enhancing client satisfaction.

4. Flexibility:

- Gives you the freedom to manage your invoicing process from anywhere.

Step 1: Customize Invoice Templates

1. Open the QuickBooks Online Mobile App and navigate to Settings.
2. Select Custom Form Styles and choose the invoice template.
3. Add your company logo, branding, and default terms (e.g., net 30 payment).

Step 2: Configure Payment Options

1. Enable online payment methods, such as:
   » Credit card.
   » ACH bank transfer.
   » PayPal or Apple Pay.
2. Go to Settings > Payments to integrate payment gateways.

Step 3: Add Customer Details

- Ensure your Customer List is up-to-date by importing contacts or manually adding new customers.

Step 1: Access the Invoicing Feature

1. Tap the + Button in the app.
2. Select Invoice from the menu of options.

Step 2: Choose a Customer

1. Select an existing customer from the dropdown list.
2. Add a new customer by entering their name, email, and billing address.

Step 3: Add Products or Services

1. Tap Add Line Item and choose a product or service from your inventory.
2. Specify details, such as:
   » Quantity or hours.
   » Rate or price.
   » Discounts (if applicable).

Step 4: Adjust Tax Settings

- Ensure sales tax is applied correctly based on your location and the client's region.

Step 5: Review and Save

- Double-check all details, including totals, payment terms, and due dates.
- Save the invoice as a draft or finalize it for sending.

1. Emailing Invoices

1. Tap Send Invoice to email the invoice directly to the client.
2. Use the pre-filled email template or customize the message to include personalized notes.

2. Sharing via Messaging Apps

- Export the invoice as a PDF and share it through apps like WhatsApp, Slack, or SMS for clients who prefer messaging.

3. Printing Invoices

- Connect your mobile device to a wireless printer to generate hard copies for clients who need physical invoices.

4. Scheduling Recurring Invoices

1. For repeat clients, set up recurring invoices by selecting Make Recurring before sending.
2. Customize the schedule (e.g., weekly, monthly) and automate delivery.

The QuickBooks Online Mobile App makes it easy to monitor the progress of your invoices:

1. Invoice Status Overview

- Access the Sales tab to view invoice statuses, such as:
  - » Unpaid
  - » Overdue
  - » Paid
  - » Partially Paid

2. Sending Payment Reminders

1. Select an overdue invoice from the list.
2. Tap Send Reminder to notify the client of the pending payment.

3. Viewing Payment History

- Check individual invoices for payment history, including partial payments or refunds.

1. Enable Online Payments

- Accept payments directly through the invoice by integrating payment gateways during setup.

2. Record Offline Payments

1. Tap the invoice and select Receive Payment.

2. Choose the payment method (e.g., cash, check).
3. Record the payment amount and save the transaction.

3. Track Payment Deposits

- Use the Banking tab to monitor deposits from online payments and reconcile them with invoices.

1. Handling Incorrect Invoices

- If you notice an error after sending, open the invoice, edit the details, and resend it.

2. Addressing Disputes

1. Use the Notes section on the invoice to document any agreements or adjustments with the client.
2. Create credit memos for refunds or discounts as needed.

3. Resolving Unpaid Invoices

- Send periodic reminders and consider charging late fees by updating your payment terms.

4. Monitoring Overpayments

- If a client overpays, record the excess amount and apply it as a credit toward future invoices.

1. Time Efficiency:

- Creates and sends invoices immediately after a service or sale, speeding up the payment cycle.

2. Reduced Errors:

- Real-time data entry minimizes errors caused by delayed recording.

3. Flexibility:

- Enables invoicing from any location, ensuring uninterrupted cash flow.

4. Better Cash Flow Management:

- Tracking invoices on the go helps you monitor receivables and plan expenses accordingly.

5. Professional Appearance:

- Delivers polished, branded invoices that build trust with clients.

1. Automate Where Possible:

- Set up recurring invoices for long-term clients to save time.

2. Use Clear Payment Terms:

- Specify due dates, accepted payment methods, and late fee policies on every invoice.

3. Follow Up Promptly:

- Send reminders for unpaid invoices as soon as they become overdue.

4. Keep Customer Records Updated:

- Ensure contact details and billing information are accurate to avoid delays.

5. Leverage Analytics:

- Use the app's reporting features to track invoicing trends, such as average payment times.

1. Sending Incomplete Invoices:

- Solution: Double-check all details before sending, including client information, itemized charges, and totals.

2. Forgetting to Attach Receipts:

- Solution: Attach supporting documents for billable expenses directly to the invoice.

3. Delayed Invoicing:

- Solution: Use the mobile app to create invoices immediately after a service or sale.

4. Overlooking Follow-Ups:

- Solution: Regularly monitor overdue invoices and send reminders promptly.

The QuickBooks Online Mobile App revolutionizes invoicing by offering a fast, efficient, and professional way to create and send invoices on the go. With its intuitive features, customizable templates, and real-time syncing, the app ensures you stay on top of your billing process no matter where you are. By mastering mobile invoicing and implementing best practices, you'll reduce payment delays, maintain a steady cash flow, and enhance your overall client experience.

Reviewing Cash Flow and Reports Anywhere

Managing cash flow effectively is vital for the financial health of any business. With the QuickBooks Online Mobile App, you can review your cash flow and generate essential reports from anywhere, ensuring you stay informed about your business's financial position even while on the move. This flexibility allows you to make timely decisions, address potential issues, and seize opportunities without being tethered to a desktop.

In this chapter, we'll explore how to leverage the mobile app's features to review cash flow and access key reports. You'll learn how to navigate cash flow insights, customize financial reports, and use these tools to monitor your business's performance in real-time.

1. Real-Time Decision-Making:

- Real-time cash flow visibility helps you decide when to invest, cut costs, or secure funding.

2. Financial Stability:

- Monitoring ensures that your business maintains enough cash to cover expenses and operate smoothly.

3. Risk Management:

- Regular reviews of financial reports highlight potential issues, such as declining revenue or rising expenses.

4. Goal Tracking:

- Reports allow you to measure progress toward financial goals, such as profitability or budget adherence.

Step 1: Sync Bank Accounts

1. Navigate to the Banking tab in the app.
2. Link your business bank accounts and credit cards to automatically import transactions.

Step 2: Enable Cash Flow Insights

1. Open the Cash Flow feature from the app's menu.
2. Set parameters, such as:
   - » Transaction categories to include.
   - » Date ranges (e.g., weekly, monthly, quarterly).

Step 3: Adjust Settings for Projections

- Customize projections based on expected inflows (e.g., receivables) and outflows (e.g., payroll or rent).

The Cash Flow Dashboard provides a quick overview of your business's liquidity.

1. Key Components of the Cash Flow Dashboard:

- Current Cash Balance: Displays the amount available in linked bank accounts.
- Cash Flow Graph: Visualizes inflows and outflows over a selected period.
- Upcoming Transactions: Lists expected payments and receivables.

2. Real-Time Updates:

- Data is updated in real-time as transactions sync with your accounts, ensuring accuracy.

3. Filtering and Customization:

- Use filters to view specific transaction categories, such as:
  - » Operating expenses.
  - » Revenue streams.
  - » Loan repayments.

The mobile app allows you to access and customize a variety of financial reports, providing deeper insights into your business.

Step 1: Open the Reports Section

1. Navigate to Reports in the app's main menu.
2. Select from pre-configured reports, such as:
   - » Profit and Loss Statement.
   - » Balance Sheet.
   - » Cash Flow Report.
   - » Sales by Customer or Product/Service.

Step 2: Customize the Report

1. Tap Customize at the top of the report screen.
2. Adjust parameters such as:

- » Date Range: View data for specific periods (e.g., this month, last quarter).
- » Accounts: Include or exclude accounts to focus on relevant data.
- » Comparison Columns: Add year-over-year or month-over-month comparisons.

Step 3: Save and Export

1. Save customized reports for future use.
2. Export reports as PDFs or Excel files for sharing or detailed analysis.

1. Profit and Loss Statement:

- Provides an overview of revenue, expenses, and net profit.
- Use Case: Track profitability and identify cost-saving opportunities.

2. Balance Sheet:

- Displays assets, liabilities, and equity at a specific point in time.
- Use Case: Evaluate financial stability and solvency.

3. Cash Flow Statement:

- Breaks down cash inflows and outflows into operating, investing, and financing activities.
- Use Case: Monitor liquidity and plan for future cash needs.

4. Sales Reports:

- Highlights sales performance by customer, product, or service.
- Use Case: Identify top-performing products or clients.

5. Expense Reports:

- Categorizes expenses by vendor or account.

- Use Case: Control spending and negotiate better terms with suppliers.

1. Real-Time Insights:

- Use real-time data to address urgent issues, such as low cash reserves or overdue invoices.

2. Strategic Planning:

- Combine cash flow projections with historical reports to plan for investments or expansions.

3. Trend Analysis:

- Identify patterns in revenue and expenses to make informed adjustments to operations.

4. Collaboration:

- Share reports with your team or accountant directly from the app for collaborative decision-making.

1. Schedule Recurring Reports:

- Set up automated delivery of key reports to your email for regular review.

2. Push Notifications:

- Enable notifications for critical updates, such as:
  - » Significant changes in cash flow.
  - » Report generation reminders.

3. Sync Across Devices:

- Access saved and automated reports seamlessly on desktop or mobile.

1. Missing Data:

- Solution: Ensure all bank accounts and credit cards are properly synced with QuickBooks Online.

2. Incorrect Projections:

- Solution: Review and adjust cash flow settings to include expected inflows and outflows.

3. Report Errors:

- Solution: Verify customization parameters to ensure accurate data.

4. Delayed Updates:

- Solution: Check for internet connectivity and ensure the app is updated to the latest version.

1. Schedule Regular Reviews:

- Review cash flow and reports weekly or monthly to stay informed.

2. Use Comparative Analysis:

- Compare current performance to previous periods to assess growth or address declines.

3. Focus on Key Metrics:

- Prioritize monitoring metrics like net cash flow, gross profit margin, and expense ratios.

4. Train Your Team:

- Ensure employees handling finances understand how to use the app for reviewing reports.

1. Accessibility:

- Access financial data anytime, anywhere for greater flexibility.

2. Time Savings:

- Quick access to reports reduces the need for desktop logins or manual data pulls.

3. Enhanced Accuracy:

- Real-time syncing ensures reports are based on the latest data.

4. Better Decision-Making:

- Provides actionable insights to guide strategic and operational decisions.

The QuickBooks Online Mobile App empowers you to review cash flow and financial reports with ease, ensuring you stay connected to your business's financial health no matter where you are. By leveraging real-time updates, customizable reports, and automation features, you can make data-driven decisions that drive success. Regularly monitoring cash flow and reports through the app will help you maintain control over your finances, optimize operations, and achieve your business goals with confidence.

CHAPTER 12

SCALING YOUR BUSINESS WITH QUICKBOOKS

As your business grows, so do the complexities of managing its financial operations. Scaling successfully requires tools that not only adapt to your increasing needs but also streamline your processes to support sustainable growth. QuickBooks Online is more than just an accounting platform; it is a scalable solution that evolves alongside your business. With its robust suite of features, add-ons, and data-driven insights, QuickBooks can help you navigate the challenges of growth and prepare for the future.

This chapter explores how to leverage QuickBooks to scale your business efficiently and effectively. From integrating specialized add-ons that expand its capabilities to using advanced financial tools for growth planning, QuickBooks provides everything you need to take your operations to the next level. We'll also delve into how to leverage data insights for strategic decision-making and ensure compliance with audit-ready records.

Scaling a business involves making informed decisions, optimizing workflows, and maintaining financial control—all of which are supported by the powerful tools and features QuickBooks offers. Whether you're planning to expand into new markets, add products or services, or hire more staff, QuickBooks serves as a central hub for managing the financial aspects of your growth. Let's dive into how you can unlock its full potential to support your journey toward business success.

Expanding QuickBooks Capabilities with Add-Ons

QuickBooks Online (QBO) is a robust accounting platform that covers a wide range of business needs, from invoicing to expense tracking. However, as your business grows, you may find that your operations require more specialized tools and features. This is where add-ons come in. By integrating third-party apps and tools, you can expand the capabilities of QuickBooks to streamline processes, enhance functionality, and support your business's evolving needs.

In this chapter, we'll explore the types of add-ons available for QuickBooks Online, their benefits, and how to select the right ones for your business. By leveraging these integrations, you can unlock new efficiencies, gain deeper insights, and create a seamless financial management system tailored to your operations.

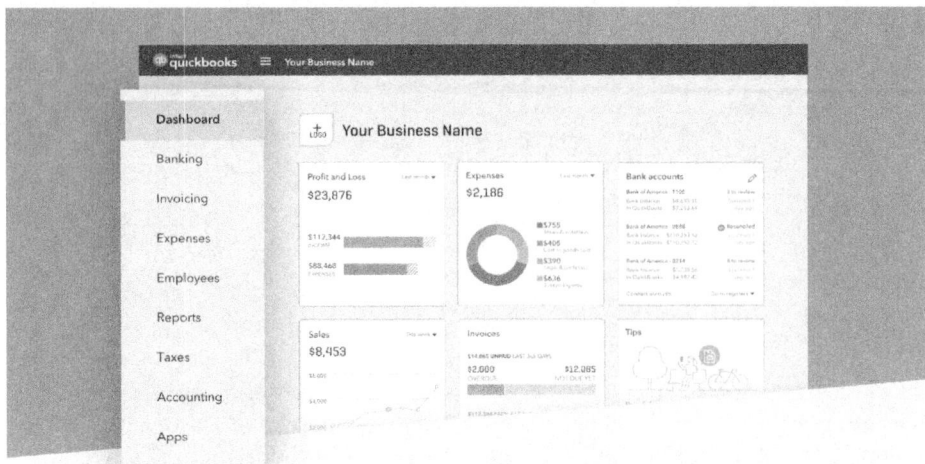

Everything organized in one place

Add-ons enhance the functionality of QuickBooks Online, providing solutions that go beyond the platform's native features. Here are the primary benefits:

1.1 Increased Efficiency

- Automate time-consuming tasks like payroll processing, inventory management, or expense tracking.

1.2 Enhanced Functionality

- Add specialized tools for industry-specific needs, such as project management or e-commerce integration.

1.3 Improved Accuracy

- Sync data across platforms to reduce manual entry and minimize errors.

1.4 Scalability

- Support business growth with tools that handle increased transaction volumes and complex workflows.

QuickBooks integrates with hundreds of third-party apps and tools. Below are some of the most popular categories and examples of add-ons:

2.1 Payroll and HR Management

- Gusto: Automates payroll processing, tax filings, and employee benefits.
- TSheets by QuickBooks: Tracks employee hours and integrates seamlessly with payroll for accurate timesheets.
- BambooHR: Manages hiring, onboarding, and employee records.

2.2 Expense Tracking and Receipt Management

- Expensify: Automates expense reporting by scanning and categorizing receipts.

- Hubdoc: Collects and organizes financial documents like receipts, bills, and bank statements.
- Fyle: Enables employees to track and submit expenses with ease.

2.3 Inventory Management

- Shopventory: Provides advanced inventory tracking and integrates with sales platforms like Shopify and Square.
- Cin7: Combines inventory and order management for businesses with large or complex inventories.
- SOS Inventory: Tracks inventory across multiple locations and integrates with QuickBooks for accurate reporting.

2.4 Customer Relationship Management (CRM)

- HubSpot CRM: Tracks customer interactions and syncs sales data with QuickBooks.
- Salesforce: Offers comprehensive CRM features for managing sales pipelines and customer data.
- Insightly: Focuses on project management and customer tracking for small businesses.

2.5 E-Commerce and Payment Processing

- Shopify: Syncs sales, inventory, and customer data with QuickBooks for seamless e-commerce operations.
- PayPal and Stripe: Integrates payment processing with QuickBooks to simplify financial reconciliation.
- Amazon Seller Central Integration: Tracks Amazon sales and expenses directly in QuickBooks.

2.6 Reporting and Analytics

- Fathom: Provides advanced reporting, visual dashboards, and KPI tracking.

- Syft Analytics: Delivers in-depth financial insights and forecasts.
- Spotlight Reporting: Offers customizable reports and forecasts tailored to your business.

When selecting add-ons, it's important to choose tools that align with your business needs and goals. Here's how to make the right choice:

3.1 Assess Your Needs

- Identify pain points in your current workflows. For example:
  - » Are you spending too much time on manual data entry?
  - » Do you need better inventory management?
  - » Is reporting and analytics a challenge?

3.2 Set a Budget

- Determine how much you're willing to spend on add-ons. While many tools offer free tiers, premium features often come with subscription fees.

3.3 Prioritize Scalability

- Choose add-ons that can grow with your business and handle increased complexity over time.

3.4 Ensure Compatibility

- Verify that the add-on integrates seamlessly with QuickBooks Online and other tools you use.

3.5 Read Reviews and Test Free Trials

- Explore user reviews and take advantage of free trials to assess the tool's effectiveness and ease of use.

Integrating add-ons with QuickBooks Online is a straightforward process. Follow these steps:

Step 1: Access the QuickBooks App Store

1. Log in to your QuickBooks Online account.
2. Navigate to the Apps tab in the left-hand menu.

Step 2: Browse or Search for Add-Ons

- Use the search bar to find specific apps or browse categories like "Payroll," "Inventory Management," or "E-Commerce."

Step 3: Install and Authorize the App

1. Select the app and click Get App Now.
2. Authorize the integration by logging into your QuickBooks account and granting permissions.

Step 4: Configure Settings

- Customize the integration by adjusting settings, such as data sync frequency and account mappings.

To maximize the benefits of QuickBooks add-ons, consider the following best practices:

5.1 Regularly Review Integrations

- Periodically evaluate whether the add-ons you're using still meet your needs. Replace outdated tools with better options as your business evolves.

5.2 Keep Data Organized

- Ensure that data sync settings are configured correctly to avoid duplicate entries or mismatches.

5.3 Train Your Team

- Provide training for employees who will be using the add-ons to ensure they understand their functionality and can use them effectively.

5.4 Monitor Performance

- Track the impact of add-ons on your workflows, such as time savings, accuracy improvements, or cost reductions.

6.1 Streamlining Payroll with Gusto

- A small business with 20 employees integrates Gusto with QuickBooks to automate payroll processing. The integration ensures accurate tax filings and eliminates manual data entry, saving hours every month.

6.2 Managing E-Commerce with Shopify

- An online retailer uses Shopify's integration with QuickBooks to sync sales, inventory, and customer data. The real-time updates simplify reconciliation and inventory tracking.

6.3 Advanced Reporting with Fathom

- A growing consultancy firm leverages Fathom's analytics to generate visual dashboards and monitor KPIs, helping leadership make data-driven decisions.

7.1 Overloading with Apps

- Adding too many tools can lead to redundant features and integration conflicts.

- Solution: Choose apps strategically to address specific needs.

7.2 Ignoring Setup and Configuration

- Incorrect setup can result in data discrepancies or inefficiencies.
- Solution: Follow setup guides carefully and test integrations before fully implementing them.

7.3 Failing to Review Costs

- Subscription fees for multiple add-ons can add up.
- Solution: Periodically review your subscriptions and eliminate unused tools.

As your business grows, your needs will change. Keep these tips in mind to ensure your add-ons remain relevant:

- Stay Updated: Regularly update your apps to access new features and maintain compatibility.
- Explore Upgrades: Many add-ons offer tiered plans with additional functionality for scaling businesses.
- Integrate New Tools: Be open to adopting new technologies as they become available.

Expanding QuickBooks Online's capabilities with add-ons is an effective way to streamline operations, improve accuracy, and scale your business. By carefully selecting and implementing the right tools, you can address your unique needs and unlock new levels of efficiency and insight. Whether you're automating payroll, enhancing inventory management, or leveraging advanced analytics, add-ons empower you to customize QuickBooks into a comprehensive financial management solution tailored to your growth journey.

Planning for Business Growth with Financial Tools

Scaling a business requires careful planning, strategic decision-making, and a deep understanding of your financial position. Financial tools play a pivotal role in helping you assess your readiness for growth, forecast future performance, and allocate resources effectively. QuickBooks Online (QBO) and its ecosystem of integrations offer powerful features for planning and executing business expansion while maintaining control over your finances.

This chapter explores how to leverage financial tools for business growth. From budgeting and forecasting to managing cash flow and tracking performance metrics, we'll discuss how QuickBooks and its add-ons can support your growth strategy. By the end of this chapter, you'll have a roadmap for using financial tools to scale your business sustainably and efficiently.

1.1 Assessing Financial Health

- Financial tools help you evaluate your current position by analyzing cash flow, profitability, and liabilities.
- Example: Use a Profit and Loss Statement in QuickBooks to assess income trends and expense patterns.

1.2 Identifying Opportunities

- Advanced reporting tools highlight areas of opportunity, such as high-performing products or untapped markets.

1.3 Reducing Risks

- Accurate financial forecasting minimizes risks by preparing you for potential challenges, such as cash shortages or increased operating costs.

1.4 Guiding Strategic Decisions

- Data-driven insights enable you to make informed decisions about hiring, expanding operations, or entering new markets.

Establishing clear, measurable financial goals is essential for effective planning.

2.1 Short-Term Goals

- Examples:
  - » Increase monthly revenue by 10%.
  - » Reduce operating expenses by 5% over the next quarter.

2.2 Long-Term Goals

- Examples:
  - » Double revenue within three years.
  - » Expand to two new markets by the end of the year.

2.3 SMART Goals Framework

- Specific: Define clear objectives, such as "Increase customer retention by 15%."
- Measurable: Use metrics, such as revenue growth or cost reduction.
- Achievable: Set realistic goals based on your financial data.
- Relevant: Align goals with your business's overall vision.
- Time-Bound: Set deadlines to measure progress effectively.

Budgeting and forecasting are critical components of growth planning. QuickBooks Online simplifies these processes with built-in tools and integrations.

3.1 Creating a Budget in QuickBooks

1. Navigate to Settings > Budgeting and select Create Budget.

2. Choose the fiscal year and set a budget for specific accounts or categories.
3. Customize budgets for revenue, expenses, and departments.

3.2 Tracking Budget vs. Actual Performance

- Use the Budget vs. Actuals Report in QuickBooks to compare your budgeted figures with actual performance.
- Adjust your budget as needed to address discrepancies.

3.3 Using Forecasting Tools

- Integrate tools like Fathom or Syft Analytics with QuickBooks for advanced forecasting.
- Example: Predict cash flow needs based on seasonal revenue trends and anticipated expenses.

Positive cash flow is essential for funding growth initiatives like hiring, inventory expansion, or marketing campaigns.

4.1 Using QuickBooks Cash Flow Tools

1. Access the Cash Flow Planner in the mobile or desktop app.
2. Review current cash balances and projections based on upcoming inflows and outflows.
3. Adjust payment schedules or invoices to maintain a positive cash flow.

4.2 Monitoring Accounts Receivable

- Use the Aging Summary Report to track overdue invoices and follow up with clients promptly.
- Offer incentives, such as early payment discounts, to improve cash collection.

4.3 Managing Accounts Payable

- Schedule payments strategically to optimize cash flow.
- Use add-ons like Bill.com to automate payment processing and maintain a clear view of liabilities.

KPIs provide measurable insights into your business's performance and growth potential.

5.1 Financial KPIs to Monitor

- Gross Profit Margin:

Gross Profit Margin=Gross ProfitRevenue×100\text{Gross Profit Margin} = \frac{\text{Gross Profit}}{\text{Revenue}} \times 100Gross Profit Margin=RevenueGross Profit×100 Indicates profitability from core operations.

- Current Ratio:

Current Ratio=Current AssetsCurrent Liabilities\text{Current Ratio} = \frac{\text{Current Assets}}{\text{Current Liabilities}}Current Ratio=Current LiabilitiesCurrent Assets Measures liquidity and ability to meet short-term obligations.

- Net Profit Margin:

Net Profit Margin=Net IncomeRevenue×100\text{Net Profit Margin} = \frac{\text{Net Income}}{\text{Revenue}} \times 100Net Profit Margin=RevenueNet Income×100 Reflects overall profitability.

5.2 Operational KPIs to Monitor

- Customer Acquisition Cost (CAC): Tracks the cost of acquiring a new customer.
- Inventory Turnover Ratio: Monitors how quickly inventory is sold and replaced.

5.3 Tracking KPIs in QuickBooks

- Use QuickBooks reports or integrate analytics tools like Fathom to track KPIs in real-time.

Efficient resource allocation is vital for scaling your business.

6.1 Workforce Planning

- Use payroll and HR tools like Gusto or TSheets by QuickBooks to manage labor costs and plan for hiring needs.

6.2 Inventory Management

- Integrate inventory tools like Shopventory or SOS Inventory to optimize stock levels and reduce carrying costs.

6.3 Marketing Budgeting

- Track marketing expenses using QuickBooks categories and evaluate ROI with tools like HubSpot or Salesforce.

Scaling a business often comes with challenges, such as increased complexity or cash flow strain. Financial tools help you prepare for these scenarios.

7.1 Managing Growth Risks

- Scenario modeling tools like Fathom allow you to simulate different growth scenarios and assess financial impact.

7.2 Securing Funding

- Use financial reports from QuickBooks to create compelling presentations for investors or lenders.
- Highlight metrics like EBITDA (Earnings Before Interest, Taxes, Depreciation, and Amortization) to demonstrate profitability.

7.3 Ensuring Compliance

- Maintain audit-ready records with QuickBooks to avoid issues with regulatory compliance.
- Use tools like Avalara to automate tax compliance.

Scenario: A retail business wants to expand to two new locations within the next year.
Solution:

1. Budgeting: Create detailed budgets for each location, including rent, payroll, and inventory.
2. Cash Flow Management: Use QuickBooks to monitor cash reserves and ensure sufficient funds for upfront costs.
3. KPI Tracking: Monitor profitability and sales growth to measure the success of the new locations.
4. Scenario Modeling: Use Fathom to evaluate risks and adjust plans as needed.

9.1 Overestimating Revenue

- Be conservative in revenue projections to avoid overcommitting resources.

9.2 Neglecting Expense Tracking

- Track all expenses to avoid budget overruns and cash flow issues.

9.3 Ignoring Data Insights

- Regularly review financial reports and adjust strategies based on the data.

Planning for business growth is a complex but rewarding process that requires strategic use of financial tools. QuickBooks Online and its integrations offer everything you need to budget effectively, manage cash flow, track KPIs, and optimize resources. By leveraging these tools, you can minimize risks, seize opportunities, and scale your business with confidence. Whether you're expanding into new markets, launching new products, or hiring additional staff, a data-driven approach will ensure your growth is sustainable and successful.

Leveraging Data Insights for Strategic Decisions

In today's competitive business environment, data is a powerful asset. When harnessed effectively, it provides a roadmap for informed decision-making, enabling businesses to identify opportunities, mitigate risks, and drive growth. QuickBooks Online (QBO) is more than just an accounting platform—it's a hub for generating actionable data insights. By leveraging its robust reporting tools and integrations, you can transform raw financial data into strategies that guide your business to success.

This chapter explores how to utilize the data insights provided by QuickBooks and its ecosystem of integrations. From tracking key performance indicators (KPIs) to advanced forecasting and scenario modeling, we'll uncover how these insights can inform strategic decisions and set your business on the path to long-term growth.

1.1 Why Data Insights Matter

- Clarity: Data provides a clear picture of your business's performance.
- Objectivity: Decisions based on data reduce guesswork and emotional bias.
- Agility: Real-time insights enable faster responses to market changes.
- Accountability: Metrics track progress toward goals, ensuring accountability.

1.2 Types of Decisions Informed by Data

- Operational Decisions: Optimize processes and resource allocation.

- Financial Decisions: Manage cash flow, pricing strategies, and budgeting.
- Strategic Decisions: Plan expansions, new product launches, or market entry.

QuickBooks Online offers a suite of reports and features that provide valuable insights into your business's financial health.

2.1 Key Reports for Strategic Insights

- Profit and Loss Statement: Tracks revenue, expenses, and net profit over time.
- Balance Sheet: Provides a snapshot of assets, liabilities, and equity.
- Cash Flow Statement: Highlights inflows and outflows, ensuring liquidity.
- Sales Reports: Identifies top-performing products, services, or customers.

2.2 Customizing Reports

1. Access the Reports section in QuickBooks.
2. Select a report and click Customize to adjust:
   - » Date ranges.
   - » Filters for accounts, customers, or vendors.
   - » Comparison columns for YOY or MOM analysis.
3. Save and export reports for presentations or further analysis.

2.3 Using Real-Time Dashboards

- Dashboards provide at-a-glance views of critical metrics like income, expenses, and overdue invoices.
- Use these dashboards for daily monitoring and quick decision-making.

KPIs are essential metrics that reflect your business's performance. QuickBooks helps you track these in real-time.

3.1 Financial KPIs

- Gross Profit Margin: Measures profitability from core operations.
- Net Profit Margin: Evaluates overall profitability.
- Current Ratio: Assesses liquidity by comparing assets to liabilities.

3.2 Sales KPIs

- Customer Lifetime Value (CLV): Tracks the revenue generated per customer over their relationship with your business.
- Sales Growth Rate: Measures the percentage increase in sales over a period.

3.3 Expense KPIs

- Expense Ratio: Compares total expenses to revenue.
- Operating Cost Per Unit: Tracks efficiency in producing goods or services.

3.4 Setting KPI Targets

1. Use historical data in QuickBooks to set realistic benchmarks.
2. Regularly monitor progress through customized reports and dashboards.

QuickBooks integrates with powerful tools that enhance its data analysis capabilities.

4.1 Fathom

- Features:
  - » Advanced financial reports and visual dashboards.
  - » KPI tracking and benchmarking.
  - » Scenario modeling for "what-if" analyses.
- Use Case: Perfect for evaluating the financial impact of strategic decisions, such as hiring or expanding.

4.2 Syft Analytics

- Features:

- » Predictive analytics and trend forecasting.
- » Automated report generation.
- » Customizable visualizations.
- Use Case: Helps businesses forecast cash flow and monitor profitability trends.

4.3 Spotlight Reporting

- Features:
  - » Consolidated financial reports for multi-entity businesses.
  - » Budgeting and forecasting tools.
  - » KPI visualization and tracking.
- Use Case: Ideal for businesses with complex reporting needs, such as franchises.

Forecasting is a powerful way to predict future performance and plan accordingly.

5.1 Cash Flow Forecasting

- Purpose: Anticipates periods of surplus or shortfall.
- Steps:

1. Use the Cash Flow Planner in Quick-Books to review projected inflows and outflows.
2. Adjust forecasts based on expected changes, such as new clients or seasonal fluctuations.
3. Take proactive steps, such as securing funding or deferring expenses, to maintain liquidity.

5.2 Revenue Forecasting

- Analyze sales trends and customer data to project future revenue.
- Use integrations like Fathom for detailed revenue models based on historical performance.

5.3 Scenario Modeling

- Simulate different scenarios, such as:

- » Launching a new product line.
- » Expanding to a new market.
- » Hiring additional staff.
- Use tools like Spotlight Reporting or Fathom to evaluate financial outcomes for each scenario.

6.1 Identifying Opportunities

- Use sales reports to pinpoint high-performing products or untapped markets.
- Example: If a region shows strong sales growth, consider focusing marketing efforts there.

6.2 Optimizing Operations

- Analyze expense reports to identify inefficiencies or cost-saving opportunities.
- Example: If a vendor's costs are rising, explore alternative suppliers.

6.3 Allocating Resources

- Review budget vs. actual reports to ensure resources are allocated effectively.
- Example: Shift funds from underperforming departments to areas with higher ROI.

6.4 Monitoring Market Trends

- Combine QuickBooks data with external market research to identify trends and adapt strategies.
- Example: Adjust pricing based on competitor analysis and sales data.

Data insights aren't just for leadership—they can inform decisions at every level of your organization.

7.1 Sharing Reports with Teams

- Export reports as PDFs or Excel files for team review.
- Highlight key insights during meetings to align strategies.

7.2 Collaborating with Advisors

- Share real-time data with accountants or financial advisors to gain expert insights.
- Example: Use collaborative tools like QuickBooks Accountant to work seamlessly with professionals.

7.3 Encouraging Data-Driven Culture

- Train employees to use data insights for decision-making in their respective roles.

8.1 Overloading with Data

- Solution: Focus on key metrics that align with your goals.

8.2 Ignoring Data Quality

- Solution: Ensure transactions are categorized correctly in QuickBooks to avoid inaccuracies.

8.3 Delayed Decision-Making

- Solution: Use real-time dashboards and automated reports to stay proactive.

8.4 Neglecting External Factors

- Solution: Combine QuickBooks insights with external market data for a holistic view.

Scenario: A retail business notices declining profit margins in one product category.

Solution:

1. Analyze Sales Reports: Identify underperforming products and compare them with inventory costs.
2. Adjust Pricing: Reassess pricing strategies based on competitor data and cost analysis.
3. Optimize Inventory: Use tools like SOS Inventory to minimize overstocking and reduce carrying costs.
4. Monitor Impact: Track the changes' effects on gross profit margin over time.

Data insights are a cornerstone of effective strategic decision-making. By leveraging the powerful tools and reports in QuickBooks Online, you can transform raw financial data into actionable strategies that drive growth. Whether it's tracking KPIs, forecasting future performance, or analyzing operational efficiency, data-driven decisions ensure your business remains agile, competitive, and poised for success. With the right tools and a focus on meaningful metrics, you'll be able to navigate challenges, seize opportunities, and scale your business with confidence.

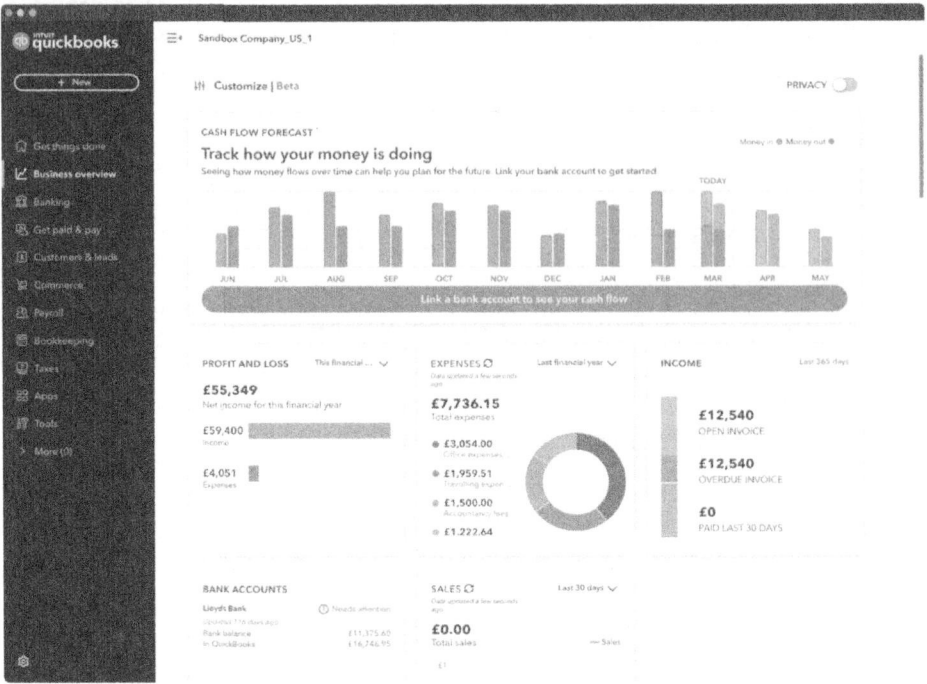

Audits and regulatory compliance are essential aspects of running a business, ensuring transparency, accuracy, and adherence to financial laws. However, the thought of preparing for an audit can often feel overwhelming. The key to a smooth audit process lies in maintaining organized financial records and leveraging tools like QuickBooks Online (QBO) to stay audit-ready year-round. By using its features for record-keeping, reporting, and tracking, you can reduce stress, avoid penalties, and instill confidence in your financial management practices.

This chapter provides a comprehensive guide on how to prepare for audits and ensure compliance using QuickBooks Online. From organizing your financial records to generating audit-ready reports and automating compliance tasks, you'll learn strategies to simplify and streamline the entire process.

1.1 Ensuring Financial Transparency

- Accurate financial records demonstrate the credibility of your business to stakeholders, investors, and regulators.

1.2 Avoiding Penalties

- Non-compliance with financial regulations can result in fines, legal repercussions, or damage to your reputation.

1.3 Supporting Business Growth

- Audit-ready financials are crucial when seeking loans, attracting investors, or planning expansions.

1.4 Building Trust

- Clear and accurate records foster trust with clients, employees, and partners.

QuickBooks Online offers several features to help you maintain organized and accurate financial records.

2.1 Automating Data Entry

1. Link your bank accounts and credit cards to QBO.
2. Enable automatic transaction imports to reduce manual errors.
3. Categorize transactions regularly to ensure proper classification.

2.2 Using Attachments

- Attach supporting documents, such as invoices, receipts, and contracts, to transactions for easy reference during audits.

2.3 Reconciling Accounts

1. Use the Reconciliation Tool to match transactions in QuickBooks with bank statements.
2. Resolve discrepancies promptly to maintain accurate balances.

2.4 Tracking Expenses and Income

- Record all income and expenses systematically to create a complete financial picture.

Compliance often requires maintaining specific records for tax and regulatory purposes.

3.1 Retaining Required Documents

- Common documents include:
  - » Invoices and receipts.
  - » Payroll records.
  - » Tax filings.
  - » Vendor and customer agreements.

3.2 Setting Up a Chart of Accounts

- Customize your Chart of Accounts in QuickBooks to align with tax reporting requirements.
- Include categories for deductible expenses, taxable income, and liabilities.

3.3 Managing Audit Trails

- QuickBooks automatically logs changes to transactions, providing a detailed audit trail that tracks who made changes and when.

3.4 Leveraging Tags

- Use tags in QuickBooks to group transactions by projects, clients, or compliance categories, simplifying data retrieval during audits.

Reports are critical for both internal reviews and external audits. QuickBooks provides several customizable reports to streamline the audit process.

4.1 Key Reports for Audits

- Profit and Loss Statement: Shows income and expenses over a period.
- Balance Sheet: Summarizes assets, liabilities, and equity.
- Cash Flow Statement: Tracks cash inflows and outflows.
- General Ledger: Provides a detailed record of all financial transactions.

4.2 Customizing Reports for Compliance

1. Access the Reports tab in QuickBooks.
2. Select the required report and click Customize.
3. Adjust filters for date range, accounts, or specific transactions.
4. Export reports as PDFs or Excel files for auditors.

4.3 Scheduling Reports

- Automate report generation by scheduling recurring reports to your email or the relevant stakeholders.

Tax compliance is a critical aspect of audit preparation, and QuickBooks offers tools to simplify this process.

5.1 Automating Tax Calculations

- Use the Sales Tax Center in QuickBooks to configure tax rates based on location or product category.
- Automate sales tax tracking for accurate calculations during audits.

5.2 Recording Tax Payments

- Track and record tax payments directly in QuickBooks to maintain a clear record.

5.3 Filing Tax Returns

- Use integrations like Avalara or QuickBooks' built-in tax filing tools to automate tax submissions.

5.4 Generating Tax-Specific Reports

- Generate reports like the 1099 Transaction Detail Report or Sales Tax Liability Report for tax filings and audits.

Being proactive and organized is essential for a smooth audit process.

6.1 Reviewing Financial Data

1. Perform a comprehensive review of your financial data in QuickBooks.
2. Check for inconsistencies, duplicate entries, or missing information.

6.2 Collaborating with Your Accountant

- Use the Accountant's Tools feature in QuickBooks to invite your accountant to review records and prepare for the audit.

6.3 Creating a Pre-Audit Checklist

- Include items such as:
  - » Updated financial statements.
  - » Reconciled accounts.
  - » Supporting documents for major transactions.

6.4 Providing Access to Auditors

- Use QuickBooks' Custom Roles feature to grant auditors access to specific reports or data while protecting sensitive information.

QuickBooks integrates with several third-party tools to enhance compliance and audit readiness.

7.1 Avalara

- Automates sales tax calculations and filings, ensuring compliance with local regulations.

7.2 Gusto

- Manages payroll taxes and filings, reducing errors in employee tax compliance.

7.3 Hubdoc

- Collects and organizes financial documents like receipts, bills, and bank statements.

7.4 Fathom

- Offers advanced financial analysis and benchmarking, helping businesses identify compliance risks.

8.1 Ignoring Regular Reviews

- Solution: Conduct monthly or quarterly reviews of your financial records to identify issues early.

8.2 Failing to Retain Documents

- Solution: Use QuickBooks' attachment feature to store all necessary documents digitally.

8.3 Overlooking Reconciliation

- Solution: Reconcile all accounts regularly to ensure data accuracy.

8.4 Waiting Until the Last Minute

- Solution: Maintain audit readiness year-round by using QuickBooks to automate compliance tasks.

9.1 Reduced Stress

- Organized records and automated tools simplify audit preparation, reducing last-minute panic.

9.2 Faster Audit Completion

- Readily available data and reports expedite the audit process.

9.3 Enhanced Credibility

- Audit-ready financials demonstrate professionalism and reliability.

9.4 Avoidance of Penalties

- Accurate records and timely filings ensure compliance with regulatory requirements.

Scenario: A small e-commerce business faces its first tax audit.

Solution:

1. Organized Records: The business uses QuickBooks to store digital receipts and categorize transactions.
2. Custom Reports: Generates tax-specific reports like the Sales Tax Liability Report.
3. Collaboration with Accountant: Grants the accountant access to QuickBooks for audit preparation.
4. Successful Outcome: The audit is completed without penalties or delays, thanks to meticulous record-keeping and the use of QuickBooks tools.

Preparing for audits and ensuring compliance doesn't have to be stressful or time-consuming. With QuickBooks Online, you can maintain accurate financial records, generate audit-ready reports, and automate compliance tasks with ease. By adopting best practices and leveraging the platform's powerful features, you can confidently face audits and regulatory requirements while focusing on growing your business. Audit preparedness not only protects your business but also strengthens its foundation for long-term success.

TROUBLESHOOTING AND COMMON MISTAKES

Even with the best tools and practices, managing business finances can sometimes lead to errors and challenges. Whether it's discrepancies in bank reconciliations, duplicate transactions, or setup issues, mistakes in QuickBooks Online (QBO) can disrupt your workflow and impact financial accuracy. Recognizing and resolving these issues quickly is essential to maintaining a smooth accounting process and keeping your business finances in order.

In this bonus chapter, we'll dive into common problems users encounter while working with QuickBooks Online and provide practical solutions to resolve them. From fixing bank reconciliation errors to avoiding duplicate transactions, we'll cover the most frequent pitfalls and how to address them effectively. Additionally, we'll explore troubleshooting tips for data entry and setup issues that can cause headaches down the road.

Staying proactive and following best practices is the key to maintaining accurate financial records. This chapter also provides a guide to ensuring your QuickBooks account remains organized and error-free. By learning to identify and correct common mistakes, you'll save time, reduce stress, and build confidence in your financial management skills. Let's tackle these challenges head-on and ensure your QuickBooks Online experience is as seamless as possible.

Bank reconciliation is a fundamental part of maintaining accurate financial records in QuickBooks Online (QBO). It ensures that the transactions recorded in QuickBooks match your bank and credit card statements. However, discrepancies between your QuickBooks records and bank accounts can arise for various reasons, leading to reconciliation errors. Identifying and resolving these errors is crucial to keeping your financial records accurate and audit-ready.

In this chapter, we'll explore common causes of bank reconciliation errors, practical steps to identify and troubleshoot them, and best practices to prevent future issues. By mastering bank reconciliation, you'll save time, reduce stress, and maintain confidence in your financial management.

1.1 What Is Bank Reconciliation?

Bank reconciliation is the process of comparing your QuickBooks transactions with your bank or credit card statement to ensure they match.

1.2 Why Is It Important?

- Accuracy: Ensures financial records reflect actual account activity.
- Fraud Detection: Identifies unauthorized or unusual transactions.
- Compliance: Maintains audit-ready records.

2.1 Missing Transactions

- Transactions recorded in the bank statement but not entered in QuickBooks.

2.2 Duplicate Transactions

- Transactions entered multiple times in QuickBooks, inflating totals.

2.3 Timing Differences

- Transactions recorded in QuickBooks but not yet cleared by the bank.

2.4 Incorrect Categorization

- Misclassified transactions can cause mismatched totals.

2.5 Adjustments or Edits

- Previously reconciled transactions modified after reconciliation.

3.1 Reviewing the Reconciliation Report

1. Navigate to Reports > Reconciliation Reports.
2. Generate the report for the account in question.
3. Look for discrepancies between QuickBooks and the bank statement.

3.2 Comparing Opening Balances

- Ensure the opening balance in QuickBooks matches the bank statement.
- Common Issue: Opening balance discrepancies often arise from transactions added or deleted after reconciliation.

3.3 Analyzing the Reconciliation Summary

- Check for:
  - » Unmatched Transactions: Trans-

actions in QuickBooks not appearing on the bank statement.
  - » Incorrect Totals: Discrepancies in ending balances.

4.1 Correcting Missing Transactions

1. Identify Missing Entries:
   - » Review the bank statement and compare it with QuickBooks.
2. Add Missing Transactions:
   - » Go to + New > Transaction and enter the missing details.
3. Reconcile the Transaction:
   - » Mark the transaction as cleared during the reconciliation process.

4.2 Deleting Duplicate Transactions

1. Locate Duplicate Entries:
   - » Search for transactions with identical details (e.g., date, amount).
2. Delete or Merge Duplicates:
   - » Open the duplicate transaction and click Delete or merge it with the correct entry.

4.3 Resolving Timing Differences

- Timing differences are common when checks or deposits haven't cleared yet:
1. Verify the transaction date in QuickBooks.
2. Confirm with the bank when the transaction is expected to clear.
3. Mark it as cleared during the next reconciliation cycle.

4.4 Correcting Categorization Errors

1. Review Misclassified Transactions:

» Identify transactions assigned to incorrect accounts.

2. Reclassify Transactions:

» Open the transaction, update the category, and save changes.

4.5 Adjusting Edited Transactions

1. Identify Edited Entries:

» Use the Audit Log to track changes made to reconciled transactions.

2. Reconcile Changes:

» Correct the transaction details or re-enter the original data.

5.1 When Ending Balances Don't Match

1. Verify Opening Balances:

» Ensure the opening balance matches the previous reconciliation.

2. Check for Unreconciled Transactions:

» Look for any transactions that were missed in previous reconciliations.

3. Adjust Bank Fees or Interest:

» Record bank fees or interest payments that may affect balances.

5.2 When Transactions Are Missing

1. Search Transactions:

» Use the Search Bar in QuickBooks to locate missing entries.

2. Check Date Filters:

» Ensure the transaction date range matches the bank statement.

5.3 When Bank Feeds Don't Sync

1. Reauthorize Bank Connection:

» Go to Banking > Update Connection to re-establish the link.

2. Manually Import Transactions:

» Download transactions from your bank and upload them to QuickBooks.

5.4 Reconciliation Still Doesn't Balance

• Use the Reconciliation Discrepancy Report to locate errors.
• Check for transactions manually marked as cleared outside the reconciliation process.

6.1 Reconciliation Tool

• Found under Accounting > Reconcile.
• Guides users through the reconciliation process step by step.

6.2 Audit Log

• Tracks changes to transactions and identifies discrepancies caused by edits.

6.3 Reconciliation Report

• Summarizes reconciled transactions, outstanding items, and discrepancies.

6.4 Bank Feeds

• Automatically imports bank transactions into QuickBooks for easy matching.

7.1 Regular Reconciliations

• Perform reconciliations monthly to catch errors early.

7.2 Automating Data Entry

• Link bank accounts to minimize manual entry errors.

7.3 Locking Reconciled Periods

- Use the Close Books feature in QuickBooks to prevent changes to reconciled periods.

7.4 Consistent Categorization

- Maintain a clear and consistent Chart of Accounts to simplify transaction matching.

7.5 Training Your Team

- Ensure employees handling transactions understand reconciliation best practices.

Scenario: A small business owner discovers a $500 discrepancy during reconciliation.

Steps Taken:

1. Review Opening Balances: Found an adjustment entry from the previous month.
2. Analyze Reconciliation Report: Identified an unmatched transaction for a $500 deposit.
3. Correct the Entry: Located and entered the missing deposit.
4. Reconcile Successfully: Balances now matched, and the issue was resolved.

9.1 Financial Accuracy

- Accurate reconciliations ensure your financial reports reflect reality.

9.2 Improved Cash Flow Management

- Clear records help you monitor available cash effectively.

9.3 Enhanced Compliance

- Audit-ready records reduce the risk of penalties during tax filings.

9.4 Fraud Detection

- Regular reconciliations highlight unauthorized transactions early.

Bank reconciliation errors can disrupt your accounting process and lead to inaccurate financial records, but they are manageable with the right approach. By understanding common causes, using QuickBooks Online's powerful tools, and implementing preventive practices, you can keep your reconciliations error-free and your financial records accurate. Mastering this essential process not only saves time and reduces stress but also ensures your business operates smoothly and confidently in its financial management.

Avoiding Duplicate Transactions and Missing Data

Accurate financial records are the backbone of any successful business. Duplicate transactions and missing data can disrupt your accounting processes, skew your financial reports, and lead to compliance issues. These common pitfalls often stem from manual data entry errors, uncoordinated workflows, or improper syncing with bank accounts. QuickBooks Online (QBO) provides powerful tools and features to help you avoid these issues and maintain clean, reliable records.

In this chapter, we'll delve into the causes of duplicate transactions and missing data, how they impact your business, and the best strategies for preventing and resolving these problems. By mastering these techniques, you can ensure that your financial records remain accurate and up-to-date.

1.1 What Are Duplicate Transactions?

- Definition: Duplicate transactions occur when the same financial entry is re-

corded more than once, inflating your income, expenses, or account balances.
- Examples:
  - » Manually entering a transaction already imported from a bank feed.
  - » Syncing the same transaction through multiple connected apps.

1.2 What Is Missing Data?

- Definition: Missing data refers to financial transactions that have occurred but are not recorded in QuickBooks.
- Examples:
  - » Unrecorded cash expenses.
  - » Missing bank feed imports.

2.1 Common Causes of Duplicate Transactions

1. Bank Feed Sync Issues:
   - » Transactions already entered manually are re-imported from the bank.
2. Multiple Integration Sources:
   - » The same transaction is imported from different apps, such as PayPal and Shopify.
3. Incorrect Matching:
   - » Mistaking one transaction for another during reconciliation.

2.2 Common Causes of Missing Data

1. Bank Feed Errors:
   - » Bank accounts fail to sync, leaving gaps in transaction history.
2. Manual Entry Omissions:
   - » Forgetting to record cash expenses or manually inputted transactions.
3. Data Overwrite:

- » Editing or deleting transactions unintentionally.

3.1 Financial Inaccuracies

- Duplicates inflate totals, while missing data understates financial results, distorting your financial position.

3.2 Reconciliation Issues

- Both issues complicate bank reconciliations and make it harder to match QuickBooks records with actual bank statements.

3.3 Tax Filing Errors

- Inaccurate records can lead to overpaying or underpaying taxes, risking penalties or audits.

3.4 Wasted Time

- Resolving errors requires time-consuming reviews and corrections.

4.1 Use Bank Feed Rules

- Create rules to automatically categorize and match transactions.
- Steps:
1. Go to Banking > Rules.
2. Set conditions for auto-categorization, such as vendor names or amounts.
3. Apply the rules to prevent duplicates.

4.2 Reconcile Regularly

- Monthly reconciliations help catch and resolve duplicates early.
- Match transactions carefully, avoiding entries that are already reconciled.

4.3 Avoid Manual and Automated Entry Overlap

- Decide whether transactions will be entered manually or imported automatically but avoid doing both for the same account.

4.4 Review Transactions Before Saving

- Check for duplicate entries before saving new transactions, especially when importing from external sources.

4.5 Sync Integrations Properly

- If using multiple integrations (e.g., PayPal, Shopify), ensure they don't duplicate each other's transactions.

4.6 Train Your Team

- Educate employees on identifying and avoiding duplicate entries during data entry.

5.1 Enable Continuous Bank Feeds

- Ensure your bank feeds are always active and syncing correctly.
- Regularly check for syncing issues in the Banking tab.

5.2 Record Transactions Immediately

- Use the QuickBooks Mobile App to record expenses and income in real-time.
- For cash transactions, create entries immediately to prevent forgetting.

5.3 Use Receipt Management Tools

- Tools like Hubdoc or QuickBooks Receipt Capture allow you to attach receipts to transactions directly, ensuring no expense is overlooked.

5.4 Review Bank Feeds for Unmatched Entries

- Regularly check the For Review tab in the Banking section for unclassified transactions.

5.5 Leverage Automation

- Automate recurring transactions, such as monthly rent or subscriptions, to ensure they are always recorded.

5.6 Perform Regular Data Audits

- Use reports like the General Ledger or Transaction Detail Report to spot missing entries.

6.1 Identify Duplicates

- Use filters in the Banking tab or run the Transaction Detail Report to find duplicates.
- Look for transactions with the same amount, date, and description.

6.2 Delete or Void Duplicates

1. Open the duplicate transaction.
2. Click More > Delete or Void to remove it.

6.3 Adjust Bank Reconciliation

- If duplicates were reconciled, delete them and reconcile the account again to ensure accuracy.

6.4 Match Imported Transactions

- Use the Match feature in the Banking tab to link imported transactions with existing QuickBooks entries instead of adding duplicates.

7.1 Import Missing Transactions

1. Log in to your bank account and download missing transactions in CSV format.
2. Go to Banking > Upload Transactions and import the file.

7.2 Re-Enable Bank Feeds

- If syncing has stopped, reconnect your bank account under Banking > Add Account.

7.3 Manually Add Entries

- For transactions that can't be imported, add them manually:

1. Go to + New > Expense (or Income).
2. Enter the details and save.

7.4 Verify Historical Data

- Review historical reports to ensure no data is missing from prior periods.

8.1 Regular Reviews

- Weekly reviews of transactions in QuickBooks ensure all data is accounted for and no duplicates exist.

8.2 Centralized Data Entry

- Limit transaction entry to a single source (e.g., QuickBooks itself) to avoid inconsistencies.

8.3 Use Tags

- Tag transactions by category, project, or customer to make tracking easier.

8.4 Regular Backups

- Regularly back up QuickBooks data to prevent loss due to accidental deletions.

9.1 Hubdoc

- Collects and organizes receipts, bills, and invoices, ensuring no expense is missed.

9.2 AutoEntry

- Automates data entry from scanned documents, reducing manual errors.

9.3 Bank Rules in QuickBooks

- Automates transaction categorization and prevents duplicate entries.

9.4 Audit Logs

- QuickBooks' audit log tracks all changes to transactions, helping identify missing or edited entries.

10.1 Accurate Financial Reporting

- Clean data ensures accurate Profit and Loss Statements, Balance Sheets, and other reports.

10.2 Improved Decision-Making

- Reliable data provides a strong foundation for business decisions.

10.3 Streamlined Reconciliation

- Accurate records simplify the reconciliation process.

10.4 Reduced Compliance Risks

- Eliminating errors minimizes the risk of issues during audits or tax filings.

Avoiding duplicate transactions and missing data is essential for maintaining accurate financial records and ensuring the integrity of your QuickBooks account. By leveraging the tools and features in QuickBooks Online, you can prevent these common pitfalls, streamline your workflows, and focus on growing your business. With consistent reviews, proper automation, and proactive management, you'll keep your records clean, reliable, and ready for any financial challenge.

Troubleshooting Common Setup and Data Entry Issues

QuickBooks Online (QBO) is a powerful accounting tool, but incorrect setup and data entry issues can create challenges for business owners and accountants. Misconfigured accounts, incorrect categorization, or overlooked settings can lead to errors that skew financial reports and disrupt workflows. Understanding how to troubleshoot and resolve these common issues ensures that your QuickBooks account operates smoothly and accurately.

This chapter provides practical guidance on identifying and resolving common setup and data entry problems in QBO. By addressing these issues early and following best practices, you'll save time, reduce stress, and maintain reliable financial records.

1.1 Incorrect Chart of Accounts

The Chart of Accounts (COA) is the foundation of your QuickBooks system, categorizing all transactions. Common issues include:

- Duplicated accounts.
- Misclassified accounts.
- Missing essential accounts.

How to Fix:

1. Review the COA:
   » Go to Settings > Chart of Accounts.
   » Compare your COA with standard templates for your industry.
2. Merge Duplicate Accounts:
   » Edit one account, then merge it with another by assigning the same name.
3. Add Missing Accounts:
   » Click New in the Chart of Accounts and select the appropriate account type and detail type.

1.2 Incorrect Opening Balances

Opening balances set the baseline for accurate financial reporting. Errors occur when:

- Incorrect amounts are entered.
- Bank accounts are linked after balances are set manually.

How to Fix:

1. Edit Opening Balances:
   » Go to Chart of Accounts and find the account with the incorrect balance.
   » Adjust the opening balance under Account History.
2. Reconcile the Account:
   » Reconcile the account to match the bank statement's opening balance.

1.3 Misconfigured Tax Settings

Errors in tax settings can lead to underreported or overreported sales tax.

How to Fix:

1. Review Sales Tax Settings:
   » Navigate to Taxes and check the tax rates and jurisdictions configured.
2. Update Incorrect Tax Rates:
   » Edit tax settings and ensure they reflect the latest regulations.

2.1 Duplicate Entries

Duplicate entries can inflate income, expenses, or account balances.

How to Identify:

- Use the Transaction Detail Report to find identical amounts with the same date and description.

How to Fix:

1. Locate Duplicate Transactions:
   - » Search for duplicates in Banking > For Review or the Transaction List.
2. Delete or Void Entries:
   - » Open the duplicate transaction and choose More > Delete.
3. Avoid Recurrences:
   - » Turn on bank rules to prevent duplicates from manual and automated entries.

2.2 Missing Transactions

Missing transactions lead to incomplete financial records, especially during reconciliation or tax preparation.

How to Identify:

- Compare bank statements with QuickBooks records using the Reconciliation Report.

How to Fix:

1. Search for Transactions:
   - » Use the global search bar in QuickBooks with filters for date and amount.
2. Manually Add Missing Transactions:
   - » Enter the transaction via + New > Expense (or Income).
3. Verify Bank Feeds:
   - » Reconnect your bank feed if it hasn't imported transactions.

2.3 Incorrect Categorization

Transactions placed in the wrong accounts or categories can distort financial reports.

How to Identify:

- Run the Profit and Loss Report and check for misclassified income or expenses.

How to Fix:

1. Review Categories:
   - » Open the transaction, select Edit, and choose the correct account or category.
2. Create Rules for Categorization:
   - » Use bank rules to automate the classification of transactions.

3.1 Bank Feed Errors

Bank feeds sometimes fail to sync, causing discrepancies.

How to Identify:

- Missing or duplicated transactions in Banking > For Review.

How to Fix:

1. Reconnect the Bank Feed:
   - » Go to Banking > Edit Account. Reconnect and refresh the feed.
2. Manually Upload Transactions:
   - » Download transactions from your bank and upload them via Banking > Upload Transactions.

3.2 Integration Sync Issues

Third-party apps integrated with QuickBooks may duplicate or omit data.

How to Identify:

- Discrepancies between app-generated reports and QuickBooks records.

How to Fix:

1. Reauthorize the Integration:

» Go to Apps > My Apps, disconnect, and reconnect the integration.

2. Check App Settings:

» Ensure the app is configured correctly to sync only unique data.

4.1 Misaligned Reports

Reports that don't match expected values often stem from categorization or data entry errors.

How to Identify:

• Compare reports like Profit and Loss with bank statements or invoices.

How to Fix:

1. Review Report Filters:

» Customize the report's date range, accounts, and filters.

2. Correct Errors:

» Trace incorrect entries back to their source transactions and edit them.

4.2 Missing Data in Reports

Missing data often occurs when transactions aren't linked to the correct accounts or are excluded from reports.

How to Fix:

1. Check Exclusions:

» Review report filters to ensure all accounts and categories are included.

2. Reconcile Accounts:

» Reconcile accounts to identify and correct missing transactions.

5.1 Incorrect Payroll Taxes

Payroll tax settings that don't align with local regulations can lead to compliance issues.

How to Fix:

1. Review Payroll Settings:

» Go to Payroll > Settings and verify tax rates and withholding amounts.

2. Update Tax Tables:

» Ensure payroll software is using the latest tax tables.

5.2 Missing Employee Information

Incomplete employee profiles can cause errors in payroll processing.

How to Fix:

1. Edit Employee Profiles:

» Add missing information under Payroll > Employees.

2. Verify Bank Details:

» Ensure direct deposit bank details are accurate.

6.1 Regular Reviews

• Conduct monthly reviews of the Chart of Accounts, transactions, and reports to catch errors early.

6.2 Automate Where Possible

• Use automation for recurring invoices, payroll, and bank feeds to reduce manual entry errors.

6.3 Establish Clear Processes

• Create standard operating procedures (SOPs) for entering data and categorizing transactions.

6.4 Train Your Team

- Provide QuickBooks training for employees involved in data entry and financial management.

7.1 Audit Log

- Tracks changes made to transactions and identifies potential setup issues.

7.2 Reconciliation Tool

- Helps identify discrepancies between bank accounts and QuickBooks.

7.3 Transaction Detail Report

- Provides an overview of all transactions, helping you identify errors quickly.

7.4 Accountant Access

- Invite an accountant to review and resolve complex setup or data entry issues.

Scenario: A small business owner realizes their opening balance for a newly added bank account is incorrect, causing discrepancies in reconciliation.

Solution:

1. Review the Opening Balance: Discovered the balance was entered incorrectly during setup.
2. Correct the Entry: Edited the account's opening balance in the Chart of Accounts.
3. Reconcile the Account: Matched transactions to the bank statement, resolving the issue.

Proper setup and accurate data entry are crucial for maintaining the integrity of your QuickBooks Online account. By identifying and addressing common issues early, you can avoid disruptions to your accounting workflow and ensure your financial records are accurate. Regular reviews, proper use of tools, and adherence to best practices will keep your QuickBooks system running smoothly, giving you confidence in your financial management and freeing up time to focus on growing your business.

Best Practices for Keeping Your QuickBooks Account Accurate

Maintaining accurate financial records in QuickBooks Online (QBO) is essential for the success and stability of any business. Accurate data ensures compliance, streamlines reporting, supports strategic decision-making, and simplifies tax preparation. However, achieving this level of precision requires consistent effort and the implementation of best practices.

This chapter provides practical tips and strategies for keeping your QuickBooks account accurate. From efficient data entry processes to leveraging automation and regular reconciliations, these guidelines will help you maintain a reliable financial management system.

1.1 Why Reconciliation Matters

Reconciliation ensures that your QuickBooks transactions align with your bank and credit card statements, identifying discrepancies early.

1.2 How to Reconcile Accounts

1. Go to Accounting > Reconcile.
2. Select the account to reconcile and match transactions with your bank statement.
3. Adjust or correct discrepancies, such as missing or duplicated transactions.

1.3 Frequency

- Perform reconciliations monthly to maintain accurate financial records.

2.1 Benefits of Automation

- Reduces manual errors.
- Saves time.
- Ensures consistency in transaction categorization.

2.2 Automation Features in QuickBooks

1. Bank Feeds:
   - » Connect your bank accounts to automatically import transactions.
2. Bank Rules:
   - » Create rules to categorize recurring transactions (e.g., utilities, rent).
3. Recurring Transactions:
   - » Automate invoices, bill payments, and other repetitive entries.

3.1 What Is the Chart of Accounts?

The Chart of Accounts (COA) is a list of categories that classify transactions. A well-organized COA ensures clarity in financial reporting.

3.2 Best Practices for COA

1. Avoid unnecessary accounts to prevent clutter.
2. Use clear, descriptive names for accounts.
3. Customize the COA to reflect your business's specific needs (e.g., industry-specific categories).

3.3 Regular Updates

- Review and update the COA periodically to ensure relevance and accuracy.

4.1 Benefits of Tags and Classes

- Provide additional layers of categorization for transactions.
- Simplify tracking of projects, departments, or campaigns.

4.2 How to Use Tags and Classes

1. Navigate to Settings > Tags to create tags for specific purposes.
2. Apply tags to transactions for better reporting and analysis.

5.1 Importance of Consistency

- Consistent data entry reduces errors and improves record accuracy.

5.2 Tips for Standardization

1. Use templates for invoices and bills.
2. Train employees on proper data entry methods.
3. Establish naming conventions for customers, vendors, and products.

5.3 Avoid Manual Entry When Possible

- Use tools like QuickBooks Receipt Capture or third-party apps like Hubdoc to automate data entry.

6.1 Why Transaction Reviews Are Crucial

- Identifies errors, missing data, or misclassifications.
- Ensures transactions are correctly categorized for accurate reporting.

6.2 How to Review Transactions

1. Access the Transaction List in QuickBooks.
2. Use filters to sort transactions by date, account, or type.
3. Review each entry for accuracy and completeness.

7.1 Reports to Regularly Review

1. Profit and Loss Statement: Tracks income and expenses to measure profitability.
2. Balance Sheet: Provides a snapshot of your financial position.
3. Cash Flow Statement: Monitors cash inflows and outflows.
4. Accounts Receivable Aging Report: Identifies overdue invoices.
5. Accounts Payable Aging Report: Tracks outstanding bills.

7.2 Customizing Reports

- Customize reports to include relevant filters and columns for deeper insights.

7.3 Frequency

- Review key reports monthly or weekly to stay informed about your business's financial health.

8.1 Benefits of Professional Assistance

- Accountants and bookkeepers bring expertise that ensures accuracy and compliance.
- They can provide insights into optimizing your financial workflows.

8.2 Inviting an Accountant in QuickBooks

1. Go to Settings > Manage Users.
2. Click Invite Accountant and enter their email address.

8.3 Conduct Regular Reviews

- Schedule quarterly or annual reviews with your accountant to validate records and improve processes.

9.1 Why User Permissions Are Important

- Protects sensitive financial data from unauthorized access or changes.

9.2 How to Set Permissions

1. Navigate to Settings > Manage Users.
2. Assign roles with appropriate access levels (e.g., Admin, Standard User).
3. Limit access to specific areas (e.g., payroll, banking).

9.3 Use the Audit Log

- Monitor user activity using the Audit Log to track changes and prevent errors.

10.1 Keep Tax Settings Accurate

- Update tax rates and jurisdictions in QuickBooks regularly.

10.2 Use Tax Reports

- Generate reports like the Sales Tax Liability Report for accurate tax filings.

10.3 Record Tax Payments

1. Go to Taxes > Record Payment.
2. Enter details for tax payments to maintain accurate records.

11.1 Importance of Data Backup

- Protects against accidental data loss or system errors.

11.2 How to Back Up QuickBooks Data

1. Use third-party tools like Rewind or ChronoBooks to schedule backups.
2. Ensure backups are stored securely and can be restored easily.

12.1 Year-End Review Checklist

1. Reconcile all accounts.

2. Review and close open invoices and bills.
3. Adjust entries for depreciation, pre-paid expenses, or accrued liabilities.

12.2 Lock the Books

- Use the Close Books feature to prevent changes to finalized periods.

13.1 Why Training Matters

- Proper training ensures that everyone involved in financial management understands best practices.

13.2 Training Topics

1. Transaction categorization.
2. Bank reconciliation.
3. Report generation and analysis.

13.3 Access to Resources

- Provide access to QuickBooks training materials, webinars, and support.

14.1 Duplicate Entries

- Use bank rules and regular reconciliations to prevent duplicates.

14.2 Missing Transactions

- Automate bank feeds and regularly check the For Review tab.

14.3 Incorrect Categorization

- Train employees and establish clear guidelines for categorizing transactions.

14.4 Skipping Reviews

- Schedule regular reviews of reports, reconciliations, and data.

15.1 Improved Financial Health

- Accurate records provide a clear picture of your business's performance.

15.2 Streamlined Tax Filings

- Proper data ensures that tax filings are completed accurately and on time.

15.3 Enhanced Decision-Making

- Reliable data supports informed strategic decisions.

15.4 Reduced Stress

- Consistent practices minimize the risk of errors and last-minute corrections.

Keeping your QuickBooks account accurate is an ongoing process that requires consistent effort, organization, and attention to detail. By implementing these best practices—regular reconciliations, leveraging automation, monitoring reports, and maintaining a well-organized Chart of Accounts—you can ensure that your financial records are error-free and reliable. Accurate financial management not only helps you avoid costly mistakes but also empowers you to make informed decisions that drive your business forward with confidence.

CONCLUSION

As we come to the end of this journey into mastering QuickBooks Online, it's worth pausing to reflect on what this powerful tool can achieve for small business owners and entrepreneurs like yourself. QuickBooks is more than just an accounting platform; it's a window into your business's financial health, a partner in streamlining your operations, and a foundation for making informed decisions. Its versatility, paired with your growing expertise, equips you to handle the complexities of financial management with confidence and precision.

Picture the day you first opened QuickBooks Online. Perhaps you felt a twinge of apprehension, overwhelmed by the tabs, charts, and reports before you. But with each passing chapter of this book, those once-daunting features have transformed into familiar tools at your disposal. From setting up your account to exploring advanced integrations and preparing for audits, you've unlocked the full potential of QuickBooks. Along the way, you've gained not only technical knowledge but also a deeper understanding of how financial clarity drives success.

Imagine your business as it stands today. There are accounts to reconcile, invoices to send, and reports to review. These tasks, which once seemed like chores, now feel purposeful. You're no longer working in the dark or guessing at your next move. Instead, your financial data tells a story—a narrative of growth, challenges, and victories. Every line item, transaction, and report adds to this story, giving you the clarity to plan your next chapter with precision and optimism.

Think about your customers, employees, and stakeholders. They, too, are part of your financial ecosystem. When you send a polished, professional invoice through Quick-Books Online, you're projecting a level of organization and credibility that inspires trust. When you track expenses meticulously, you're safeguarding the resources that keep your business running. And when you use the data insights QuickBooks provides to make strategic decisions, you're laying the groundwork for sustainable growth. Each step, no matter how small, contributes to a stronger, more resilient business.

Consider the moments when QuickBooks helped you overcome challenges. Perhaps it was during tax season, when automated reports and well-organized records saved you hours of stress and positioned you for compliance. Or maybe it was the seamless integration with a payroll tool that stream-lined your employee management process, giving you more time to focus on growing your business. These victories, while perhaps unnoticed by the outside world, are monumental to you as a business owner. They mark the transformation of your financial management from a source of anxiety to a well-oiled machine.

And yet, this isn't the end of your Quick-Books journey—it's just the beginning. Mastery of this tool doesn't mean perfection. Mistakes will happen, and unforeseen challenges will arise. But now you have the knowledge and confidence to troubleshoot those issues with efficiency and grace. Bank reconciliation errors? Duplicate transactions? Missing data? These are no longer insurmountable obstacles but opportunities to refine your processes and strengthen your understanding of your business's financial landscape.

The tools you've learned to wield—customized reports, bank rules, integrations, and automation—aren't static. QuickBooks evolves alongside your business. As you scale your operations, hire more employees, or venture into new markets, QuickBooks will adapt, providing the capabilities you need to manage complexity with ease. And as you grow, so will your ability to leverage its features creatively, finding new ways to save time, cut costs, and uncover opportunities.

Reflecting on the time and effort you've invested in mastering QuickBooks, it's clear that this journey has been about more than just software. It's about empowerment. You've equipped yourself with a skill set that transcends QuickBooks and applies to the very core of running a successful business. Financial literacy, strategic thinking, and a commitment to accuracy are the hallmarks of any thriving entrepreneur. These qualities, honed through your work with QuickBooks, will serve you in every aspect of your business life.

But let's not overlook the personal growth that has occurred along the way. The confidence you've gained from taking control of your finances is invaluable. That confidence extends beyond the numbers—it shapes how you approach challenges, make decisions, and communicate with your team and clients. It's a quiet yet profound transformation, one that empowers you to lead your business with clarity and purpose.

As you close this book, take a moment to celebrate your progress. Whether you're just starting out or have been running your business for years, your commitment to mastering QuickBooks is a testament to your dedication and vision. Running a business is no small feat, and every step you take toward better financial management is a step toward a stronger future.

In the weeks and months ahead, QuickBooks will continue to be a steadfast ally. Use it not just to manage your day-to-day tasks but to dream bigger. The reports you generate are not just numbers on a page; they are insights into what's possible. The tools you use are not just shortcuts; they are enablers of efficiency and growth. And the time you save by streamlining your workflows is not just convenience; it's freedom to innovate, strategize, and build the business you envision.

Let your journey with QuickBooks inspire others. Share your insights with fellow entrepreneurs, encourage them to embrace financial literacy, and remind them of the power that comes from understanding their numbers. In doing so, you'll not only reinforce your own mastery but also contribute to a community of business owners who are stronger together.

Finally, as you move forward, remember that QuickBooks is a tool, but you are the driver. The decisions you make, the processes you implement, and the goals you set are what truly shape your business's trajectory. QuickBooks is here to support you, but your vision and determination are what make success possible. So trust yourself, embrace the challenges, and celebrate the milestones. Your business's future is bright, and you are more prepared than ever to navigate it.

Thank you for allowing this book to be a part of your journey. The knowledge you've gained, the confidence you've built, and the tools you've mastered are just the beginning. With QuickBooks Online at your side and your entrepreneurial spirit guiding the way, there's no limit to what you can achieve.

ENHANCE YOUR QUICKBOOKS JOURNEY

Take your QuickBooks experience to the next level with our exclusive bonus materials! Designed to complement the content of this book, these resources include hands-on video tutorials and printable guides to help you master QuickBooks Online efficiently.

Video Tutorials

Step-by-Step Guidance

Watch visual tutorials that walk you through QuickBooks Online features and workflows. From setup to advanced reporting, these videos are perfect for learning QuickBooks in action.

Access the Playlist:

Printable Guides

Your Quick Reference Toolkit

Download and print these guides for instant access to essential QuickBooks knowledge:

1. QuickBooks Reference Guide – A comprehensive overview of key features and shortcuts.
2. FAQ Guide for Beginners – Answers to common questions and troubleshooting tips.
3. AI-Powered QuickBooks Guide – Insights into using AI tools for smarter financial management.

Download the Guides:

Maximize your QuickBooks mastery with these tools! Scan the QR codes to start learning today.

APPENDIX

Glossary of QuickBooks Terms

- Account Register: A detailed list of all transactions within a specific account, similar to a checkbook ledger.
- Accounts Payable (A/P): Money your business owes to vendors or suppliers for goods and services received.
- Accounts Receivable (A/R): Money owed to your business by customers for goods or services sold.
- Audit Log: A feature that tracks changes made in QuickBooks, showing who made changes, what was changed, and when.
- Bank Feeds: Automated connections between QuickBooks and your bank accounts that import transactions in real time.
- Chart of Accounts (COA): A list of all accounts used to categorize your business's transactions.
- Class Tracking: A feature that allows you to categorize transactions by department, project, or location for more detailed reporting.
- Closing Date: The date that marks the end of an accounting period, after which changes to transactions are restricted.
- Expense: Any cost incurred by your business, such as rent, utilities, or office supplies.
- Invoice: A bill sent to a customer for goods or services provided, detailing the amount owed.
- Liability: Obligations or debts your business owes, such as loans, taxes, or accounts payable.
- Profit and Loss Report (P&L): A financial statement summarizing revenues, costs, and expenses during a specific period.
- Reconciliation: The process of matching QuickBooks transactions with your bank statement to ensure accuracy.
- Recurring Transactions: Pre-scheduled transactions like invoices or expenses that are automatically generated in QuickBooks.
- Sales Receipt: A record of an immediate payment for goods or services.
- Trial Balance: A report showing all accounts and their balances to verify that total debits equal total credits.

Shortcuts and Keyboard Tips for QuickBooks Online

Maximize your efficiency in QuickBooks Online with these handy shortcuts and tips:

General Shortcuts:

- Alt + N: Create a new transaction (invoice, bill, etc.).
- Alt + R: Reconcile accounts.
- Alt + H: Open the Help menu.
- Alt + P: Open the Print dialog box.

Navigation Shortcuts:

- Ctrl + Alt + F: Search for transactions or accounts.
- Ctrl + Alt + A: Open the Chart of Accounts.

- Ctrl + Alt + I: Go directly to the Invoice screen.
- Ctrl + Alt + E: Open the Expense screen.

Data Entry Shortcuts:

- Tab: Move to the next field.
- Shift + Tab: Move to the previous field.
- Ctrl + Enter: Save a transaction.
- Esc: Close a window or cancel an action.

Date Shortcuts:

- T: Enter today's date.
- Y: Enter the first day of the year.
- R: Enter the last day of the year.
- M: Enter the first day of the month.
- H: Enter the last day of the month.
- + or -: Increment or decrement the date by one day.

Report Shortcuts:

- Ctrl + Alt + R: Open the Reports tab.
- Ctrl + Alt + S: Generate a Profit and Loss report.

Tips:

- Customize your toolbar with frequently used features for quicker access.
- Use browser shortcuts (e.g., Ctrl + T for a new tab) to manage multiple QuickBooks screens.

Contacting QuickBooks Support

QuickBooks offers a range of support options to help you resolve issues or learn more about its features.

1. QuickBooks Help Center

- Access FAQs, guides, and trouble-shooting tips.
- Visit: https://quickbooks.intuit.com/learn-support/

2. Live Chat and Call Support

- Get real-time assistance from Quick-Books experts.
- Log in to your QuickBooks account, go to Help > Contact Us, and follow the prompts to chat or request a callback.

3. QuickBooks Community

- Connect with other users and experts to discuss features, ask questions, or share solutions.
- Visit: https://quickbooks.intuit.com/community/

4. QuickBooks ProAdvisor Program

- Work with certified QuickBooks ProAdvisors for personalized support and training.
- Learn more: https://quickbooks.intuit.com/find-an-accountant/

5. Social Media Support

- Follow QuickBooks on platforms like Twitter (@QuickBooks) for updates, tips, and customer service.

6. QuickBooks Desktop and Mobile App Help

- For app-specific issues, use the in-app Help feature or contact support through the mobile app.

7. Support Hours

- QuickBooks offers support during standard business hours. For urgent issues, check their site for after-hours availability or support plans.

Printed in Great Britain
by Amazon